It's a shore thing – surf at Sennen Cove and (previous page) catching a wave at Porthcurno.

ornwall is special. It gets hold of you in a big sandy hug, and won't let go. If you went there on holiday as a child, you'll be wanting to take your own kids there. Cornwall stays with you for life. It epitomizes the childhood holiday idyll.

North Cornwall offers a frothy cocktail of Atlantic breakers, surf schools and beach cafés, sprinkled with legends of King Arthur at Tintagel Castle. You can kayak from rocky coves, hike to cliff-top lookouts or cycle the Camel Trail from Padstow to Bodmin – gateway to a wonderfully wild and woody side of Cornwall.

By contrast, South Cornwall is for messing about in boats and delving in gardens. The Fal and Fowey estuaries are ideal for canoeing, Falmouth has the shipshape National Maritime Museum, while St Austell is the gateway to leafy gems like the Eden Project and Heligan Gardens.

Undecided? Then go to West Cornwall where you'll find the best of both worlds – surfing at Whitesand Bay, smugglers' coves on the Lizard Peninsula, fine art and fine food at St Ives, boat trips on the Helford River, plus the big attractions of Land's End and St Michael's Mount.

Award-winning writer and photographer **William Gray** is also the author of Footprint's *Travel with Kids*, *Europe with Kids* and *Britain with Kids*.

Digging the beach at Kynance Cove.

About the book

Just like an RNLI beach lifeguard *Cornwall with Kids* is good looking and useful to have around. It will happily grace a coffee table for winter evening perusal, just as it can slip into a coat pocket or the glovebox of your car for on-the-spot holiday reference (all entries for attractions, accommodation and places to eat have postcodes to help you find your way by Sat Nav). On this page you'll find background information on getting the most out of the book, plus some important safety information.

Beach safety
The 'FLAGS' code by the RNLI (rnli.org.uk/beachlifeguards) is a handy checklist for staying safe at the beach:
F Find the red and yellow flags and swim between them.
L Look at the safety signs.
A Ask a lifeguard for advice.
G Get a friend to swim with you.
S Stick your hand in the air and shout for help if you get into difficulty. See also page 201.

Family rates
Unless otherwise specified, family rates quoted in *Cornwall with Kids* are for two adults and two children. If you have more than two children it's always worth checking if there are special deals for larger families. Similarly, some attractions have rates specifically for single-parent families.

Members' perks
Throughout *Cornwall with Kids*, look out for nature reserves, gardens and historical sites that are free to members of English Heritage, the National Trust or the Royal Society for the Protection of Birds (RSPB). Family membership of these charities represents excellent value for money when travelling in Cornwall, and also helps to support conservation work.
English Heritage T0870-333 1181, english-heritage.org.uk. Annual adult membership costs £48, including free entry for up to six children.
The National Trust T0844-800 1895, nationaltrust.org.uk. Annual family membership is £97 (two adults and their children under 18, free for under fives), while a direct debit rate of £72.75 is available for the first year's membership. For single-parent families, membership costs £60.50 or £45.37 by direct debit.
The RSPB T01767-693680, rspb.org.uk. Wild Families membership costs from £5 per month and includes magazines for different age groups and free entry to over 100 reserves.

Blue Flag awards
Please note that these awards (given to beaches with outstanding water quality) are given for one season only and are subject to change. For details of current Blue Flag beaches, visit blueflag.org.uk or keepbritaintidy.org.

Tourist Boards
The official website of the Cornwall Tourist Board can be found at visitcornwall.com. Details for local tourist boards are given in the Grown-ups' section, see page 203. You can also find information about visiting Cornwall at visitengland.com, while a good starting point for overseas visitors is visitbritain.co.uk.

Symbol Key

Beaches
- 😎 Blue Flag award
- 🍴 Café/pub/restaurant
- 🏖 Beach shop
- 🏝 Deckchairs
- 🏠 Beach huts
- 🏄 Water sports
- 🎡 Amusement arcade
- ➕ Lifeguards (summer)
- 🚻 Toilets nearby
- 🅿 Car park nearby
- ❗ Warning!

Campsites
- ⛺ Tents
- 🚐 Caravans
- 🏪 Shop
- 🎠 Playground
- 🍽 Picnic area
- ♿ Disabled facilities
- 🐕 Dogs welcome
- 🏖 Walk to beach
- 🔌 Electric hook-up
- WC Family bathroom
- 🍼 Baby care area
- 🚲 Bike hire
- 🍔 Café/takeaway van
- 🔥 Campfires permitted

It is up to parents to assess whether the information given in *Cornwall with Kids* is suitable or appropriate for their children. While the author and publisher have made every effort to ensure accuracy with subjects such as activities, places to stay and food, they cannot be held responsible for any loss, injury or illness resulting from advice or information given in this book.

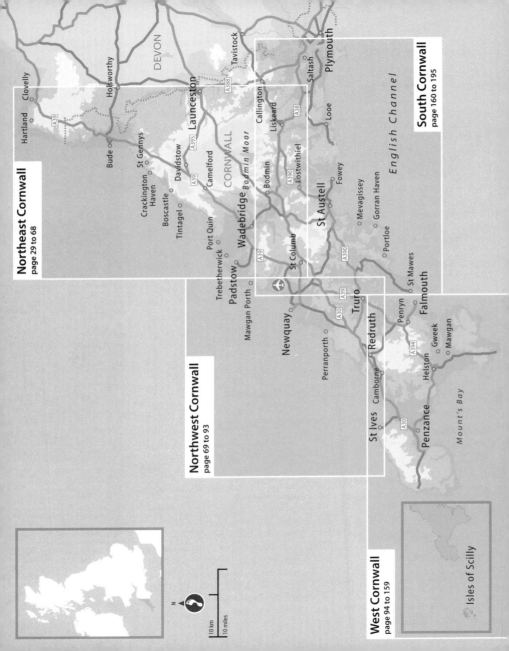

Northeast Cornwall
page 29 to 68

Northwest Cornwall
page 69 to 93

West Cornwall
page 94 to 159

South Cornwall
page 160 to 195

DEVON

CORNWALL

Bodmin Moor

English Channel

Mount's Bay

Isles of Scilly

N

10 km
10 miles

Clovelly
Hartland
Holsworthy
Bude
St Gennys
Crackington Haven
Boscastle
Tintagel
Port Quin
Trebetherwick
Padstow
Mawgan Porth
Davidstow
Camelford
Wadebridge
St Columb
Launceston
Tavistock
Callington
Liskeard
Bodmin
Lostwithiel
St Austell
Fowey
Mevagissey
Gorran Haven
Portloe
St Mawes
Falmouth
Penryn
Gweek
Mawgan
Helston
Truro
Redruth
Camborne
St Ives
Penzance
Perranporth
Newquay
Saltash
Plymouth
Looe

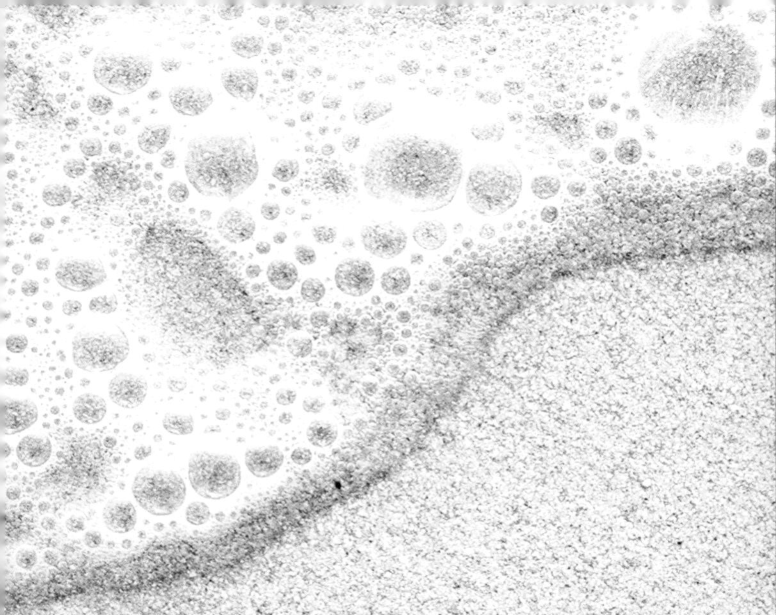

Contents

8   Family favourites
20   Kids' stuff

28   North Cornwall
30   **Northeast Cornwall**
34   Out & about
50   Sleeping
53   Eating

56   **Padstow**
60   **Bodmin Moor**
66   **Launceston**

68   **Northwest Cornwall**
72   Out & about
87   Sleeping
91   Eating

94   West Cornwall
98   **The Far West**
100 Out & about
116 Sleeping
119 Eating
122 **St Ives**

128 **The Lizard**
130 Out & about
142 Sleeping
145 Eating

148 **Isles of Scilly**

160 South Cornwall
164 **Southeast Cornwall**
166 Out & about
180 Sleeping
184 Eating

186 **The Roseland**
190 **Falmouth**
194 **Truro**

196 Grown-ups' stuff
196 Inroads
200 Tots to teens
202 Essentials

204 **Index**
208 **Credits**

10 Gwel an Mor

12 Feather Down Farms

14 Classic Cottages

16 Forest Holidays

18 Bosinver Farm Cottages

Family favourites

Gwel an Mor

Cornish for 'view of the sea', Gwel an Mor certainly gets a good eyeful of the Atlantic, its Scandinavian-style timber lodges and state-of-the-art Residence holiday homes occupying a grandstand position above Portreath on the north coast. Fling open the doors to your balcony and you can gaze dreamily at the blue horizon and hear the swish of surf.

Sea views are almost a happy coincidence at this resort where luxurious accommodation, great facilities and friendly staff have set it on course to becoming one of Cornwall's holiday hotspots.

The traditional two- and three-bedroom lodges have been designed upside down with living rooms upstairs to make the most of the views. Some have hot tubs and log fires. The contemporary lodges are open-plan and very stylish, with plasma TVs, mood lighting, underfloor heating and wrap-around decks.

The Clubhouse at Gwel an Mor boasts an indoor pool, gym, sauna and outdoor adventure play area, while the Wellbeing Spa offers a range of treatments using marine inspired products.

When not self-catering, you can dine at the superb Terrace Restaurant which uses ingredients that are almost exclusively Cornish. Local knowledge also shines through at Gwel an Mor's reception where staff provide a tailormade booking service for whatever activities take your fancy – from surfing to horse riding.

If there's just one thing you do while staying here, however, make sure it's a walking safari with Gary Zammit, the wildlife ranger at Gwel an Mor's adjacent Feadon Farm. Cornwall's Dr Doolittle, he'll have your kids' eyes on stalks as he reveals slow worms, slugs and sparrowhawks in the woods and meadows below Gwel an Mor. You'll go pond dipping, rock-pooling, badger watching and – best of all – get to meet Gary's rescued foxes and fly his barn owl, Sly, and Harris hawk, Harry.

Portreath, TR16 4PE, T01209-842354, gwelanmor.com. Year round. Lowena Lodge (sleeps 4/5) £469-1639/wk, Residence two-bedroom lodge £609-2489/wk.

Feather Down Farms

Safari chic with wellies on, Feather Down Farm tents lead the herd when it comes to luxury camping. Lift the flap on these canvas creations and you step into a snug den complete with wood stove, oil lanterns, three bedrooms (including a secret cubbyhole for kids) and everything you need for a relaxing farmstay – including a flush toilet and kitchen sink.

A working dairy farm near Penzance, Boswarthen is the only Feather Down Farm location in Cornwall – its six tents enjoying glorious views towards Mount's Bay. Like all Feather Down Farms, there's an outdoor clay oven for baking potatoes or pizzas and an honesty shop stocked with local produce and a range of food hampers and barbecue packs. Boswarthen Farm also has a rustic, outdoor hot tub, a farm trail, maize maze and the option of renting a private chicken coop.

A typical day starts with children hurrying outside in pyjamas and wellies to collect chicken eggs, while you grind fresh coffee beans and clunk the kettle on top of the stove. Breakfast is always late – it will take the kids at least an hour to check on the pygmy goats and help Farmer Nicholls feed the calves. With your car parked out of sight (and mind) in the farmyard, and with no electricity to bring radio, television or computer games crashing into your consciousness, time at Boswarthen Farm ebbs and flows to a calming, rural rhythm.

Later in the day, you might plan a picnic or cycle ride (bikes are available to hire), play hide and seek, walk the goats, watch swallows flitting to and from their nests in an old barn or set off on a pilgrimage to St Michael's Mount or the Tate Gallery in St Ives. Some fine beaches, like Porthcurno and Whitesand Bay, are also nearby.

At meal times, cooking becomes a family affair and a chance to indulge in the often-neglected pleasures of a good old chat, while bedtime stories are infused with the magical glow of candlelight.

T01420-80804, featherdown.co.uk. Apr-Nov. £445-975/wk, £315-655/weekend, £245-645/midweek (Mon-Fri).

Classic Cottages

They're not the only cottage agents in Cornwall, but Classic have a knack of finding those 'X-Factor' properties with all the star qualities that discerning families look for – great location, beautifully furnished, child-friendly inside and out, plus that extra little touch – a sunny terrace or a path to the beach perhaps – that ensures everyone gives it an emphatic 'yes'. In short, they are the kind of cottages you hate to leave.

Classic Cottages have specialized in the West Country holiday cottage business for over 35 years, so they've had time to build an impressive portfolio of properties (around 600 in Cornwall alone). Take your pick from stone cottages in Mousehole and Coverack, waterside apartments in Falmouth and Newquay, houses overlooking St Ives Bay and the Fowey Estuary, character barns tucked away in the Cornish countryside and farms with sweeping views of Bodmin Moor.

The collection shown here is a mere taster. An ideal property to share with another family, Glossop Farmhouse (main photo and photo 1, £756-2700/wk) sleeps up to 12 and has a wonderful courtyard garden surrounded by stone outbuildings containing a separate annexe, wet room and children's playroom. The well-furnished holiday home is within easy walking distance of Nanjizal cove, Porthcurno and the Minack Theatre.

In Sennen Cove, the New-England-style Atlantic House (photo 2, £579-1620/wk, see also page 118) accommodates seven and has a bespoke kitchen and raised garden with views to Cape Cornwall.

Sleeping six, Penally Cottage (photos 3 and 4, £447-1170/wk, see also page 52) overlooks Boscastle Harbour and is the perfect retreat for a smuggler's cove-style holiday.

Combining coast and country, Trewane Barn (photos 5 and 6, £492-1329/wk) is hidden away in a wooded valley just three miles from Port Isaac. With room for five, it has a sheltered walled garden.

Helston, TR13 8NA, T01326-555555, classic.co.uk. Year round. Mon-Fri 0900-2000, Sat 0900-1700, Sun 1100-1600.

Forest Holidays

A partnership between the Forestry Commisson and the Camping & Caravanning Club, you'd expect Forest Holidays to know a thing or two about running campsites in beautiful woodland locations. But its select group of cabin sites, including Deer Park, near Liskeard, might come as a surprise.

Branching out into cabin holidays has come as easily to Forest Holidays as falling off a log. Not only has it infused this secluded patch of Cornish forest with home comforts, but it has done so in such a way as to preserve the elemental thrill of sleeping deep in the woods. You'll hear tawny owls hooting – but from the comfort of your deck, a wood stove glowing in the lounge behind you. And chances are, your best sightings of woodpeckers will be in the treetops directly above your open-air hot tub.

Each cabin is carefully sited so that you feel an intimate part of the woodland – and many have the added bonus of overlooking a lake (you can almost feed the ducks without leaving your bed). Double-storey windows flood open-plan living areas with tree-dappled sunlight. Kitchens come with all the mod cons; most cabins have barbecues, flatscreen TVs and DVD players, while a few have an en-suite treehouse attached by an adventurer's bridge. You'll even find a Wii games console in Golden Oak cabins, but don't fret – children get ample opportunity to live in the real world thanks to ranger-led activities that include bat watching and forest survival skills. You can book them at the Forest Retreat, an information hub at the heart of each site, where you can also buy local food and arrange activities such as mountain biking, fishing, sailing and pony trekking. Don't miss the duck race – a great way to meet the lively, fun staff at Deer Park before racing yellow bath ducks along a stream through the woods.

T0845-130 8223, forestholidays.co.uk. Year round. Cabins include Copper Beech (sleeping 2-4) £268-1370/wk, Silver Birch (sleeping 4-6) £420-2095/wk and Golden Oak (sleeping 6) £580-2265wk or sleeping 8 with attached treehouse. Midweek and weekend breaks also available.

Bosinver Farm Cottages

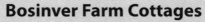

Tucked into a hidden valley between St Austell and Mevagissey, this fabulous holiday bolthole, akin to a small hamlet, combines the rural idyll of a farmstay with the flexibility of a self-catering cottage agency and the facilities of a top-notch holiday park. A frequent winner in the Cornwall Tourism Awards, Bosinver's collection of 20 highly individual, lovingly furnished and well equipped cottages (sleeping 4-12) is set on a 30-acre farm with wildflower meadows and woodland.

There are plenty of attractions nearby, but chances are you'll want to spend most of your time around the farm. Included in the cost of your holiday there are daily animal feeding sessions and egg-collecting with Farmer Dave, as well as pony rides and a weekly Wild Kids club, with activities ranging from den building and bug safaris to woodland art and pond dipping. It's all about reconnecting kids with nature. At Bosinver, children can run free, safely, on adventures of their own – whether it's tracking wildlife on a farm trail or taking a more adrenaline-charged journey on Bosinver's zip wire.

Kids also love the play barn, games room, adventure playground, tennis courts and new indoor, solar-heated swimming pool. They can try their luck fishing on the farm's lake, borrow Nanny Pat's baking box, containing everything they need for a cake-making session, or hop on bikes and pedal the three-mile, car-free Pentewan Valley Trail that starts close by.

Bosinver's self-catering properties range from cosy thatched cottages with inglenook fireplaces to a stunning zero-carbon, energy self-sufficient eco-home. Each one has a fully-equipped kitchen, plenty of baby and nursery equipment, Wi-Fi, toy box, barbecue... everything, in fact, that you need for a carefree family holiday, no matter what age you are.

Trelowth, nr St Austell, PL26 7DT, T01726-72128, bosinver.co.uk. £400-3555/wk, check website for live availability. Short breaks mid-Sep to mid-May (from £160 for 2 nights); dogs permitted at some properties.

22 Sandcastles

23 Books

25 Seaside safari

26 Crabbing

THE
MOUSEHOLE
CAT

Dig for glory
Make the perfect sandcastle

1 Location is crucial. Site your castle near a stream so it's easy to divert water into the moat. Also, make sure the sand is neither too dry nor too sticky.

2 A moat without a boat is no fun at all. Create a harbour on one side of your castle, using a piece of driftwood as a gate. Periodic dredging will be required.

3 Using a spade, carve steps and terraces on the flanks of the castle. Add pebbles and shells for windows and seagull feathers for medieval banners.

4 Don't overlook your outer defences. At least one tide-restraining wall will be required outside your moat. This should feature crenellations or 'dribble sand' towers.

5 Main access should always be via a bridge with pebble parapets (or a drawbridge using flat driftwood). Cobbles make ideal stepping stones across the moat.

6 Special features can include jetties to outlying towers and lighthouses, or tunnels scooped by hand through sturdy bastions of the main castle.

Beach games

Beach bowling Using a bucket and spade, make 10 sand skittles arranged in a triangle and take turns in bowling a ball at them.

Frisbee golf You'll need a big sandy beach at low tide for this one. Mark out as large a circle as you dare and dig a shallow, frisbee-sized hole in the middle of it. Throw the frisbee from the circle and see how many 'shots' you take to get it in the hole. Move around the circle until you've completed nine holes, taking a few steps inside or outside the circle to lower or raise the par for each hole.

Rapid runners Many Cornish beaches have a shallow stream flowing across them at low tide. Buy model boats (or build your own from picnic containers or strandline debris) and race them through the rapids. First one to reach the sea wins.

Boredom busters

Car bingo Give players a sheet of paper and ask them to write down 25 different numbers between one and 99. The person in the front passenger seat calls out the last one or two digits from the licence plates of passing cars. The winner is the first to cross off all their numbers and shout "Bingo!"

Licence to thrill Make up phrases based on the letters of licence plates. For example, 234 IFS 00 could be 'Ice-cream for Sally', 'Ian fancies Susan' or 'I feel sick!'

Buzz words Pick a word, then turn on the radio or play a story CD and try to be the first to shout "buzz" when the word is mentioned.

Good read
10 great children's books set in Cornwall

Early years

Cat on the Hill
by *Michael Foreman* (Andersen Press)
A simple, but poetic, season-by-season account of the life of a stray cat in St Ives.

Dolphin Boy
by *Michael Morpurgo* (Andersen Press)
A close bond between a boy and a dolphin brings life and energy back to a Cornish village.

The Mousehole Cat
by *Antonia Barber* (Walker Books)
The classic tale of fisherman Tom and his faithful cat Mowzer. Take a copy with you to the fishing village of Mousehole, near Penzance, where the adventure is set. See page 100.

The Sand Horse
by *Ann Turnbull* (Andersen Press)
One windy summer day, an artist makes a beautiful sand sculpture of a horse at St Ives. It's much admired by everyone on the beach, but as they leave at the end of the day, the Sand Horse hears the surf calling to him and he longs to join the white horses.

The Seashore
(Usborne)
Essential reference book for all rock-pool detectives (of any age) with colour illustrations and short descriptions of 200 seashore species, from gobies to gulls. A Naturetrail guide to the seashore is also available.

Shanti The Wandering Dog of Sennen and the Land's End
by *Janeta Hevizi* (Cornish Cove Publishing)
A free-spirited dog goes walkabout around Sennen, exploring the village, the beach and the cliffs around Land's End.

Ages 6-12

Children's History of Cornwall
by *Peggy Burns* (Home Town World)
A colourful insight into Cornish history, with timelines and accounts of life in the mines, smuggling and Celtic mythology.

The Wreck of the Zanzibar
by *Michael Morpurgo* (Egmont books)
It is 1907 in the Scilly Isles and a time of extreme hardship. Laura Perryman's diary tells of a violent storm and the unexpected harvest that it brings.

The True Story of Bilbo the Surf Lifeguard Dog
by *Janeta Hevizi and Steve Jmo* (Cornish Cove Publishing)
Get to know adorable Bilbo, a 14-stone chocolate Newfoundland, who became the world's first qualified surf lifeguard dog at Sennen Cove.

Teens

Rebecca
by *Daphne du Maurier* (Virago)
A classic tale of love, jealousy and intrigue, set in the fictional stately home of Manderley on the south Cornish coast.

Super surfer

You can't go to Cornwall and not try surfing – even if it's just mucking about with a bodyboard. A proper surf lesson, though, is not only fantastic fun, but you'll gain a real sense of achievement standing up and riding waves like a proper little dude (even if it is only for a few seconds before you wipe out!). Instructors will also teach you about the beach flag system, how to avoid dangerous situations and even how to fall off safely.

10 more things you've got to try on holiday

Fly a kite Low tide on a big sandy beach is best.
Catch a crab Try your luck off the harbour wall.
Take a boat trip Fish for mackerel or search for seals.
Look for treasure Scour the strandline for mermaids' purses, cuttlefish bones, shells and feathers.
Go rock-pooling Compulsory! See the guide opposite.
Become an ice cream expert There are lots of local ones to try, like Roskilly's, Kelly's and Callestick.
Plan a picnic Stock up on local goodies from a farm shop and set off for the sand dunes.
Go snurfkling Paddle a surf board with a mask and snorkel and see what lies beneath.
Hold back the tide Build a massive sandy wall and see how long it takes the sea to knock it down.
Visit a lifeboat station Check out the cool gear and don't forget to drop some coins in the donation box.

Cool kayaker

Sit-on kayaks are all the rage in Cornwall. They're easy to paddle and great fun for messing about in calm, shallow seas or exploring sheltered estuaries on the south coast. You can hire them at several locations or, better still, join a guided kayaking trip. Remember to keep safe by always wearing a lifejacket (and helmet if it's choppy) and staying close to shore.

Snazzy snorkeller

Follow these steps to happy, safe and leak-proof snorkelling: Get gear that fits properly (hold the mask up to your face and breathe in through your nose – it should stick to your face) • Rub some spit on the inside of the glass to stop it misting over • Start in calm, shallow water and make sure you're happy with everything before swimming out of your depth • If water seeps into your mask, tread water and pull the lower edge of the mask away from your face to allow it to drain out • Check every few minutes to make sure you haven't drifted too far from shore • Be sun smart – wear a wetsuit and lots of sunblock.

Seaside safari

Join an organized rock-pool ramble or set off on your own, equipped with a good guidebook, such as *Seashore* (Dorling Kindersley, 2011). Remember to check tide times to ensure that you do not become trapped by the rising tide. Wear shoes with good grip, take care to disturb animals and plants as little as possible – particularly when looking under rocks – and leave creatures where you find them. Find out more about the Seashore Code from the Marine Conservation Society (mcsuk.org).

Common blenny or shanny.

Barnacle rock pool/harbour

Beadlet anemone rocky shore/rock pool

Blue-rayed limpet rock pool

Brown shrimp sandy shore/rock pool

Common cockle sandy shore

Common blenny or shanny rock pool

Common goby sandy shore/rock pool

Common limpet rock pool/harbour

Common mussel rock pool/harbour

Common periwinkle rock pool

Common ragworm sandy shore

Common starfish rocky shore

Dog whelk rock pool

Flat periwinkle rock pool

Green sea urchin rock pool

Hermit crab rock pool

Painted top shell rock pool

Razor shell sandy shore

Rock goby rock pool

Shore crab rock pool/harbour

Snakelocks anemone rock pool

Velvet swimming crab rock pool/harbour

Common limpet.

Flat periwinkle.

Dog whelk.

Painted top shell.

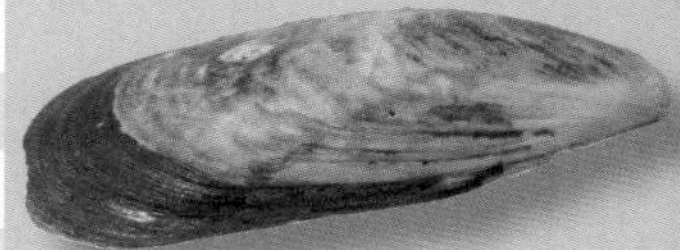

Common periwinkle.

Common mussel.

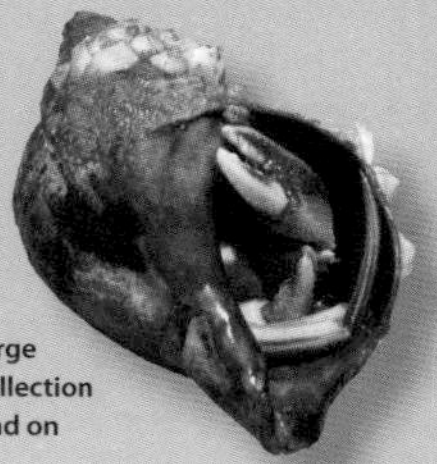

Think twice before bringing shells home with you – they may look empty, but are often home to other animals. This old whelk shell, for example, is not only covered in barnacles, but is also inhabited by a large hermit crab. Why not make a digital collection of shells using the close-up mode found on many digital compact cameras.

Catch a crab
A nifty guide to netting nippers

There are some great spots to dangle a crab line in Cornwall. On the north coast, Boscastle, Padstow and Port Isaac are probably the best; in the south, try Fowey, Looe, Mevagissey or Polperro – you can stake out a patch of harbour wall (taking care of steep drops and slippery, seaweed-covered steps) and try scrounging some fish scraps from local fishermen to use as bait. You could even ask ice-cream sellers for empty plastic tubs – ideal for storing your crabs in. A net is useful for holding under your line as you haul crabs in (there are always one or two crafty nippers which let go of the bait just as you're about to swing them ashore). You can buy a crab line (with either hooks or a mesh bag that you stuff with bait). Alternatively, you could make one for practically nothing. Just get some old string, weight it with a pebble or two, tie a hook-shaped piece of wire to the end and hey presto – you've just saved yourself a few pounds. Shore crabs will dominate your catch but, with luck, you might be able to hook a red-eyed velvet swimming crab. Take care – they're much more feisty than shore crabs. Hold one by the back of its carapace and you should be able to spot three distinguishing features – red eyes, paddle-shaped back legs for swimming and soft, fuzzy carapace. Remember not to let the water in your bucket overheat in the sun, and always carefully return your crabs to where you caught them.

Shore crabs are easy to catch – they feed on worms, molluscs, small crabs, seaweed and carrion (so fish scraps or bacon make ideal bait). Just watch out for those pincers! Hold a crab gently at the back of its carapace. Shore crabs often fight with each other. As a result, typically about five per cent of individuals in any one population have only one claw.

Contents

31 Northeast Cornwall
32 Map
34 Fun & free
38 Best beaches
43 Action stations
46 The Camel Trail
48 Big days out
50 Sleeping
53 Eating

56 Padstow

60 Bodmin Moor

66 Launceston

68 Northwest Cornwall
70 Map
72 Fun & free
74 Best beaches
80 Action stations
84 Big days out
87 Sleeping
91 Eating

North Cornwall

Main photo: On the trail of King Arthur – doorway to Tintagel Castle. Opposite from top: The net result at Port Quin, a coasteering cliffhanger and the Rock–Padstow ferry.

Northeast Cornwall

From tales of King Arthur and the Beast of Bodmin to Bude's surf beaches and Stein's fish & chips, northeast Cornwall is the stuff of legends. You won't find mightier sea cliffs anywhere in the county, while A-list attractions like Tintagel, Boscastle and the Camel Trail are not to be missed.

Heading south from the Devon border on the A39 Atlantic Highway, you'll barely last four miles before **Bude** lures you to the coast. You can almost hear the rattle of spades on buckets as you approach Summerleaze, Bude's big family beach with its seawater pool and miles of sand.

Instead of rejoining the Atlantic Highway, continue south past the surf beach at **Widemouth Bay**, following coastal lanes to **Crackington Haven** – a rollercoaster ride along the rugged backs of Cornwall's highest sea cliffs (reaching 224 m). You won't find another decent sandy beach until **Trebarwith**, south of Tintagel. Instead there are some spectacular, if thigh-twanging, clifftop walks, and two of Cornwall's most enduring and engaging highlights – the definitive smugglers' hideout that is **Boscastle** (lovingly restored after the floods of 2004) and the mysterious ruins of **Tintagel Castle**, legendary birthplace of King Arthur. Both will have your kids wide-eyed with wonder, whether they're creeping into Merlin's Cave or clambering above Boscastle's axe-stroke harbour.

Another glorious stretch of coast, Tintagel Head to Pentire Point extends south in a wide bite of undulating cliffs studded with fishing villages like **Port Gaverne**, **Port Isaac** and **Port Quin**. At **Polzeath**, surfers get another crack at the white stuff, then it's all plain sailing in the sheltered waters of the Camel Estuary, where a ferry shuttles back and forth between **Rock** and **Padstow**. Cornwall's gastronomic capital ever since Rick Stein opened a restaurant here in the 1970s, Padstow is also the perfect spot to burn calories on the **Camel Trail** – a superb 18-mile cycling and walking trail to the edge of **Bodmin Moor**.

Often overlooked, but easily accessible from the coast, the moors have everything from woodland walks and watersports centres to standing stones and steam trains.

Here to there

For the purposes of this book, Northeast Cornwall covers the county's Atlantic shoreline from the Devon border to Padstow, including beaches like Daymer Bay and Rock in the Camel Estuary. For Trevose Head and attractions south of Padstow (such as Crealy Great Adventure Park), refer to the Northwest Cornwall chapter (see page 68). Inland, coverage extends to Launceston and Bodmin Moor, although many attractions in this region are just as accessible from South Cornwall (see page 160).

Bude – Padstow

You must

1. **Track down** the legend of King Arthur at Tintagel Castle.

2. **Get goosebumps** at Boscastle's Museum of Witchcraft.

3. **Catch a wave** at Summerleaze Beach, Bude.

4. **Jump off a cliff** while coasteering at Port Quin.

5. **Cycle the Camel** Trail between Padstow and Wadebridge.

6. **Conquer the** Cheesewring Tor on Bodmin Moor.

7. **Watch the otters** being fed at Tamar Otter Park.

8. **Ride the ferry** from Padstow to Rock and walk to Polzeath Bay.

9. **Watch the surf** roll in at glorious Trebarwith Strand.

10. **Munch Stein's fish** and chips beside the harbour at Padstow.

N

5 km
5 miles

DEVON

Hartland Point • Titchbury • Windbury Point
Hartland Quay • Stoke • Hartland • Clovelly
Milford • Philham • Higher Clovelly
Elmscott • Woolfardisw
South Hole • Tosberry
Knaps Longpeak • Hartland Forest • Ashmans
Welcombe • Meddon
Gooseham • Eastcott • Youlstone • Dinworth
Morwenstow • Shop • Bradwo
Sharpnose Point • Woodford • Bradworthy Cross
Stanbury Mouth • Kilkhampton • Alfardisworthy • Sole Cro
Lower Sharpnose Point • Coombe
Duckpool • Stibb • Holswe Beac
Sandy Mouth • Poughill • Hersham
Northcott Mouth • Grimscott
Crooklets • Bude Haven • Flexbury • Stratton • Pancraswe
3 Summerleaze • Launcells • Holsw
Bude Castle • **Bude** • Derril
Heritage Centre • Upton • Bridgerule
Marhamchurch • Pyworthy Derri

Bude Bay
Widemouth Bay
Millook • Coppathorne • Budd's Titson
Dizzard Point • Tregole • Treskinnick Cross • Whitstone • Lewe
Cambeak • St Genny's • Trewint • Week St Mary • North Tamerton • Tet
The Strangles • Crackington Haven • Wainhouse Corner • B3254 • West Curry
Fire Beacon Point • Beeny • South Wheatley • Maxworthy • Cha V
Tresparrett Posts • Tresparrett • Canworthy Water • Brazacott • Bennacott
2 **Museum of Witchcraft** • Boscastle • Lesnewth • Otterham • North Petherwin • Langdon
Bossiney Head • Trevalga • Warbstow
Bossiney Haven • Trelash • Davidstow • Tresmeer • 7 **Tamar Otter Park** • Yeolmbrid
1 **Tintagel Castle** • Bossiney • Cold Northcott • **Launceston** **Launce**
Tintagel Head • Tintagel • Treknow • **North** • Trewassa • **Steam Railway**
9 Trebarwith Strand • **Cornwall** • St Clether • **Hidden Valley** • **Launce**
Trebarwith • **Museum** • **Discovery Park** • **Cast**
Tregardock • Treligga • Delabole • Helstone • Rough Tor (400m) • Altarnun • **Trethone** • South Petherwi
Port Isaac Bay • Valley Truckle • High Moor • **Leisure Park** • Lewannick
4 Port Quin Bay • **Camelford** • Garrow Tor (331m) • Brown Willy (420m) • Codda • Trewint • Congdon's Shop • Trebulle
Pentire Point • New Polzeath • Port Gaverne • St Teath • Treveighan • Bolventor • **Jamaica Inn** • Trebartha • Coad's Green
Padstow Bay • Port Isaac • Trelill • Michaelstow • North Hill • B3257 • Bra Sho
Gulland Rock • Hawkers Cove • Polzeath • Port Quin • St Endellion • St Tudy • St Breward • Kilmar Tor (396m) • Bathpool
Trevose Head • Trebetherick • Daymer Beach • Chapel Amble • St Kew • Row • **Bodmin Moor** • Ria Mill
Rock Beach • Pityme • Wenfordbridge • **Colliford** • Dozmary • Upton Cross
Trevone • 8 • St Kew Highway • **Lake Park** • Pool • 6 **Cheesewring** • Pensilva
10 **Padstow** • **National** • St Mabyn • Blisland • Temple • Minions • Golberc
Shop • **Lobster** • **Pencarrow** • **Colliford** • **Siblyback** • Siblyback Lake
Porthcothan • Little • **Hatchery** • **Wadebridge** • **House** • Helland • Lake • **Watersports** • St Cleer • Newb
Petherick • St Issey • Cardinham • **Cardinham** • **Centre** • Tremar
Park Head • Penrose • St Breock • Washaway • **Woods** • Warleggan • **Golitha Falls** • Merrymeet • St Ive
Trenance • St Ervan • St Jidgey • **Bodmin** • Cardinham • Mount • **National Nature** • Dobwalls • **Liskeard** • Quethio
Trevarrian • St Eval • **Crealy Great** • Ley • **Reserve** • Pengover Green
Watergate Bay • Talskiddy • **Adventure Park** • Ruthernbridge • Nanstallon • **Bodmin &** • Fowey • West • Doublebois • Menheniot
Newquay • St Columb • Rosenannon • **Wenford** • Taphouse • East • St Keyne
Lane • Major • Withiel • **Railway** • Taphouse • St Keyne
Cornish Birds • **Goss Moor** • Lanivet • **Lanhydrock** • Trerule Foot
of Prey Centre • **National** • Trebyan • Couch's Mill • Trewidland • Widegates
Kestle Mill • St Columb • **Nature** • Victoria • Sweethouse • **Restormel Castle** • Duloe
Road • **Screech Owl** • **Reserve** • Lockengate • **Lostwithiel** • Quethio
• **Sanctuary** • Tregoss • Lanjeth • **Museum**
Trevarren • Indian Queens • Roche • Bilberry • **Lostwithiel**
• Bugle

From top left: cottage at Port Quin, flotsam sculpture at Trebarwith Strand, tea room in Port Isaac, Port Gaverne at low tide, beach gear for sale at Crackington Haven, Tintagel Head, strandline treasures on a door in Bude.

Out & about Northeast Cornwall

Track down a legend

You have to pay to visit Tintagel Castle (see page 48), legendary birthplace of King Arthur (and it's money well spent). On Tintagel's Fore Street, **King Arthur's Great Halls** (T01840-770526, visitboscastleandtintagel. com), with its round table, granite throne and 72 stained glass windows depicting the Arthurian legend, also charges a small admission fee (£8 family). However, there are many other locations in northeast Cornwall where you can follow in King Arthur's footsteps for free. The waterfall at **St Nectan's Glen** between Tintagel and Boscastle, for example, is said to be the site where the mighty monarch was blessed before undertaking his quest for the Holy Grail. Just to the south is **Slaughterbridge**, where some believe Arthur was fatally wounded by Mordred in

the Battle of Camlann. Just to the south, **Camelford** has been linked to Camelot, while Bodmin Moor has several Arthurian sites, including **Dozmary Pool** where Excalibur was returned to the mysterious Lady of the Lake.

Befriend a blenny

Top spots for rock-pooling along Cornwall's northeast coast include Crackington Haven, Port Isaac and Port Quin. If you're feeling slightly more adventurous, however, set off for **Lundy Bay**, a secluded rocky cove just to the west of Port Quin. To reach it, turn right off the B3314 between St Minver and Trelights, following the lane for a short distance until you reach a small parking area on the left. Alternatively, follow Bishop's Hill Road out of Polzeath. A short path crosses fields to the coast. Bear right and take the upper path to Lundy Hole, a spectacular sea arch,

Check out the events listings in the free *Coast Lines* newspaper or at the Boscastle Visitor Centre. Many of the rock-pool rambles, beachcombing walks and treasure hunts are free or have a nominal charge.

beyond which a trail descends into Lundy Bay. Be aware that the bay fills with water at high tide, so you will have to plan your rock-pooling expedition with the help of tide tables.

Fly a kite

Judging by its popularity with windsurfers and kitesurfers, **Daymer Bay**, just inside the Camel Estuary, is a good bet for flying a kite. Also try big, breezy beaches like **Summerleaze**.

Visit Trevathan

Why? As well as all the scrummy local food on sale at Trevathan Farm Shop near Port Isaac, there's loads of outdoor space for kids to run around and let off steam. Football goals, ride-on tractors (coin operated), sand pit, swings, climbing frame and a speedy zip wire should keep most kids occupied for an hour or two – and there are also goats, rabbits and wallabies to pet. See page 53 for contact details, opening times and information on farm shop produce and restaurant menu.

Explore Port Isaac

North Cornwall's favourite poster pin-up, Port Isaac (see also page 41) is well worth a morning or afternoon amble. Walking towards the village from the clifftop car park, you join the top of Fore Street where the Old School (now a hotel) was closed in 1978 for fear of the playground slipping into the sea. Continue down the hill, pausing to browse in Boathouse Stores. The low wall here offers a good vantage point over the harbour. Where the road bends right at the bakery, continue straight on into Temple Bar and what locals call Squeeze Belly Alley (for reasons that will become clear). Turn right into Dolphin Street and right again into Middle Street to reach the harbour. There's a lifeboat station here, as well as a small aquarium next to the fish market. Follow the lane up Roscarrock Hill to join the coast path, which hugs the cliffs all the way to Port Quin.

Cross the footbridge over to the left side of the famous dog-leg harbour and you are suddenly faced with dramatic vistas of sea cliffs, surging waves and wild Meachard Island. At low tide you can witness the Devil's Bellows blowhole at the base of the cliffs near the harbour entrance. Seals are often seen here too.

Explore Boscastle

This fascinating north coast village made headlines during the devastating floods of 2004. It's sobering to stand in the renovated visitor centre (where a sign at ceiling level marks the extent of the floodwaters) and watch video footage of cars and campervans being swept downstream. There are also displays on geology and wildlife, as well as children's brass-rubbing activities and a giftshop. Nearby, you'll find a National Trust shop and the spooky Museum of Witchcraft (see page 49), while the village centre has craft shops, galleries, a bakery, cafés and restaurants. However, don't get too waylaid in browsing Boscastle's tourist traps. To fully appreciate the village's dramatic setting you need to hike the short, but fairly steep, footpath up to the coastguard lookout. Start by crossing the footbridge over to the left side of the famous dog-leg harbour, beyond which you are suddenly faced with dramatic vistas of sea cliffs, surging waves and wild Meachard Island. At low tide you can witness the Devil's Bellows blowhole at the base of the cliffs near the harbour entrance. Seals are often seen here too. Continue along the path, skirting a deep cleft where fulmars nest on narrow ledges, until you reach the lookout. Volunteers man this lonely outpost 365 days a year and you may well be invited inside the hut for a brief squint through powerful binoculars. On a clear day you can make out the buildings on distant Lundy Island. Another lovely walk follows the opposite side of Boscastle, past the little row of whitewashed cottages, to the vertiginous Pennally Point – a strictly hand-held adventure if you have young children!

Out & about Northeast Cornwall

The beaches described here are found east to west, from the Devon border to Padstow. For Trevose Head, see page 74.

Duckpool
🌊 🅿️ ♻️ ‼️

Hemmed in by cliffs and raked by strong currents, Cornwall's far-north beaches are wild and rugged. Forget Stanbury Mouth a few miles south of the Devon border – it has no facilities, tricky access and dangerous swimming. Further south, Duckpool is more inviting. Nuzzled beneath the dramatic headland of Steeple Point, it's a sandy cove with rocky reefs at low tide (don't forget your shrimping nets). Surfers will find a fairly decent beach break, but remember to stay well clear of the rocks, particularly at the northern end of the cove.

Sandy Mouth
🌊 🏄 🅿️ ♻️ ‼️

As with Duckpool, above, you need to take extra care at Sandy Mouth. Not only are the cliffs unstable, but there are strong undercurrents and a real danger of getting cut off by the tide. On the plus side, there's a lifeguard service during summer and a great little café/shop in the National Trust car park, selling drinks, snacks and beach gear, and renting out wetsuits and bodyboards. The beach itself

is a stunner: pebbles strewn with flotsam at high tide and then, as the tide ebbs, a broad swathe of golden sand and wave-smoothed reefs of rock pockmarked with pools. It's a good option for escaping the busier beaches near Bude and the surf can be just as good. Be wary of fierce riptides though.

Northcott Mouth
🌊 🏄 🅿️ ♻️ ‼️

A sandy precursor to the 'Bondi beauties' of Bude just to the south, Northcott Mouth actually merges with Crooklets at low tide. It's a great beach for strandline-roaming (tide tables to hand) and you can also reach it by following the coast path from Bude. Although the surf is consistently good at Northcott Mouth, the huge beach break is prone to rip tides.

Crooklets
🌊 🏄 🅿️

One of Bude's main beaches and home to Britain's first life-saving club (founded in 1953), Crooklets often has superb surf with breakers pounding a wide expanse of firm sand. Just don't expect to have it all to yourself.

Summerleaze
🌊 🏄 🅿️

Bude's spectacular downtown beach, Summerleaze has all bases covered. Sea too rough? Opt instead for the large saltwater pool scooped from

the base of the cliffs. It overflows into shallow sandy lagoons that are quick to warm under the sun. Then it's just a short sprint across hard, rippled sand to a stretch of lifeguard-patrolled surf. There's no shortage of surfing schools, if you feel like tackling the big stuff, but the beach is so wide and flat that even young children can have fun riding bodyboards in the frothy remnants of spent breakers. Higher up the beach, the sand gets softer, rucking up into dunes by the main beach car park and RNLI shop. To the north, Summerleaze blends with Crooklets; to the south it wraps around the harbour where the remaining mile or so of Bude Canal (dug in 1823) delves

Sandy Mouth at high tide.

inland. Here you'll find Bude's gentlest waters, with rowing boats for hire, cafés, craft shops, Bude Castle (see page 49) and a lovely, grassy canal-side walk – the perfect way to get the sand off your feet.

Widemouth Bay
🏄 🚶 🏊 ➕ 🚻 Ⓟ

South of Bude, Widemouth Bay has over a mile of sand and promises fine surfing for beginners to pros. There's a surf school and board hire here, plus rock pools at low tide.

Crackington Haven
🏄 🚶 🏊 ➕ 🚻 Ⓟ

A dramatic beach snug between 130-m-high headlands with cliffs striped black and white like humbug mints, Crackington Haven has a mixture of shingle, rock and sand. A stream flows across the pebbles, spreading out across darkish sand at low tide, when the time is ripe for building dams or rock-pooling. The Bude–Wadebrige bus calls here and there are also two excellent cafés (see page 54), one of which hires out westuits and surf boards.

Bossiney Haven
🚶 Ⓟ 🏄

Park in Bossiney, near Tintagel, then follow the footpath to steep steps leading down to this sandy cove, wedged in a narrow cleft in the cliffs. You'll be wasting your time at high tide when there is little or no beach.

Locals claim Bossiney is a good spot for mussel collecting.

Trebarwith Strand
🏄 🚶 🏊 ➕ 🚻 Ⓟ 🏄

With no sand at high tide, beach-goers stake out the flat rocks at Trebarwith waiting for the tide to ebb. Families with young children might find getting across the rocks tricky (wetsuit booties are recommended), but once you're on the beach at low tide, Trebarwith is a gem with plenty of sand, excellent surf, rock pools and natural paddling pools. Right behind the beach there's a cluster of beach shops, cafés (see page 54) and a surf shop with wetsuits and bodyboards for hire. After a long surfing

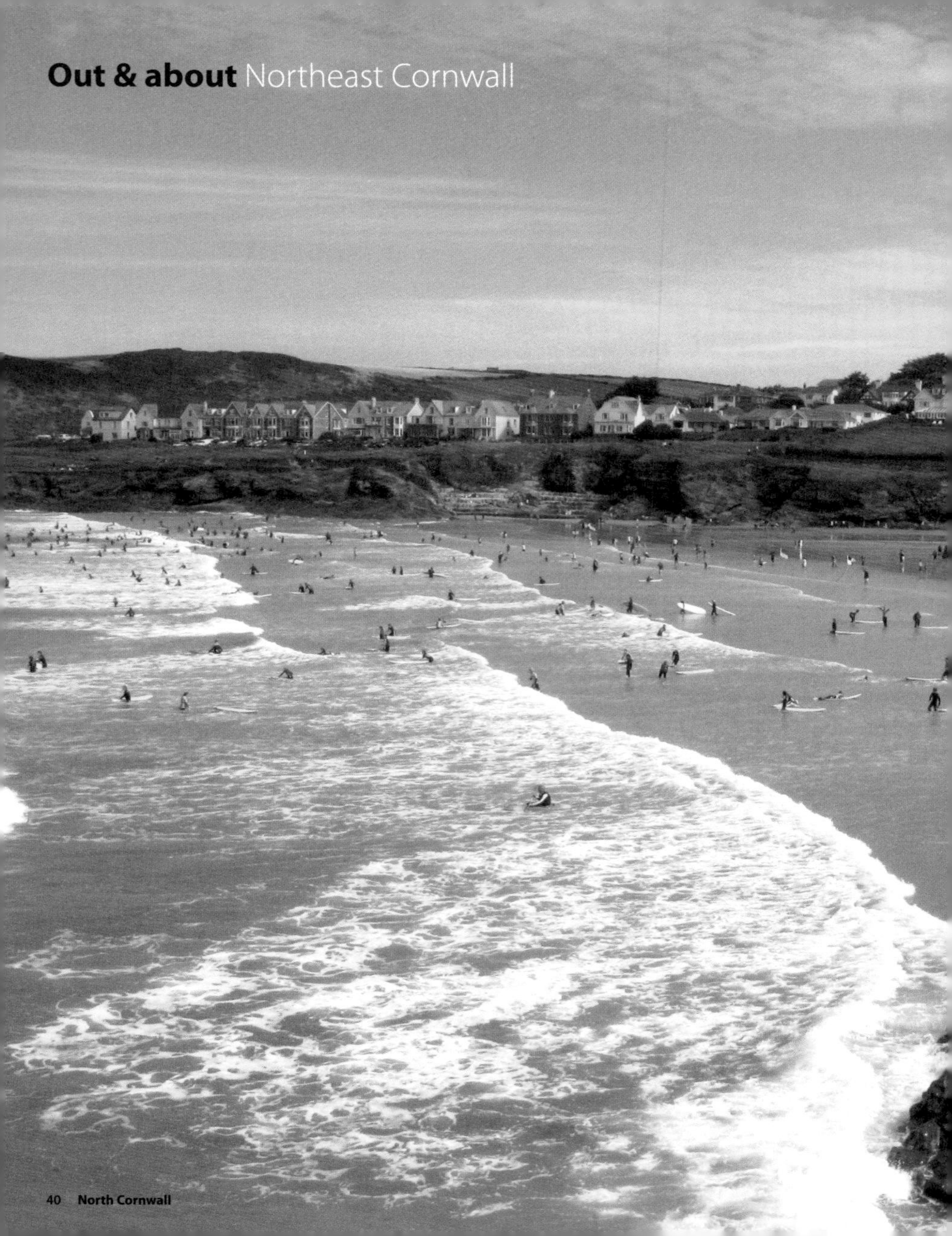

Out & about Northeast Cornwall

Mighty surf at Polzeath.

session, bundle the kids up in towels and stop by the Shop in the Strand Café for freshly made doughnuts dunked in steaming hot chocolate. Holiday heaven!

Port Gaverne

Pilchard-fishing smacks and two-masted luggers laden with coal, lime and salt jostled for space in this haven during the mid-19th century. Nowadays, you'll still find a handful of fishing boats hauled up on the pebbles, but it's the prospect of sea kayaking that draws many visitors to this sheltered cove. Along with Port Quin, it's one of the best paddling spots on the north coast (see page 44 for operators). Rock-pooling is also rewarding at Port Gaverne and, although the beach is narrow, you still get a fair wedge of (wet) sand at low tide.

Port Isaac

You can park on the beach at Port Isaac, but it's far easier (and less prone to tides!) to leave your car in the cliff-top car park. The harbour town of Doc Martin fame is only a 10-minute walk from here, and the views across the bay to Tintagel Head are glorious. Strolling down through the narrow lanes, you'll pass numerous gift shops and cafés (see pages 53-54) before reaching the harbour – cluttered with fishing boats and lobster

pots and the site of a small fish market and aquarium. As you'd expect from a busy fishing village, the beach is strewn with ropes and crab shells. It's weedy and whiffy, but fun to explore – particularly if you follow the concrete walkway on the right-hand side of the beach where there are some large rock pools.

Port Quin

A few houses, a small National Trust car park, a tiny snack shack and that's about it. Port Quin may be small on facilities but it's big on adventure. A sheltered rocky inlet west of Port Isaac, this is an excellent location for sea kayaking, snorkelling or coasteering (see page 43). There's not much of a beach at high tide (try crabbing off the slipway) but, as the sea ebbs, you'll find rock pools shimmering with green and purple snakelocks anemones.

Polzeath

Cool Cornwall's surf central, Polzeath squirms with neoprene during the height of summer when wetsuited bodies take to the sea in such numbers it can resemble a crowded seal colony. This superb family beach is so popular that part of it has long been commandeered as a car park. Everything crowds in on the beach: cars, surf shacks, snack bars – even ice cream

Mere ripples at Daymer Bay.

vans drive out across the bay! There are good surf breaks along the beach, with waves for all abilities. If the sea gets too crowded, try New Polzeath on the northeast side of the bay. Alternatively, swap surf board for frisbee – there's usually plenty of unclaimed sand in the middle of the bay at low tide. You can also follow the coast path north to rugged Pentire Point, a good vantage point for spotting seabirds and marine wildlife.

Daymer Bay

Sheltered from the surf that pummels Polzeath a mile or so to the north, sandy Daymer Bay is an ideal spot for young children to go paddling. Low tide exposes acres of beautifully rippled (but hard) sandflats that will test the backs and spades of sandcastle-builders – or form a challenging wicket for beach cricket. Rock-poolers, meanwhile, should check out the north side of the bay. The tide sweeps in fast at Daymer Bay, so be prepared to beat a hasty retreat to the softer sand and dunes above the high-water mark. If it's windy, bring a kite or watch the windsurfers and kitesurfers tacking back and forth across the Camel Estuary.

Rock Beach

A long sandy beach stretching from Porthilly Cove to Daymer Bay on the east side of the Camel Estuary, Rock is linked to Padstow (see pages 56-59) by a landing-craft-style passenger ferry (return tickets around £3 adult, £2 child). Depending on the tide, you land either on the slipway at Padstow Harbour or on Lower Beach just to the north of the town. Rock Beach is a popular and trendy spot for sailing and windsurfing, and there's a lovely coastal walk north to Daymer Bay and Polzeath (see left).

Boat trips
See also Cornish Rock Tors, page 44, and Padstow, page 58.

Orcades II
Port Isaac Harbour, T01208-880716, carn-awn.co.uk/orcades. Call for rates. Sightseeing and mackerel fishing.

Winnie the Pooh
Port Isaac Harbour, T01208-880421. Call for rates. Mackerel fishing and wildlife trips.

Canoeing
Atlantic Pursuits
20 Priestacott Park, Kilkhampton, Bude, EX23 9TH, T01288-321765, atlanticpursuits.co.uk. Half-day £25, full day £45.
Paddle a three- or four-seater Canadian canoe along Bude Canal's 'Jungle Run'. Surfing and bodyboarding are also available.

Coasteering
Cornish Coast Adventures
Scarrabine Farm, Port Quin PL29 3ST, T01208-880280, cornishcoastadventures.com. Coasteering £40 (minimum age 10) or £35 if in a family group. Sea kayaking family fun session (2-3 hrs) £30 (minimum age 10).

Leap of faith – coasteering at Port Quin.

Throw caution (and yourself) to the wind and sea on a three-hour coastal romp, leaping from ledges, swimming into sea caves, spinning in whirlpools and generally behaving like a crazed mermaid. Relax – you're in safe hands. CCA's coasteering trips are led by beach lifeguards or lifeboat crew members and are suitable for beginners. You'll be kitted out with wetsuits, helmets and lifejackets on the slipway at Port Quin before taking the plunge and entering 'seal mode'. Sea kayaking trips (on two-person sit-on kayaks) are also available, nosing about the inlets and sea caves at Port Quin and, if conditions allow, venturing along the coast in search of deserted coves, seals and basking sharks. Flop overboard for a cooling swim or have a go at fishing by trawling a mackerel line behind your kayak or pulling up one of CCA's lobster pots.

⚙ **Natural** cycle
Most people experience Goss Moor as a 60-mph blur from the A30 just before they reach Indian Queens. But this 480-hectare national nature reserve is crying out for more leisurely exploration by bicycle. A relatively flat seven-mile circular trail winds its way around a widlife-rich patchwork of heathland and scrub that, according to legend, was once a hunting ground for King Arthur.

Cycling
See page 46 for the Camel Trail.

Horse riding
Efford Down Riding Stable
Efford Down Farm, Vicarage Rd, Bude, EX23 8LT, T07817-033092, efforddown.co.uk/stables. Easter-Sep Mon-Fri, plus Sundays during school holidays. 1hr trek £24 (minimum age 5, maximum weight 15 stone).
There's a horse or pony for everyone at Efford Down – from a diminutive Shetland to a 16-hand Shire cross. Escorted

Out & about Northeast Cornwall

riding takes place on the farm with fantastic views along the north coast.

Gooseham Barton Farm

Morwenstow, Bude, EX23 9PG, T01288-331204, gooseham-barton. com. Rides from £25/hr.
Hacks of up to three hours are available for experienced riders, while novices can join half-hour-long walks with children taken on a leading rein for safety.

Tredole Trekking Stables

Trevalga, Boscastle, PL35 0ED, T01840-250495. Call for rates.
Family groups and all abilities for beginners' lessons or romantic sunset canters along the coast.

Multi activity
Cornish Rock Tors

Polzeath, PL27 6SS, T07791-534884, cornishrocktors.com. Coasteering £40 (minimum age 10), climbing £60, sea kayaking £30 (minimum age 8), Sea Safaris powerboat tours £40 adult, £30 child.
As well as three-hour coasteering and sea kayaking tours, Cornish Rock offers full-day rock-climbing trips (suitable for all abilities) and two-hour boat trips on the *Mor Cannow*. Operating from Rock, this high-speed RIB can whisk you to The Rumps (via Pentire Head), to Gulland Rock (a nursery ground for seals) or to Tintagel Castle, via teeming seabird cities and the cathedral-like caves of Cartway Cove.

Outdoor Adventure

Widemouth Bay, Bude, EX23 0DF, T01288-362900, outdooradventure. co.uk. Adventure family holidays, mid Jul-late Aug, 5 days all-inclusive from £624 adult, £503 child.
With the added bonus of a wild cliff-top setting, this residential centre offers family holidays packed with pursuits, such as surfing, bodyboarding, kayaking, Canadian canoeing, archery, climbing, abseiling, windsurfing, coasteering, orienteering and coastal traversing (boulder-hopping along rocky shores). See also page 198.

Shoreline Extreme Pursuits

Crooklets Beach, Bude, EX23 8NE, T01288-354039, shorelineactivities. co.uk. Half-day abseiling £24.50, archery £22, canoeing £35 (per boat), coasteering £29, kayaking on Bude Canal £24.50, rock climbing £24.50, sea or surf kayaking £29. Beach ecology and geology sessions £10.95 (minimum 5 people).
A one-stop shop for adrenaline junkies with introductory sessions and qualification courses in a range of activities. Most can be tailored to all abilities, except surf kayaking where you need some paddling experience – perhaps from one of Shoreline's more gentle sojourns on the Bude Canal. Also on offer are beach ecology safaris where you can expect another, albeit milder, adrenalin rush if you spot the elusive Celtic sea slug, *Onchidella celtica*.

Tamar Lakes Watersports

Kilkhampton, Bude, EX23 9SB, T01288-321712, swlakestrust.org.uk. Canadian canoe £18/hr, dinghy sailing £15/hr (Pico) £20/hr (Feva), £30/hr (Wayfarer), kayak £10/hr, pedalo £12/hr, rowing boat £15/hr, surf ski £10/hr, windsurfer £15/hr; call for details of RYA courses.
The antithesis to Bude's surf scene, the calm waters of Upper Tamar Lake are perfect for learning to sail or windsurf. For camping, see page 50.

Sea kayaking
Camel Canoe & Kayaks

The Pontoon, Rock PL27 6LD, T07791-533569, ccak.co.uk. Sit-on kayaks £25/day (single), £50/day (double), guided estuary trips £35.
Sales, hire, tuition and guided kayaking tours on the Camel Estuary and beyond.

Cornish Coast Adventures

See page 43.

Surfing

See opposite.

Waterskiing
Camel Ski School

The Pontoon, Rock, PL27 6LQ, T01208-862727, camelskischool. com. Ski/wakeboard £27.
Learn how to waterski or wakeboard on the calm waters of the Camel Estuary – or go for a bit of 'Costa del Cornwall' with a high-speed banana boat ride. Stand-up paddleboards and kayaks are also available to hire.

Surf schools

Atlantic Pursuits
Bude, T01288-321765,
atlanticpursuits.co.uk. £20/2-hr
lesson, £40/day (2 lessons).
Also offers bodyboarding, sea
kayaking and canoeing.

Big Blue Surf School
12 Summerleaze Crescent, Bude,
EX23 8HH, T01288-331764,
bigbluesurfschool.co.uk.
£30/2½- to 3-hr lesson, £50/day (2
lessons), from £75/weekend (3-4
lessons), £110/long weekend.

Bude Surfing Experience
Adventure International, Belle Vue,
Bude, EX23 8JP, T0777-911 7746,
budesurfingexperience.co.uk.
£29/2½-hr lesson on Summerleaze
Beach, 5 lessons £110, private one-
to-one lesson £90.
Also offers stand-up paddleboarding
lessons and group accommodation.

Harlyn Surf School
23 Grenville Rd, Padstow,
PL28 8EX, T01841-533076,
harlynsurfschool.co.uk.
£40/2-hr lesson, 1-hr lessons for
kids 5-8 £25, family package £130.
Also offers coasteering, stand-up
paddleboarding, guided kayak tours
and rental of boards, kayaks etc.

Outdoor Adventure
Widemouth Bay, Bude, EX23 0DF,
T01288-362900, outdooradventure.
co.uk. £30/2½-hr lesson.
Also runs family holidays and
coasteering (see opposite).

Padstow Surf School
Harlyn Bay, T07531-364036,
padstowsurfschool.co.uk. Operates
from beaches in the Padstow area.
£30/2-hr lesson.

Raven Surf School
32 Seawell Rd, Poughill, Bude,
EX23 8PD (or EX23 0AW for beach
location), T01288-353693 or 07860-
465499, ravensurf.co.uk. £35/2½-hr
lesson, discounts for families.

Shoreline Extreme Sports
Crooklets Beach, Bude, EX23 8NE,
T01288-354039 or 0780-5288
689, shorelineactivities.co.uk.
£24.50/2½-hr lesson.
Also offers sea kayaking, canoeing,
rock climbing and other activities.

Surf's Up Surf School
21 Trenant Close, Polzeath,
PL27 6SW, T01208-862003 or
07760-126225, surfsupsurfschool.
com. £26/2½-hr lesson, £16/1½-hr
taster lesson (kids aged 7 and under).

Trebarwith Surf School
Trebarwith Strand,
T01840-770535 or 07528-436760,
surftrebarwith.co.uk. £25/2-hr lesson.

Wavehunters
6 Fore St, Port Isaac, PL29 3RB,
T01208-880617 or 07969-660014
(beach mobile), wavehunters.co.uk.
£28/2-hr lesson at Polzeath.
Also runs Kids Club, daily 0945-1230
during school holidays (minimum
age 6), Girls Only Diva Days and
Grom Club, Tue & Sun, for ages 6-16.

Waves Surf School
St Merryn, Padstow, PL28 8NW,
T01841-521230 or 07792-574749,
wavessurfschool.co.uk. £40/2-hr
lesson, £130 family package.

Don't miss The Camel Trail

Cornwall's most popular cycling adventure, the 18-mile Camel Trail links Padstow, Wadebridge, Bodmin and Wenfordbridge via a largely traffic-free route that follows an old railway track alongside the River Camel.

The trail is divided into three main sections: Padstow to Wadebridge, five miles, flat all the way; Wadebridge to Bodmin, six miles, with a small climb to Bodmin; and, finally, the slightly more challenging seven-mile sector between Bodmin and Wenfordbridge. You could also try a circular route to Rock and catch the ferry back to Padstow.

Allow 45 minutes each way for the estuary-side pedal between Padstow and Wadebridge. You can hire bikes at either town (see box right). This often busy section (used by walkers and birdwatchers as well as cyclists) follows the south bank of the estuary, crossing the old iron bridge over Little Petherick Creek and ducking under the A39 bypass before reaching Wadebridge. Stop en route for a picnic or encourage tired legs with the promise of Granny Wobbly's fudge in Wadebridge or ice cream at Stein's Deli if you're Padstow-bound.

Intrepid cyclists can push on past Wadebridge to Bodmin, where the Camel Trail delves into beautiful riverside woodland. For refreshments, stop at the Camel Valley Vineyard or Camel Trail Tea Gardens near Nanstallon or make for the picnic tables at Grogley Halt, where there's access to the river. Look out for a steam train at Boscarne Junction, the western terminus of the Bodmin and Wenford Railway (see page 64).

From Dunmere (near Bodmin), the Camel Trail loops north towards Poley's Bridge and Wenfordbridge. This is the quietest section of the trail, climbing gently through beech woodland with views of the river below. There is a seasonal tea room at Tresarrett, while the Blisland Inn makes a worthwhile one-mile detour off the trail.

Bike hire

Bike Smart
Eddystone Rd, Wadebridge, PL27 7AL, T01208-814545, bikesmart.eu. Daily from 0900.

Bridge Bike Hire
Wadebridge, PL27 7AL, T01208-813050, bridgebikehire.co.uk. Daily 0900-1700.

Padstow Cycle Hire
South Quay, Padstow, PL28 8BL, T01841-533533, padstowcyclehire.com. Daily 0900-1700, plus evening hire mid July-end Aug.

Trail Bike Hire
South Quay, Padstow, PL28 8BL, T01841-532594, trailbikehire.co.uk. Daily 0900-1800.

Expect to pay: Adult bike £11-15, adult trike £12-14, tandem £24-28, bike and child seat £14-15, bike and tag-a-long £18-20, trailer £6-7, dog trailer £5-6, junior 24-in bike £8-9, junior 20-in bike £6-7, junior 16-in bike £4-5. Helmets, locks, pump, toolkit and map usually free of charge.

Watch the birdies

A nutrient-rich medley of sandbanks, mudflats and salt marsh makes the Camel Estuary a favourite spot for a wide variety of birds. Cycle the stretch of the Camel Trail between Padstow and Wadebridge at low tide for your best chance of sighting common waders like the little egret, curlew, heron and oystercatcher. During summer, shelduck young venture out onto the mudflats and occasionally fall prey to marauding peregrines. If you're really lucky, you might spot an osprey, spoonbill, or glossy ibis. Mute swans nest at several locations on the estuary, while kingfishers are more frequently seen further upriver.

Encourage tired legs with the promise of Granny Wobbly's fudge in Wadebridge or ice cream at Stein's Deli if you're Padstow-bound.

No need to get the hump – the section of the Camel Trail between Padstow and Wadebridge promises effortless cycling on a level track.

Out & about Northeast Cornwall

Big days out

For the Bodmin and Launceston area, see pages 60-67.

Cornish Birds of Prey Centre
Nr St Columb Major. See page 86.

Crealy Great Adventure Park
Nr Tredinnick. See page 84.

Screech Owl Sanctuary
Nr Indian Queens. See page 86.

Tintagel Castle
Tintagel, PL34 0HE, T 01840-770328, english-heritage.org.uk. Year-round daily from 1000. £5.90 adult, £3.50 child (5-15), £15.30 family.
Like St Michael's Mount (see page 114), a large part of Tintagel's appeal lies in its location – perched on surf-scoured cliffs where the only access is by a long flight of uneven steps and a dramatic footbridge. In fact, at Tintagel you won't find much of a castle at all. Crumbling walls are all that remain of the 13th-century fort. It's what Tintagel could have been, however, that puts a spring in the step of all who venture there.

The discovery of the inscribed sixth-century Artognou Stone fuelled tantalizing speculation that Tintagel was the birthplace of King Arthur – a great excuse for the riveting myths and legends recounted during summer by a local storyteller. You can also

delve into Tintagel's mysterious past at the excellent little visitor centre where a short film, *Searching for King Arthur*, turns "the forensic eye of archaeology on Arthur's bond with Tintagel".

Sorry kids, but the evidence is pretty scratchy. What you will find, having scaled the steps onto Tintagel Head, are the remains of a medieval castle built by Richard, Earl of Cornwall, between 1233 and 36 – some 500 years after the supposed reign of King Arthur.

None of this, however, detracts from the thrill of exploring the network of skeletal walls clinging to the clifftop or venturing inside Merlin's Cave (reached from the cove below). Interpretation boards reconstruct what life was like at Tintagel, while free quiz sheets challenge children to devise the best way to lay seige to the castle. There's also a beach café (see page 54) and a giftshop selling Arthurian nick-nacks, Callestick Farm ice cream and other local goodies.

Looking across the cove to Tintagel Castle, with Merlin's Cave at the base of the cliff. Above left: Exploring the ruins.

● Walk this way

Park in the free car park at St Materiana's Church (signposted from Tintagel village to Glebe Cliff), from where it's a fabulous 10-minute cliff-top walk to Tintagel Castle – by far the best way to appreciate the natural spectacle of the Atlantic-gnawed headland rearing 80 m above the sea.

About half a mile inland, Tintagel village will make short work of pocket money thanks to Merlin's Gifts, Granny Wobbly's Ice Cream Parlour and other irresistible temptations. Try to find time for the Old Post Office (see right) – a medieval yeoman farmhouse with a slate roof that 'heaves and rolls' like the sea. It's delightfully dingy and atmospheric inside.

It's what Tintagel could have been that puts a spring in the step of all who venture here.

More family favourites

Bude Castle Heritage Centre

Bude, EX23 8LG, T01288-357300, bude-stratton.gov.uk. Year round daily 1000-1600. £3.50 adult, £2.50 child (5-15), £10 family.
Small but captivating, this quirky museum covers everything from the geology of north Cornwall and the making of Bude Canal to shipwrecks, Civil War costumes and the inventions of 'forgotten genius' Sir Goldsworthy Gurney.

Museum of Witchcraft

The Harbour, Boscastle, PL35 0HD, T01840-250111, museumofwitchcraft.com. Easter-Hallowe'en Mon-Sat 1030-1800, Sun 1130-1800. £5 adult, £4 child.
Get face to face with 'horrible history', wise up on witchcraft and curses, peruse torture instruments (used for extracting confessions from witches) and meet Harry the tarred head.

Tintagel Old Post Office

Fore St, Tintagel, PL34 0DB, T01840-770024, nationaltrust.org.uk. Feb-Nov daily from 1100. £3.60 adult, £1.80 child (5-17), £9 family.
See Tintagel Castle, left.

Trevigue Wildlife Conservation

Trevigue, Crackington Haven, EX23 0LQ, T01840-230730, wild-trevigue.co.uk. Call for details.
Join a guided walk to learn how modern agriculture can co-exist with wildlife. Learn about shipwrecks and smuggling at Strangles Beach, watch badgers and bats and search for dormice. Luxury cottages also available.

Rain check

Cinemas

Cinedrome
Lanadwell St, Padstow, T01841-532344.

Rebel
Treskinnick Cross, Bude, T01288-361442.

Regal
The Platt, Wadebridge, T01208-812791.

Indoor play & amusements

Harlequinns Leisure
Stucley Rd, Bude EX23 8AR, T01288-355366, harlequinns.com. Weekends and school holidays daily 0930-2300. Huge indoor play zone for under-12s, ten-pin bowling, café.

Porteath Bee Centre
See page 53.

Indoor swimming pools

Budehaven Leisure Centre
Stratton Rd, Bude, EX23 8AW, T01288-353714.

Camelford Leisure Centre
Sportsmans Rd, Camelford, PL32 9UE, T01840-213188.

Dragon Leisure Centre
Lostwithiel Rd, Bodmin, PL31 1DE, T01208-75715.

Phoenix Leisure Centre
Coronation Park, Launceston, PL15 9DQ, T01566-772551.

Splash Leisure Pool
Stucley Rd, Bude, EX23 8AR, T01288-356191.

Wadebridge Leisure Centre
Bodieve Rd, Wadebridge, PL27 6BU, T01208-814980.

Museums

North Cornwall Museum
The Clease, Camelford, T01840-212954. Apr-Sep Mon-Sat 1000-1700. £2 adult, £1 child. Showcase for the old days, with exhibits on farming, wagon-making and other trades, as well as pottery, crafts and paintings.

Wonder Years Toy Experience
27 Queen St, Bude, T01288-359979, Year round, daily 1000-1700. Toys galore from the '60s-80s.

Sleeping Northeast Cornwall

Pick of the pitches

Cornish Coasts
Middle Penlean, Poundstock, EX23 0EE, T01288-361380, cornishcoasts. co.uk. Apr-Oct. £12-16/pitch, plus £3-4 extra adult, £2-3 extra child.

⚫ 🎏 🅿 🐕 🔥 ♿ 🛒 🚰 🍽

Quiet site with terraced pitches overlooking Widemouth Bay.

Lower Pennycrocker Farm
Nr Boscastle, PL35 0BY, T07967-605392, pennycrocker.com. Easter-Oct. £6 adult, £4 child.

⚫ 🎏 🔥 🐕 🚰

Close to Cornwall's highest cliffs, this small family-run campsite (with 40 pitches sheltered by wildlife-rich hedgerows) is located on a dairy farm, so no shortage of fresh eggs or milk.

Southwinds
Polzeath, PL27 6QU, T01208-862215, polzeathcamping.co.uk. Apr-Sep. £20-28/pitch.

⚫ 🎏 🅿 🐕 🔥 ♿ 🛒 🚰 🍽

Half a mile from the sea, Southwinds offers a peaceful (families and couples only) alternative to its sister site, Tristram, which is perched right above Polzeath's beach.

Upper Tamar Lake
Kilkhampton, Bude, EX23 9SB, T01288-321712, swlakestrust.org.uk. £13-16/pitch, camping pods from £35.

⚫ 🅿 🐕 🔥 ♿ 🚰

This slightly sloping site runs right down to the lake with its beach, pedaloes and watersports centre (see page 44).

Wooda Farm Park

⚫ 🎏 🅿 🐕 🔥 ♿ 🛒 🚰 🍽

Poughill, nr Bude, EX23 9HJ, T01288-352069, wooda.co.uk. Apr-Oct. £12-33/pitch (2 adults), plus £5-7 extra adult, £2.50-4.50 extra child (3-15). A holiday park with a rural twist, Wooda Farm has tractor rides, woodland walks, fishing, golf, archery and a mini-menagerie of chickens, goats and lambs. Some pitches have views of the coastline at Bude. There's a well-stocked shop and a bar serving home-cooked food. Facilities are top-notch – there are even private family bathrooms for hire and a new toddler play zone.

Wooda Farm.

⚫ Go glamping
Belle Tents (Owls Gate, Davidstow, Camelford, PL32 9XY, T01840-261556 belletentscamping.co.uk) adds comfort, style and a touch of theatre to camping with its stripy-topped belle tents – each one lavished with beds, duvets and furniture. Campfires add to the atmosphere and there's also a fully equipped kitchen tent.

Feel the sea breeze at
Southwinds, near Polzeath.

Pirate play at Sandymouth.

Holiday parks

Bossiney Bay
Nr Tintagel, PL34 0AY, T01840-770325, haulfryn.co.uk.
Smart country lodges and luxury cottages with hot tubs.

Hentervene Holiday Park
Crackington Haven, EX23 0LF, T01840-230365, hentervene.co.uk.
Peaceful park with lodges and caravans for hire.

Juliot's Well Holiday Park
Camelford, PL32 9RF, T01840-213302, juliotswell.com.
Rural setting with heated pool.

Little Bodieve Holiday Park
Wadebridge, PL27 6EG, T01208-812323, littlebodieve.co.uk.
Friendly family park with lots of facilities; close to Camel Trail.

St Minver Holiday Park
Nr Rock, PL27 6RR, T0844-335 3450, parkdeanholidays.co.uk.
Beautiful parkland setting, quality lodges and caravans, heated indoor pool and free kids' club.

Sandymouth Holiday Park
Nr Bude, EX23 9HW, T0800-717707, sandymouthbay.co.uk.
Coastal views, excellent facilities; located up a steepish lane from Sandymouth Bay.

Widemouth Bay Holiday Village
Bude, EX23 0DJ, T01288-362171, widemouthbayholidays.com.
Well-equipped chalets with views across the bay; indoor pool.

Cool & quirky

Cornish Tipi Holidays

Tregeare, Pendoggett, St Kew, PL30 3LW, T01208-880781, cornishtipiholidays.co.uk. Apr-Oct. From £485-1100/wk in tipis sleeping 3-7. Short breaks also available. Wild camping £15/adult, £7.50/child.

Tipis have popped up all over Britain, but not only was this the first site to add a touch of 'pow-wow' to camping holidays, it is arguably still the best. That probably has something to do with the setting – a 16-acre woodland surrounding a spring-fed quarry lake where kids can play real-life *Swallows and Amazons*: swimming, fishing, boating or simply watching the dragonflies whizz past. Then there's the tipi experience itself – ducking inside to flop on cosy rugs and rolling on to your back to gaze up at the 18-ft high cone of canvas and locally sourced poles, lashed together with twine and hessian and daubed with authentic Native American designs. There are 40 tipis here, sleeping up to 10 and arranged either in village fields (complete with totem poles) or tucked away in private clearings. Each one comes with its own cooking fire and woodpile. There's a gas stove for back-up (plus flush toilets and hot showers at either end of the site), but essentially this is no-frills, back-to-nature camping where, in the absence of electricity, tipis take on a warm, magical lantern glow at night. A friendly warden that lives on site will be able to point you in the direction of Port Isaac, 10 minutes' drive away.

Sleeping Northeast Cornwall

Cottages

Eastcliffe
Port Isaac, Pl29 3RN, T01208-880355, portisaaccottage.com. £350-900/wk.
Two-bedroom cottage with a terrace overlooking the harbour at Port Isaac. Parking is a bonus.

Gooseham Barton Cottages
Gooseham, Morwenstow, nr Bude, EX23 9PG, T01288-331204, gooseham-barton.com. Cottages (sleeping 4-7) £300-625/wk, farmhouse (sleeping 8-10) £600-1110.
Large traditional farmhouse and three cosy cottages on a 50-acre farm with its own stable offering riding in the Marsland Valley.

The Olde House
Chapel Amble, Wadebridge, PL27 6EN, T0844-7700 420, theoldehouse.co.uk. £380-1495/wk.
Wide choice of lovingly restored cottages (sleeping 2-8) on a 500-acre working farm with indoor pool and play barn, adventure playground, farm trail, bird hide, tennis courts and pets corner.

Penally Cottage
Boscastle, available from Classic Cottages, T01326-555555, classic.co.uk. £447-1170/wk.
Sleeping six, Penally is the first in a row of fishermen's cottages perched above Boscastle Harbour. Traditional features like wooden shutters and window seats haven't been compromised by a slick makeover, which includes a useful utility/shower room for post-beach wash-downs.

Trevathan Farm
St Endellion, nr Port Isaac, PL29 3TT, T01208-880248, trevathanfarm.com. 2- and 3-bedroom cottages £300-1100/wk, 4-bedroom cottage £520-1530.
Well-equipped cottages on a working farm just three miles from the sea. Lambs, bunnies and other cuddlies for the kids.

Wooldown Farm Cottages
Marhamchurch, nr Bude, EX23 0HP, T01288-361216, wooldown.co.uk. Call for rates.
Although half of the properties on this immaculate complex are luxury escapes for adults only, that leaves four family-friendly self-catering cottages sleeping up to eight. All come with stylish features like spa baths and four-poster beds.

Cottage agents
See also page 198.

Cornish Horizons
T01841-533331, cornishhorizons.co.uk.
Cottages in and around Padstow, Wadebridge and Newquay.

Harbour Holidays
T01841-533402, harbourholidays.co.uk.
150 properties in Padstow area.

Padstow Cottage Company
T01841-532633, padstowcottagecompany.co.uk.
Select group of over 40 cottages.

Gooseham Barton Farmhouse.

Port Isaac.

Best of the rest

Forda Lodges
Nr Kilkhampton, EX23 9RZ, T01288-321413, forda.co.uk. £345-1425/wk.
Ten Scandinavian-style lodges in a tranquil woodland setting with fishing lakes and indoor pool.

Hengar Manor Country Park
St Tudy, PL30 3PL, T01208-850382, hengarmanor.co.uk. Lodges £226-1574/wk, bungalows £163-734/wk, villas £226-1045/wk.
Wide range of accommodation, including smart, open-plan lodges, in 35 acres of landscaped gardens, woodland and lakes. Facilities include crazy golf, kids' club, adventure playground and indoor leisure complex.

Ivyleaf Combe Lodges
Stratton, Bude, EX23 9LD, T01288-321323, ivyleafcombe.com. Lodges (sleeping up to 6). Call for rates.
Timber lodges, some with hot tubs, tucked in a wooded valley.

Eating Northeast Cornwall

Carruan Farm
Polzeath, PL27 6QU, T01208-869584,
carruan.co.uk. Call for opening times.
Farm centre £1 adult, £3.50 child
(2-16), tractor tours £3.
Around 1000 Poll Dorset ewes
and 90 dairy cows – that's
the mainstay of Mike and
Clare Parnell's farm but, like
so many farmers, they've also
diversified into tourism with
tractor tours and play areas etc.
The Parnells stand out from
the herd, however, with their
superb restaurant which serves
breakfasts (including a Young
Farmer's Breakfast of sausage,
hash brown, baked beans and
egg), light lunches, cream teas,
homemade cakes and dinners.
Barbecues are held during the
summer, when special events
like sheep racing, storytelling,
sheepdog trials and bird of prey
handling are run alongside a
feast of lamb chops, burgers
and steaks. Carruan's farm shop
sells (and delivers) local goodies,
while The Farm Centre has a
soft play barn, go karts and an
indoor Big Bale Assault Course.

Market days
Bude Farmers' Market
Lower Wharf,
every other Friday 1000-1400.
Launceston Farmers' Market
St Mary's Hall, Friday 0930-1400.
Wadebridge Country Market
Town Hall, Thursday 0845-1230.

Dennis Knight
Fish Cellars, Port Isaac, PL29 3RB,
T01208-880498. Mon-Sat 0930-1300,
1400-1700.
With daily catches landed
straight into the cellars by the
slipway, fish simply doesn't
come any fresher. You'll also find
Just Shellfish here.

Ice cream
Decadent and delicious, Treleavens
(treleavens.co.uk) has an ice cream
shop in Tintagel, while Helsett Farm
in Boscastle churns out its own
organic ice creams and sorbets.

Porteath Bee Centre

St Minver, PL27 6RA,
T01208-863718,
porteathbeecentre.co.uk. Easter-Oct.
Try hive-fresh honey in fudge,
jams, ice cream or dripping
from the end of a spoon. And,
as if that wasn't a sweet enough
temptation, this busy little
centre has a Living Honey Bee
Exhibition (where you can peer
at beehives housed in glass-
fronted cabinets), a Winnie the
Pooh shop, a tea room serving
light lunches and cream teas
and a chance for children to
make their own beeswax rolled
honeycomb candles (£1).

St Kew Harvest Farm Shop
St Kew Highway, PL30 3EF, T01208-
841818, stkewharvest.co.uk. Tue-Sat
1000-1700 (café until 1600).
Vegetables are picked daily
from the field next to this
organic farm shop, which uses

Pick your own at Trevathan.

composted seaweed to enrich
the soil. You can also buy fresh
baked bread and cakes, smoked
bacon from Truro and free-range
chicken from Bude.

Trevathan Farm Shop
St Endellion, nr Port Isaac (on B3314),
T01208-880164, trevathanfarm.com.
Year round daily from 0900.
The pick of the bunch when
it comes to North Cornwall's
farm shops, Trevathan almost
warrants a day out in its own
right. For starters there is a
pick-your-own (raspberries,
strawberries, blackcurrants etc)
and a shop crammed with local
produce, including home-made
quiches, jams and chutneys,
farm-fresh bacon, sausages and
steak, Treleavens ice cream and
Cornish blue cheese. You could
easily buy everything you need
for a beach barbecue at nearby
Port Quin or Port Gaverne –
trouble is, Trevathan also has a
restaurant with a tempting array
of dishes, from Sunday roasts to
crab salads. The home-baked
cakes are a meal in themselves.
Outside, there's a picnic area,
playground, ride-on tractors, a
wicked zip slide and a collection
of rabbits, goats and wallabies
(see also page 34).

Eating Northeast Cornwall

Cabin Café

Crackington Haven, EX23 0JG
T01840-230238, cabincafe
crackington.co.uk. Summer daily.
Colourful and trendy, the Cabin
Café sells Kelly's and Callestick
ice cream and smoothies, plus
pasties (with local cliff-reared
beef), freshly baked cakes,
paninis, salads and cream teas.
There's a surf shop downstairs
offering wetsuits and boards for
hire. **Haven Café** (across the car
park) has fresh crab sandwiches,
cream teas and tasty dishes like
oak-roasted chicken.

Life's a Beach

Summerleaze Beach, Bude, EX23
8HN, T01288-355222, lifesabeach.
info. Dinner from 1900, ice cream
parlour and café open during the day.
The daytime menu here features
freshly baked baguettes and
bruschettas from £5, burgers
from £4.75, salads from £8.50,
plus various other snacks such
as cheesy nachos (£6.50) and
shell-on prawns (£8.50). It's
during the evening, however,
that this café/bistro really gets

Fish & chips

Port Isaac's **Takeaway** (T01208-
880281) fries cod and haddock
fresh from village fishermen. Also
recommended are **Barny's Fish &
Chip Restaurant** (Wadebridge),
**The Port and Starboard Café Fish
& Chip Shop** (Indian Queens) and
Peck Fish & Chips (Camelford).

its creative juices flowing. Main
courses are changed weekly,
but typically include local sirloin
steak (£20) and sublime seafood
dishes like prosciutto-wrapped
halibut with Cornish asparagus
and creamy mash (£19).

Nicki B's Deli & Bakery

Fore St, Port Issac, PL29 3RB,
T01208-880099.
Freshly made coffee, pasties,
cakes and local produce. The
Pea Pod, also in Port Isaac, is a
small deli offering pies, cakes,
sandwiches and baguettes
– just the job for picnic supplies.

Pilchard Cellar Café

National Trust Visitor Ctr, Boscastle,
T01840-250353, nationaltrust.org.uk.
Apr-Nov daily 1030-1700; Dec-Mar
daily 1100-1600.
Occupying a former pilchard
cellar where fish were packed
in salt, this busy café adjoins
the National Trust shop near
Boscastle's slipway. It serves
good-value snacks, such as
soups, sandwiches, pasties and
cakes. You can also pick up
children's picnic boxes. If you
want a more refined cream tea,
head to the quaint Harbour
Light Tea Gardens opposite.

The Strand Café

Beach Rd, Trebarwith, PL34 0HB,
T01840-779109, thestrandcafe.co.uk.
Easter-Sep 1000-1800.
Just yards from the stunning
beach at Trebarwith, The Strand
Café has a menu packed with

Trebarwith's beachside café.

bacon rolls, crab sandwiches,
salads, ciabattas, soups, burgers,
chips and cream teas – to eat
in or take away. Expect to pay
around £3 for a pasty or £10 for
a Cornish crab salad. Across the
road is the more basic Shop in
the Strand Café, where surfers
queue up for pasties followed
by fresh doughnuts dunked in
creamy hot chocolate.

Tintagel Beach Café

Tintagel Castle, T01840-772101,
english-heritage.org.uk.
Daily 1000-1730.
Located just above the cove
at Tintagel Castle, this popular
café has a small terrace with
views of King Arthur's legendary
stronghold. Standard café fare,
including sandwiches, soup,
baguettes, cakes, cream teas,
pasties and jacket potatoes,
are all available, along with
local specials such as crab
linguine and beer-battered
Port Isaac cod and chips with
home-made tartare sauce (both
around £8). Kids' meals include
fish goujons and shepherd's
pie. Work off the calories with
a jaunt on the coast path 2¼
miles to Trebarwith or 4½ miles
to Boscastle. The café sells
children's picnic boxes for £3.50.

The Waterfront Café Bar

Beach Rd, Polzeath, PL27 6SP, T01208-869655, waterfrontpolzeath. co.uk. Summer daily 0900-2300.
This excellent restaurant has a great selection of seafood – the platters are perfect for a family free-for-all and there's also a kids' menu. Dishes range from a £7.95 bowl of Porthilly mussels to a £19.95 sirloin steak, and there's everything inbetween, from crab sandwiches to home-made burgers. For informal beachside snacks, head to The Sandbar.

Also recommended
Antie Avice's Pasty Shop

St Kew Highway (next to Costcutter supermarket and garage).
Handy spot (just off the A39) to pick up a decent pasty.

Blue Tomato Café

Ferry Point, Rock, PL27 6LD, T01208-863841, bluetomatocafe. co.uk. Daily 0900-1700.
Bright and breezy café with mezze, pastas and some excellent burgers, including a butterbean and Tintagel smoked cheddar option.

King Arthur's Arms

Fore St, Tintagel, T01840-770831, kingarthursarms.co.uk. From 0900.
Family-friendly pub opposite the National Trust's Old Post Office.

The Castle Restaurant

Bude, T01288-350543. From 1000.
Coffee, lunch or dinner. Terrace overlooking Summerleaze beach.

Posh nosh

Elements Hotel Bistro

Marine Drive, Bude, EX23 0LZ, T01288-352386, elements-life.co.uk. Daily, food served from 1200.
Using locally sourced ingredients from Bude fishing boats and Cornish farmers, Elements prepares simple yet sophisticated food in a stunning location overlooking Widemouth Bay. Pick a window seat (or sit out on the terrace) and enjoy specials such as whole baked Megrim sole or lobster and king prawn spaghetti. There's also a good range of pizzas and pastas, from around £9, while desserts include gelato, cheesecake, Eton mess and panna cotta.

The Mill House Inn

Trebarwith, PL34 0HD, T01840-770200, themillhouseinn.co.uk. Daily.
Excellent gastropub with specials like pan-fried Trebarwith sea bass with lemon butter, fennel and wild rocket (£18.95). The bar menu (with kids' options) has more basic, cheaper meals, such as fish and chips.

Salt Water Café Bistro

Tristram Cliff, Polzeath, PL27 6TE, T01208-862333. Daily from 1145, children's menu served until 1900.
With a prime spot overlooking Polzeath Bay, friendly service and excellent food, the Salt Water Café Bistro has established itself among Cornwall's culinary elite. You won't taste better fish and chips anywhere, while more sophisticated seafood dishes, like the platter of smoked salmon, mackerel, pilchards and potted Newlyn Harbour crab, are always beautifully presented. The steaks and vegetarian mezze are also delicious.

Seven Bays Bistro

St Merryn, nr Padstow, T01841-521560, sevenbaysbistro.co.uk. Mon-Sat (plus Sun during school holidays) from 1830.
Seven Bays cooks up classic seafood dishes like fish pie, scallops and baked sea bass, as well as more daring concoctions with a Mediterranean twist. The pizzas are excellent.

The Slipway Hotel

The Harbour Front, Port Isaac, PL29 3RH, T01208-880264, portisaachotel.com.
As you'd expect with Port Isaac's fish cellars practically next door, the Slipway's menus are dominated by seafood. For dinner in the atmospheric oak-beamed restaurant, start with Cornish scallops or Porthilly mussels, followed by sea bass served with a crayfish and herb mousse. The lunch menu, served alfresco on the terrace, includes sandwiches and salads, as well as plenty of local favourites such as Cornish steak pasty, mussels with garlic, white wine and cream, grilled haddock and seafood tagliatelle.

Let's go to...

Padstow

This is not just fish and chips. This is a succulent fillet of cod gently fried in a thin, crispy coating of beef dripping and served with hand-cut potato chips, a wedge of lemon and home-made tartare sauce. This is Stein's Fish & Chips...

Will you taste the difference? Quite possibly. Rick Stein has liberally seasoned Padstow with his gastronomic flare, transforming a pilchard port at the mouth of the Camel Estuary into a mecca for foodies. As well as a posh chippie, the celebrity chef's culinary empire includes three restaurants, a deli and a patisserie. Cafés, bistros, bakers, fudge shops and ice cream parlours have turned the knot of streets around the harbour into the most concentrated source of calories (and pasty-toting tourists) in Cornwall.

There's more to Padstein than food though. Look beyond the batter and you'll find a charming old fishing port, historic buildings, great crabbing, an estuary teeming with wildlife and beaches that are more golden than one of Stein's hand-crafted chips.

Get your bearings

Padstow's quayside car parks fill up quickly, but there are two great ways to arrive here without driving. The **Black Tor Ferry** (T01841-532239, padstow-harbour.co.uk, daily from 0800, return fares £3 adult, £2 child) shuttles back and forth across the estuary to Rock (see page 42), while the **Camel Trail** (see page 46) connects Padstow with Wadebridge – a five-mile cycle ride (or walk) that you can use to compensate for your inevitable pasty binge. If you do drive to Padstow during peak season, use the park and ride.

Located on the north side of the harbour, the **Padstow Tourist Information Centre** (Red Brick Building, North Quay, PL28 8AF, T01841-533449, padstowlive.com) is chock-a-block with leaflets, while the nearby Harbour Shop is a handy place to buy beach gear or crab lines. The safest spot for crabbing is on the harbour slipway.

Walk north out of town to sandy estuary beaches (or catch the ferry to Rock and hike to

Nip to the lobster hatchery

National Lobster Hatchery
South Quay, Padstow, PL28 8BL, T01841-533877,
nationallobsterhatchery.co.uk. Daily from 1000.
£3.50 adult, £1.50 child (5-17), £7.50 family.
This quirky quayside attraction at the head of the
Camel Trail is good for nippers of both the curly-
haired and crustacean variety. Lobsters are hatched
and reared here before being released into the wild
to replenish stocks around Cornwall. You can peer
through portholes into the high-tech laboratory
where planktonic lobster larvae swirl about inside
giant glass cylinders, and tiny juveniles squat in
ice-cube size containers. It takes up to seven years for
them to reach maturity – if given the chance, lobsters
can live for 100 years and grow to nearly 2 m in
length! Dai the Claw is already halfway there. He's one
of the hatchery's resident lobsters, inhabiting a small
display of immaculate tanks, along with Charlie the
albino lobster, Thermidor the orange-coloured lobster
(a one-in-10-million occurrence), Sennen the spider
crab, Gordon the edible crab and a trio of sponge
crabs called Sponge Bob, Sponge Bill and Sponge
Bert. Crustaceans have never seemed so cuddly and
your children may never want to eat seafood again
(parents, meanwhile, will be drooling over the recipe
suggestion – grilled lobster with pernod and olive
oil dressing – that's been sneaked into the display).
Don't miss the rock-pool tank where domed glass
provides a magnified view of blennies, crabs and
anemones. There's also a small craft table with puzzles
and colouring sheets, some fun interpretation boards
about lobster life cycles and marine conservation, plus
a chance to adopt a lobster – a snip at just £2.50.

Stein's Fish & Chips
South Quay, Padstow, T01841-532700, rickstein.com.
Daily 1200-1500, 1700-2000.
You can eat in or take away at Stein's, but be prepared
to queue. Cod and chips costs £9.50 in the restaurant or
£7.85 in a box; children's cod bites and chips cost £6.25
eat-in, £5.25 takeaway. Is it worth it? You could save by
not splurging on the home-made tartare sauce (85p/
pot). The lemon wedge and, if you're lucky, a sprig of
parsley, are complimentary. Portions are a bit measly,
but the flavour really does set it apart. The batter is
thin and doesn't hit your stomach like a depth charge;
the fish is fresh and moist, and the chips, of course, are
proper spuds and not too soggy. Other seafood on offer
includes haddock, sea bream, tiger prawns and scallops.

Daymer or even Polzeath, see page 41). To hire
bikes for the Camel Trail, walk to South Quay,
where you will also find the **National Lobster
Hatchery** (see box opposite). The Elizabethan
manor and deer park at **Prideaux Place** (Padstow,
PL28 8RP, T01841-532411, prideauxplace.co.uk,
Easter-Oct Sun-Thu from 1230) is a short walk from
the harbour along Duke Street, Cross Street and
Fentonluna Lane.

Local celebrity – Dai the Claw.

Let's go to... Padstow

Retreat to a beach

Escape the harbour crowds by taking a low-tide stroll along the beaches that fringe the mouth of the Camel Estuary. To reach **St George's Cove** allow 20 minutes to walk from the quay, past the war memorial to the ruined Napoleonic fortifications at Gun Point where, at low tide, St George's extends to **Harbour Cove** and **Hawker's Cove**. Quite tricky to find, Hawker's Cove is just beyond the Old Lifeboat Station – a secluded, sandy haven for a picnic.

Take to the water

The 200-passenger **Jubilee Queen** (T07836-798457, padstowboattrips.com, Easter-Oct, check boards around harbour for rates and departures) explores offshore islands and potters upriver to Wadebridge on a high evening tide. Mackerel fishing boats include the **Celtic Warrior** (T01841-532639) and **Emma Kate** (T07970 595244), while **Padstow Speedboats** (T0781-111 3380, padstowboattrips.com, Easter-Oct daily, £6) offers 15-minute flits around the Camel Estuary. **Padstow Sealife Safaris** (T01841-521613, padstowsealifesafaris.co.uk, £39 adult, £25 child) runs two-hour tours in search of seals, dolphins, seabirds and basking sharks. See page 44 for details of the **Camel Ski School**. Padstow's nearest surf beaches are at Polzeath (see page 41) and Trevose Head (see page 74). See page 45 for surf schools.

Canvas & cottages

Overlooking the estuary, **Dennis Cove Camping** (Padstow, PL28 8DR, T01841-532349, denniscove campsite.co.uk, Apr-Sep, from around £18/pitch) is a small, sheltered campsite within easy walking or cycling distance of Padstow. For a more solid roof over your head, the **Padstow Cottage Company** (T01841-532633, padstowcottagecompany.co.uk) has a portfolio of over 40 cottages in and around the town, including Harbour's Reach – a four-bedroom cottage just 20 m from the water's edge.

Grab a bite

The ultimate Padstow snack – a hot, flaky (and award-winning) Cornish pasty fresh from the **Chough Bakery** (The Strand, PL28 8AJ, T01841-532835, cornishpasty.com, Mon-Sat 0900-1700) – is best nibbled while dangling your legs over the quayside. Try the Cornish beef and blue cheese one.

A diner offering simple, tasty food for breakfast, lunch and supper, **Custard** (The Strand, PL28 8AJ, T0870-1700 740, custarddiner.com, daily 0900-1500, 1900-2130) serves crab sandwiches and other local dishes. Padstow's best pizzas can be found at **Rojano's** (Mill Square, PL28 8AE, T01841-532796, rojanos.co.uk), while sweet options in the harbour area include **Roskilly's Ice Cream**, **The Fudge Shop** and **Stein's Patisserie**. If you just want to pick up a sandwich, pop into **Simply Sandwiches** or **Doorsteps Sandwich Shop**.

Heading out of town, **Padstow Farm Shop** (Trethellick Farm, PL28 8HJ, T01841-533060, padstowfarmshop.co.uk, Tue-Sat 1000-1600) sells locally reared meat, Cornish cheeses, seasonal vegetables, honey, jams, chutneys and ice cream.

In nearby St Merryn, **Fryer Tucks** (T01841-520724) is a popular chippie, while **Seven Bays Bistro** (see page 55) offers fresh Cornish cuisine with a Mediterranean zing. Also in St Merryn, Rick Stein is a happy tenant of **The Cornish Arms** (no reservations, Mon-Sat 1200-2100, Sun 1200-1800) serving British pub classics and Sunday roasts.

Padstow harbour.

SCALLOPS
£1 EACH.

GRADE 'A'
MUSSELS
(ST AUSTELL)
£5.0?

HAKE
FILLET £12.?

Stein's Deli
South Quay, Padstow, T01841-532700, rickstein.com.
Mon-Sat 1000-1700, Sun 1000-1600.
A gastronomic Aladdin's Cave, Stein's Deli is a feast for
the eyes, with fresh seafood and seasonal fruit and
vegetables arranged on counters like natural works
of art. There is also a good range of local meat (try
the lamb and mint sausages on your barbecue), lots
of preserves, a cookshop and a selection of luxury
Treleaven's ice cream. The Deli Kitchen Table offers soup,
quiche, cake and coffee. Anyone with a genuine sweet
tooth should make for Stein's Patisserie on Lanadwell
Street where the shelves are packed with cakes and
pastries. For a sit-down treat, visit Stein's Café or The
Seafood Restaurant. See page 57 for Stein's Fish & Chips.

HADDOCK £15.12/kg
FILLET

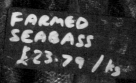

COD
£1?.?

FARMED
SEABASS
£23.79/kg

Let's go to...

Bodmin Moor

You can have too much of a good thing in Cornwall, so when you feel 'surfed out' or just yearn for a beach-free day that doesn't resort to an expensive family attraction, head inland to Bodmin Moor for walks, woods and wonderful views. You can go sailing on one of the moor's reservoirs or cycle the Camel Trail from Bodmin. The town's other attractions include a steam railway and historic jail, while the splendid manor house of Lanhydrock is nearby.

Get your bearings

Remember Bodmin Moor? It was that hilly bit with the wind turbines and speed cameras that slowed you down on the A30 as you rushed to get to your seaside bolthole. It's the one part of Cornwall that most visitors see, but few ever explore. That's a shame because, not only is this a wild and beautiful place, but it's easily accessed – not only from the bisecting A30, but also from the A390/ A38 (linking Callington, Liskeard and Bodmin) and the A39 (running between Bude and Wadebridge).

If you don't fancy venturing straight onto the moors, pop into the visitor centre in Bodmin's 19th-century Shire Hall for information on walks. This is also where you'll find the dastardly **Courtoom Experience** (join the jury in a Victorian murder trial) and **Town Museum** (Easter-Sep Mon-Fri 1030-1630, Sat 1030-1430, free) – an ideal combo for a rainy afternoon. Bodmin Library has storytelling and activities for under-fives every Wednesday at 1400, while the Dragon Leisure Centre (see page 49) has a heated indoor pool.

Walk in the woods

Signposted from the A38 between Bodmin and Liskeard, **Cardinham Woods** is managed by the Forestry Commission (T01594-833057, forestry.gov. uk). Four waymarked trails weave through a woodland of oak, rowan, alder, willow and beech, including the two-mile, 45-minute bike- and buggy-friendly Lady Vale Walk.

Remember Bodmin Moor? It was that hilly bit with the wind turbines and speed cameras that slowed you down on the A30 as you rushed to get to your seaside bolthole.

Rock fan – the granite tors of the Cheesewrings are a magnet to adventurous children.

Let's go to... Bodmin Moor

Woods Café, Cardinham.

This easy path follows a stream frequented by birds such as dippers, wagtails and kingfishers. You might also spot buzzards spiraling above the treetops or glimpse a deer tiptoeing through the dense undergrowth.

Wheal Glynn Walk (1 mile, 45 mins) involves a short strenuous climb from Lady Vale Bridge to a long-abandoned lead and silver mine where you can still spot the old engine house and chimney stack amongst the trees. Lidcutt Valley Walk (3½ miles, 2 hrs) is a long loop leading off the Lady Vale walk, with a picnic area at Scotch Pine, while the moderately strenuous Callywith Wood Walk (2½ miles, 1½ hrs) skirts a wildlife research area where dormice are being studied.

Off-road biking is also available in Cardinham Woods – choose from the moderate 12-km Bodmin Beast trail or two challenging red graded routes.

There is a picnic area and playground near the car park (£3/day) or you could treat yourself to soup, salad, sandwiches or a cream tea at the idyllic Woods Café. Summer events include bushcraft, wildlife detectives, fireside tales and bat-watching nights from around £6 child (free for accompanying adults).

Further east on the southern flanks of Bodmin Moor, **Golitha Falls National Nature Reserve** (T01726-891096, naturalengland.org.uk) is another shady woodland retreat that's popular with walkers. Several trails (including a buggy-friendly one) probe a steep-sided valley where the River Fowey tumbles and froths between ferns, fallen logs and moss-covered boulders – a hideout for woodland pixies if ever there was one.

Head for the hills

There are numerous walks on Bodmin Moor, but one of the most engaging for children is the 2½-mile **Cheesewring Trail**, which starts and finishes at the car park in Minions (signed 'The Hurlers').

To begin with, the easy path weaves across springy moorland pockmarked with tea-coloured pools and roamed by wind-tussled sheep and cattle. You'll soon reach a ring of standing stones with the higgledy-piggledy outcrop of Cheesewring Tor visible ahead. It's a short scramble through bracken before the impressive scale of these giant 'stone hamburgers' becomes clear. Adventurous kids will be bounding all over them, scrambling up their chiselled flanks and even reaching the top of one or two of the more accessible ones – arms spread wide, pretending to fly in the breeze. It's great fun, accessible, not too arduous, the views are tremendous and there's even a bit of geological and historical intrigue thrown in for good measure.

In Minions there's a tea room, shop and toilet, plus the Cheesewring Hotel – Cornwall's loftiest inn. Hurlers Halt offers B&B and self-catering, plus hot meals and cream teas.

Another high point for the kids, **Helman Tor** (Cornwall Wildlife Trust, T01872-273939, cornwallwildlifetrust.org.uk) was once a Neolithic hill fort and has far-reaching views towards Bodmin Moor's high-point, Brown Willy (417 m). A 13-km walking trail (download a leaflet from the wildlife trust's website) takes you through woodland and heath, following in the footsteps of Cornwall's mining pioneers..

Alternatively, make a beeline for **Bodmin Beacon**, a great spot to fly a kite in the shadow of the 44-m-tall obelisk raised in memory of Sir Walter Raleigh Gilbert, a distinguished officer of the British East India Company.

Top: Plain sailing at Siblyback Lake; steaming along on the Bodmin & Wenford Railway; pretending to fly at Cheesewring Tor. Middle: Woodland stream at Golitha Falls. Bottom: Cardinham Woods, standing stones at The Hurlers and a view from Bodmin Moor across the Tamar Valley.

Let's go to... Bodmin Moor

Get afloat

Siblyback Lake (Common Moor, PL14 6ER, T01579-346522, swlakestrust.org.uk) has a wide range of activities on offer. You can hire Canadian canoes, kayaks, windsurfers, rowing boats, sailing dinghies and pedaloes for £10-30/hour, enrol on a two-day RYA Junior Stages 1-4 sailing course (from £135) or stick to dry land with archery, high ropes and climbing. You can also hire bikes at Siblyback and tackle the family-friendly off-road cycle paths.

If that all sounds too energetic, Siblyback is also a lovely spot for a picnic with views across the lake and surrounding hills. Other facilities include a playground, tea room, shop and campsite.

Pitch your tent

The meadow campsite at **Siblyback Lake** (see above for contact details) is open April to October and has pitches for £13-16 (plus £4 for eelctric hook-up and/or hard standing).

Set on a 200-acre organic farm, the sheltered campsite at **South Penquite Farm** (Blisland, nr Bodmin, PL30 4LH, T01208-850491, southpenquite. co.uk, May-Oct, camping £8 adult, £4 child (5-16), yurts £250-390/wk) has solar-powered showers, family bathrooms and a children's play area. For a Mongolian twist try one of the four yurts (sleeping up to 5). Each has a wood-burning stove, rugs, futons and a roof light for star-gazing. Local burgers and sausages are available for your barbecues, while a lovely farm walk takes you to a Bronze Age settlement and ancient woodland.

Cosy up in a cottage

One of the best set-ups for families, **Bamham Farm Cottages** (Higher Bamham, Launceston, PL15 9LD, T01566-772141, bamhamfarm.co.uk. from around £400-1600/wk) is an attractive farm complex with seven cottages (sleeping 4-8), a 12-m indoor heated swimming pool, games room and play barn.

Another sound choice, **Glynn Barton Cottages** (Cardinham, PL30 4AX, T01208-821104, glynnbarton.co.uk, from around £580/wk for a 2-bedroom cottage) are a collection of beautifully restored 18th-century properties with light, contemporary interiors and lots of family-friendly features – from farm animals and a softplay barn to farm shop and indoor swimming pool.

Also try **Coombe Mill** (St Breward, PL30 4LZ, T01208-850344, coombemill.com) and **Mount Pleasant Farm** (nr Bodmin, PL30 4EX, T01208-821342, mountpleasantcottages.co.uk).

Refuelling

Collect your picnic supplies from **St Kew Harvest Farm Shop** (see page 53) and walk to Delphi Bridge, a secluded spot near the village of St Breward. Immortalized in Daphne du Maurier's novel, the legendary **Jamaica Inn** (Bolventor, PL15 7TS, T01566-86250, jamaicainn.co.uk) is open most days for breakfast, lunch and dinner and has the added attractions of a pirate museum and playground.

Siblyback Lake.

Lanhydrock.

Don't miss

Bodmin & Wenford Railway
Bodmin General Station, Bodmin, PL31 1AQ,
T01208-73555, bodminrailway.co.uk.
Mar-Dec. All-day rover tickets £12 adult,
£6 child (3-16), £33 family.
This six-mile train ride on Cornwall's only full-size
railway operated by steam locos links directly with
the Camel Trail (see page 46) at Boscarne Junction,
Cardinham Woods (see page 60) via a footpath from
Colesloggett Halt or Lanhydrock (see below) via a path
from Bodmin Parkway. Restored to 1950s nostalgia,
the main station is in Bodmin (Bodmin General), where
you'll find a souvenir shop and workshop viewing area.

Carnglaze Caverns
St Neot, PL14 6HQ, T01579-320251, carnglaze.com.
Year round Mon-Sat 1000-1700 (Aug till 2000).
£6 adult, £4 child, £17.50 family.
Join a 45-minute guided tour to a subterranean lake
deep within old slate-mining caves.

Lanhydrock
Nr Bodmin, PL30 5AD, T01208-265950, nationaltrust.
org.uk. Garden year round daily from 1000;
house Mar-Nov Tue-Sun from 1100.
£11 adult, £5.45 child (5-17), £27.50 family.
A magnificent estate with vast grounds and an
imposing gatehouse, the interior of Lanhydrock itself
is surprisingly unpretentious and reflects the day-
to-day – albeit very wealthy – lifestyle of a Victorian
family. Children can follow a quiz trail to explore the
50-odd rooms which include a nursery and the servants
quarters 'below stairs'. Craft activities are held in the old
stables across the courtyard from the café, while paths
weave through park and woodland to the banks of the
River Fowey (keep your eyes peeled for otters). Back
near the car park there's a woodland play area.

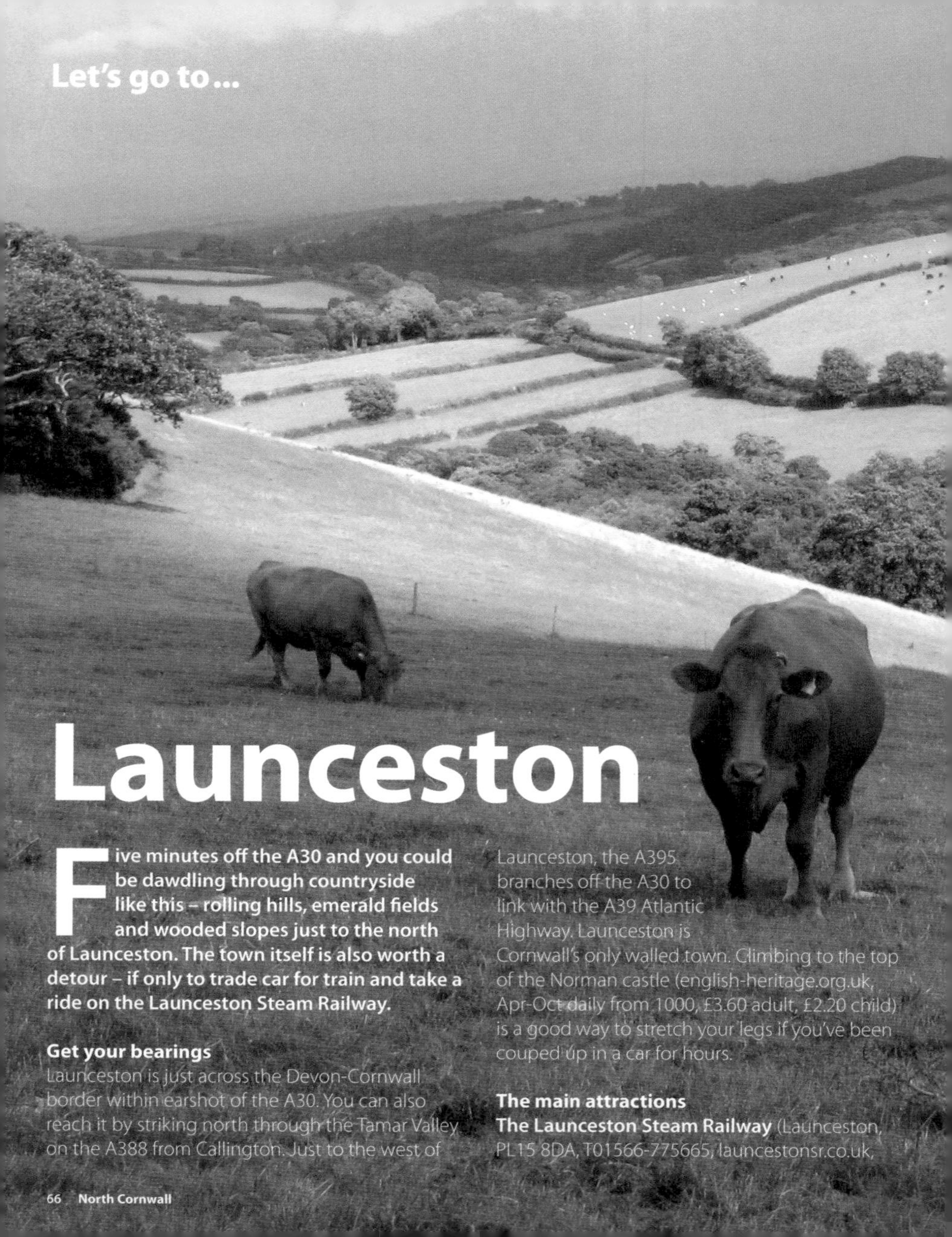

Launceston

Five minutes off the A30 and you could be dawdling through countryside like this – rolling hills, emerald fields and wooded slopes just to the north of Launceston. The town itself is also worth a detour – if only to trade car for train and take a ride on the Launceston Steam Railway.

Get your bearings

Launceston is just across the Devon-Cornwall border within earshot of the A30. You can also reach it by striking north through the Tamar Valley on the A388 from Callington. Just to the west of Launceston, the A395 branches off the A30 to link with the A39 Atlantic Highway. Launceston is Cornwall's only walled town. Climbing to the top of the Norman castle (english-heritage.org.uk, Apr-Oct daily from 1000, £3.60 adult, £2.20 child) is a good way to stretch your legs if you've been couped up in a car for hours.

The main attractions

The Launceston Steam Railway (Launceston, PL15 8DA, T01566-775665, launcestonsr.co.uk,

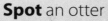

Spot an otter

Tucked away in beautiful rolling countryside, the Tamar Otter & Wildlife Centre is just a few miles north of Launceston and makes a welcome diversion off the relentless A30. You'll see two types of otter here – European and Asian short-clawed. Both are shy and secretive, so try to visit during feeding times (1200 and 1500), when keepers do their rounds of the enclosures, handing out offcuts of cod from local fish and chip shops and offering titbits of information on each otter's life history. The otters emerge from their hiding places, chattering excitedly, squirming like eels in their pools and pestering the keepers for food. Peacocks, guineafowl and geese amble around the park and there are also various owls and hawks in aviaries. You can attempt to hand-feed fallow deer and wallabies on a woodland walk – and even spot Scottish wildcats (part of a reintroduction project). The centre has a café, gift shop and picnic area.

Tamar Otter & Wildlife Centre
North Petherwin, Launceston PL15 8GW, T01566-785646, tamarotters.co.uk. Apr-Oct daily 1030-1800. £7.50 adult, £4 child (3-15), £20 family.

European otter.

Easter and Oct half term, plus May-Sep Sun-Fri, from 1100, £9.50 adult, £6.20 child, £27 family) operates narrow gauge steam locos through the Kensey Valley back and forth to **New Mills Farm Park** (Launceston, PL15 8SN, T01566-777106, newmillsfarmpark.com, Easter-Sep 1030-1700, £3). You can also reach New Mills by car (not nearly as much fun). Once there, kids can get stuck into good-value food at the Hungry Farmer Café before running riot in the indoor/outdoor play areas.

Three miles west of Launceston, there's more fun and games at **Trethorne Leisure Park** (Kennards House, PL15 8QE, T01566-86324,

trethorneleisure.com, Feb-Nov daily from 1000, from £6.50) – one of Cornwall's biggest play zones with a huge amount to do whatever the weather.

Nearby, at **Hidden Valley Discovery Park** (Tredidon, PL15 8SJ, T01566-86463, hiddenvalleydiscoverypark.co.uk, Apr-Oct 1000-1700, £8.95 adult, £7.95 child (5-15), £30 family) you can explore the secret passageways of the Forbidden Mansion, solve clues on a Crystal Maze style adventure trail, step inside a Hobbit House, ride a miniature railway through the beautiful grounds of the park, get lost in the Beech Maze and then relax in Mrs Sproggett's Tea Room.

Main photo: The white stuff –
shark biscuit at Gwithian Sands.
Opposite: The last stand at Treyarnon
Beach; sailing at Stithians Lake.

Northwest Cornwall

It doesn't matter if you're shark biscuit (surf speak for bodyboarder), a grommet (young surfer) or a macker-carving dude (someone pretty good cutting smooth turns on big waves), the northwest coast is Cornwall's surf central, with fantastic beaches almost non-stop from Trevose Head to the Hayle Estuary.

Newquay hogs the limelight. It's one of Europe's premier surf spots with legendary Fistral Beach hosting international competitions. The sprawling resort is awash with teenage surf heads lured by a frothy cocktail of Atlantic breakers, alcopops and nightclubs. But don't let Newquay's brash reputation put you off. There are plenty of quiet family beaches here, while attractions like the Blue Reef Aquarium and Newquay Zoo top the must-do lists of most children. New developments are driving the resort up-market, while Newquay's airport ensures that the resort remains well and truly on the map.

It's not without stiff competition though. A few miles to the north, **Watergate Bay** comes up trumps for many families, thanks to its superb beach, adrenaline-charged Extreme Academy and family-friendly hotel – not to mention the culinary delights of Jamie Oliver's Fifteen restaurant.

Further north still, **Mawgan Porth** has the Bedruthan Steps Hotel (about as family-orientated as they come) and is close to both the Crealy Great Adventure Park and the spectacular beach at Bedruthan Steps (where adventures are inspired by nature). More sandy beaches fringe the granite headland of **Trevose Head**, near Padstow, where you can learn to surf at sheltered Harlyn Bay or run wild in the dunes at Constantine while the Atlantic beats its steady thunder on the rocky reefs offshore.

Six miles south of Newquay, **Holywell Bay** is another sensational, dune-backed beach with the added family appeal of a fun park. **Perranporth** is a busy resort, while **St Agnes** – or 'Aggie' – spills down to pretty Trevaunance Cove in a tumble of rose-clad cottages, galleries and cafés.

Porthtowan has a thriving surf scene and one of the region's most hip beach cafés, in contrast to the quieter beach at **Portreath**. Continue south past this former mining port and you enter a spectacular stretch of National Trust coastline, dramatic cliffs finally bowing to the stoic little lighthouse at **Godrevy Head**, where several miles of glorious beach curl west along broad St Ives Bay.

Here to there

The Northwest Cornwall chapter of *Cornwall with Kids* covers the Atlantic shoreline from Trevose Head to St Ives Bay, including beaches as far west as Hayle. For Carbis Bay and the beaches of Porthminster and Porthmeor, see the section on St Ives (page 122). Inland, Northwest Cornwall coverage extends roughly to the A39/A30 and south beyond Redruth to Stithians Lake. The Coast-to-Coast cycle trail between Portreath and Devoran is also covered in this chapter (see page 80). For Truro, see page 194.

Trevose Head – St Ives Bay

N

2 km
2 miles

You must

1 Learn to surf at Harlyn Bay.

2 Cycle the Portreath Tramroad through Cornwall's World Heritage mining site.

3 Follow in a giant's footsteps at Bedruthan Steps.

4 Run wild and get wet at Crealy Great Adventure Park.

5 Count seals at Godrevy Point.

6 Talk to the animals at Paradise Park.

7 Scoff Jamie Oliver's pasta at Fifteen.

8 Get savvy with surf and beach safety at Lusty Glaze beach, Newquay.

9 Sail a dinghy at Stithians Lake.

10 Sprint across the vast sands at Perranporth or Holywell Bay.

Pentire Point
Padstow
Bay Pola
Trebeth
Hawkers
Cove
Mother
Ivey's Bay
Harlyn
Bay
Trevone
Bay
Trevone
Crugmeer
Padst
C
Es
Trevose Head
Constantine Bay
Treyarnon Bay
Constantine
Bay
Trevone
St Merryn
Treyarnon Shop
A389
Little
Petheri
Porthcothan Beach
Porthcothan
Penrose
St Isse
Rumford
Tred
Park Head
St Ervan
Crealy Great
Adventure Park
4
3 Bedruthan Steps
Trenance
St Eval
A3274
Cornish B
of Prey Ce
Berryl's Point
Mawgan Porth
St Mawgan
Trevarrian
Talskiddy
A39
Watergate
Bay
7
Tregurrian
St Colum
Major
Newquay
Bay
8
Newquay
Newquay
Porth
A3059
St Columb Minor
Trebudannon
Fistral Bay
Crantock
Beach
Pentire
Blue Reef
Aquarium
Mountjoy
Screech
Sanctu
Porth Joke
West Pentire
Gannell
Estuary
Newquay
Zoo
Quintrell
Downs
A392
St Columb
Road
A
10 Holywell Bay
Crantock
Kestle Mill
A3058
Dairyland
Farm World
Indian Que
Penhale Point
Holywell
Holywell Bay
Fun Park
Lappa Valley
Railway
Gummow's
Shop
Fraddon
Retew
Trevi
Penhale Sands
Cubert
St Newlyn
East
Ligger or
Perran Bay
Mount
A3076
Summercourt
Treti
Perranporth Beach
Rejerrah
A3075
Newlyn
Downs
Mitchell
Brighton
A30
St Ste
Perranporth
Goonhaven
Carland
Cross
Trevaunance
Cove
Bolingey
B3285
Perranzabuloe
Zelah
New Mills
B3275
St Agnes Head
Trevellas
Mithian
Callestick
St Allen
A39
Trispen
St Erme
Ladock
Trelassick
Chapel Porth
St Agnes Museum
St Agnes
B3284
Marazanvose
A30
Allet
Probus
Grampo
Porthtowan Beach
Goonbell
Mount
Hawke
B3277
Shortlanesend
Tresillian
A390
Tresawle
Trego
Porthtowan
Three Burrows
Mawla
Blackwater
Kenwyn
Truro
Godrevy
Lighthouse
Navax
Point
Hell's
Mouth
Portreath
Feadon Farm
2
Treasure
Park
Chacewater
Scorrier
Threemilestone
Malpas
St Michael
Penkevil
Ruan
Lanihorne
A3078
Godrevy
Towans
5
B3301
Illogan
Coast to Coast Cycle Route
Twelve
Heads
Baldhu
A39
Playing
Place
Lamorran
Gwithian
Towans
Roscroggan
Cornish Mines
& Engines
Redruth
St Day
Bissoe
Carnon
Downs
Treworga
Veryan
Gwithian
Kehelland
Pool
Carnbrea
Carharrack
Trelissick
Philleigh
Connor
Downs
Cambourne
Mineral
Tramways
Lanner
Gwennap
Devoran
Feock
Treworlas
Carne
Phillack
Roseworthy
Carnkie
A393
Perranarworthal
Trewithian
Gerrans
Bay
Copperhouse
B3303
Troon
Four Lanes
Penhalvaen
Mylor Bridge
Hayle
6
Paradise Park
Barripper
Carnhell Green
9
Stithians
Lake
Stithians
Ponsanooth
Burnthouse
B3280
B3297

From top left: kite flying at Constantine Bay; beach lifeguard on patrol at Gwithian Sands; bucket of crabs; Gwithian Towans; surfing at Harlyn Bay; living jewels in a Portreath rock pool; getting the sand and sea between your toes at Watergate Bay.

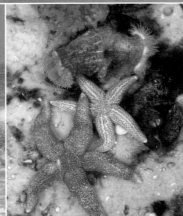

Out & about Northwest Cornwall

Fun & free

Fly a kite
The strongest gust ever recorded at a low-level site in England was at Gwennap Head, the most southerly headland on Cornwall's Penwith peninsula, where wind speeds reached 118 mph on 15 December 1979 (tip: don't pitch your tent here). The coast of Cornwall is officially the windiest place in England, which also makes it prime kite-flying territory. On the northwest coast unwind your strings at beaches like **Gwithian**, **Perranporth** and **Watergate Bay**.

Watch the birdies
During spring and autumn the **Hayle Estuary RSPB Reserve** is a magnet for migrant waders and gulls, while in summer you may be lucky enough to spot an osprey. It's winter, however, that really sees the estuary getting all of a flutter as up to 18,000 birds (from lapwings to teals) descend on the mudflats.

Run wild in the dunes
The sand dunes at **Constantine Bay** on Trevose Head are scribbled with paths – an open invitation to a picnic and a mega-game of hide and seek.

> I've lived in Cornwall for over 20 years. I came here on holiday and married a Cornish girl. Portreath is my favourite beach – it's good for swimming and has rock pools full of wildlife. For something fun and free, take a field guidebook to one of the Cornwall Wildlife Trust's nature reserves – they're all over the county and you'll learn loads. My top three places to see wildlife are Godrevy for seals, Portreath's North Cliffs for peregrine falcons and Gwithian Towans for adders. As for the best fish and chips in Cornwall – it has to be Mac's Fish Bar, 9 Higher Fore St, Redruth.

Gary Zammit
Wildlife ranger, Feadon Farm, Gwel an Mor, nr Portreath, T01209-842354, gwelanmor.com.

Keep your eyes (and ears) open for the Gannel Crake, a mysterious creature whose terrible cry echoes across Newquay's Gannel Estuary.

Spot a seal
Walk to **Godrevy Head**, find a safe place to sit on the cliffs and train your binoculars on the rocky shore below. Grey seals can often be seen 'spy-hopping' or squirming in the surf.

Delve into Cornish history
A little gem, **St Agnes Museum** (Penwinnick Rd, T01872-553228, stagnesmuseum.org.uk, Easter-Oct daily 1030-1700) covers everything from fishing and folklore to tin mining and turtles.

Visit Tehidy Country Park

Why? Sometimes you just feel like a change from the beach. Carpeted in bluebells during spring, this woodland oasis is bursting with wildlife. Stroll the pushchair-friendly Pink Trail around North Cliffs and you will discover majestic beech trees over 200 years old. Tehidy was formerly the estate of the Bassett family, which developed Portreath as a port for exporting tin ore. The easy Purple Trail loops around ornamental lakes near the Bassett mansion.

Where? From the A30, take the Pool exit and follow brown tourist signs. The Mineral Tramways cycle trail (see page 80) also passes through the park.

How? Visitor Centre & Café daily during summer 1000-1700, winter Tue-Sun 1000-1600. Cornwall County Council, T0300-1234 202, cornwall.gov.uk.

Hell & back

The B3301 between Portreath and Hayle condenses everything that is fabulous about Cornwall's coast into a few miles. Dawdle and stop often. There's a small car park at Hell's Mouth Café where, after crossing the road, you are just a few steps from dizzy cliff-top views of smugglers' coves and rocky islets wrapped in filigrees of surf. Fulmars pirouette on updraughts, basking sharks tack back and forth through turquoise waters, while flowers – thrift in spring, heather in summer – blush the cliffs pink. A little further on, the road unravels from the cliff tops; a right-hand turn leads past surfing bays and a string of sandy coves to Godrevy Head and its offshore lighthouse.

Out & about Northwest Cornwall

The beaches described here are found east to west, from Trevose Head to the Hayle Estuary. For St Ives' beaches, see pages 124-127.

Trevone Bay

Just two miles west of Padstow, Trevone is a small sandy bay that's popular with families and surfers. Walk up on to the cliffs to the north and you can peer into Round Hole – the result of a collapsed sea cave roof.

Harlyn Bay

Tucked into the lee of Trevose Head, Harlyn Bay is often sheltered when west-facing beaches are being pummelled by breakers. A perfect family beach, it has gorgeous golden sand, shallow streams to dam, a surf school and snack bar.

Mother Ivey's Bay

Overlooked by two caravan parks (Harlyn Sands and Mother Ivey's – see page 89), this beautiful bay faces northeast and, like Harlyn Bay, is a sheltered option for young families. The Padstow lifeboat station is at the far end of the beach, but there are no facilities (unless you're staying at one of the caravan parks), so you will need to park at Harlyn Bay and walk 20 minutes or so along the coast path.

Booby's & Constantine Bay

South of Trevose Head (where you can walk along the cliffs to the lighthouse), the beaches feel the full brunt of the Atlantic and take on a more rugged appearance. Booby's is the first – and probably the least family-friendly – in a long string of spectacular sandy beaches extending all the way to Newquay and beyond. Rocky reefs and strong currents make swimming dangerous at Booby's, but at low tide the beach merges with Constantine where you're as likely to hear the piping of oystercatchers as the scream of excited children surfing, flying kites or running wild across acres of pristine sand. Parking and facilities are located at the Constantine end of the bay.

Treyarnon Bay

A popular surf beach south of Constantine Bay, Treyarnon has a mixture of sand and rocky outcrops. Be wary of strong currents. There's a Snak Attak beach bar in the car park and a good choice of accommodation nearby, including the Treyarnon Youth Hostel (see page 88).

Porthcothan

A narrow wedge of sand backed by dunes, Porthcothan has decent surf, but take care at low

tide when dangerous currents can whip around the headlands.

Bedruthan Steps

Cornwall's very own Twelve Apostles, Bedruthan Steps might not be quite on the scale of Australia's natural wonder, but it is still an impressive beach, dominated by gnarled sea stacks. Be warned, though, that not only is access via a very steep flight of steps, but

View from the top – Bedruthan Steps.

swimming is dangerous due to strong currents. A fine beach to explore, but be alert to tides as it's easy to get cut off. There's a National Trust car park with shop and tea room at Carnewas. Paths lead from here across flower-speckled cliff tops to a vantage point overlooking the beach.

Mawgan Porth

A shark-fin-shaped wedge of sand between Bedruthan Steps and Watergate Bay, Mawgan Porth is a favourite spot for swimmers and surfers, but usually remains less crowded than beaches further south. There is easy access to the beach, with toilets and parking nearby. The family-friendly Bedruthan Steps Hotel (see page 90) is perched above.

Watergate Bay

This glorious stretch of surf-raked coast sees stylish Cornwall riding the crest of a wave. Not only is it home to Jamie Oliver's Fifteen restaurant (see page 93), but the upmarket Watergate Bay Hotel (see page 90) and adrenaline-charged Extreme Academy (see page 82) also preside over its two-mile stretch of pristine sand. Watergate Bay is not a particularly pretty beach – there are no interesting nooks and crannies and it's backed by crumbling cliffs that march

Towans Beach – Newquay

austerely northwards – but it is one of those run-wild-and-free Atlantic beaches that are a signature of north Cornwall. The B3276 loops down to the beach at the Watergate Bay Hotel and a car park that backs onto the main beach complex – a grandstand-style building that houses the excellent Beach Hut and Venus Café (see pages 92-93) as well as Fifteen. You certainly won't go hungry at Watergate Bay. Burning off calories shouldn't be a problem either – the Extreme Academy organizes surf lessons, there are trampolines set up by the lifeguard station and you can also try your luck at kite surfing. Newquay's attractions, meanwhile, are just a few miles away across the bay.

Porth Beach

Practically a northern suburb of Newquay, Porth is a busy coastal resort with several good hotels. The beach has a good-size swathe of sand even at high water. When the tide ebbs, it's sometimes possible to walk around the headland into neighbouring Lusty Glaze beach. A wide stream flows along the northern edge of Porth beach, which is bordered by Porth Island – connected to the mainland by a footbridge and the site of an Iron Age settlement. Smugglers' caves near the base of the island are

well worth exploring at low tide when Whipsiderry beach (just to the north of Porth) is revealed.

Newquay

From east to west, Newquay's main town beaches are **Lusty Glaze**, **Tolcarne**, **Great Western** and **Towan** – all four merging into a continuous ribbon of sand at low tide. From quiet pilchard fishing village to bustling (some would say rowdy) holiday resort, Newquay has everything from holiday parks and plush apartments to boat trips and attractions like the Blue Reef Aquarium and Newquay Zoo (see pages 84-85). And then, of course, there's the surf. Located on the town's western outskirts, Fistral, see below, is Newquay's prime spot for serious wave-riding. Try the more sheltered town beaches if Fistral is too fiesty. Not only are they ideal for novice surfers, but they are also good, albeit frequently crowded, family beaches. As well as surfing lessons, Lusty Glaze Adventure Centre (see page 81) runs a Junior Baywatch programme of basic surf rescue techniques and beach safety for children aged eight to 14. Tucked next to the harbour, Towan is usually the most sheltered of the town beaches and also has excellent facilities: a sound choice for young families. Tolcarne and Lusty Glaze have a dog ban, May to September.

Out & about Northwest Cornwall

Fistral Beach

If the surf's up, Fistral will be packed. Europe's most famous surfing beach, this iconic strip of sand is located just to the west of Newquay's Towan Head. Fistral has probably the most reliable surf of any beach in Cornwall with waves typically peaking at around 4 to 8 ft. South Fistral tends to be more protected than the northern end of the beach, where large barrelling waves can develop at low tide. With big swells and a southeast offshore breeze, Fistral's legendary Cribbar (a monster wave reaching up to 30 ft in height) pounds the reefs off Towan Head. Located right on the beach, the International Surf Centre at Fistral is a surfer's paradise – book a surf lesson or watch the action from the comfort of the Blu Bar.

Crantock Beach

Located at the mouth of the Gannel Estuary, Crantock has plenty of sand and dunes (ideal for beach games and a picnic), but swimming is dangerous due to strong currents. During summer, a ferry runs to the beach from near the Fern Pit Café on Pentire Head.

Porth Joke

Tiny Porth Joke (or 'Polly Joke') is wedged between West Pentire and Kelsey Head. A lovely little cove with good surf – but no facilities and a 15-minute walk from the car park.

Holywell Bay

Just three miles down the coast from Newquay, this large sandy beach is given a family-friendly boost by the nearby fun park (see page 84), which features a range of pay-as-you-play attractions, such as F1 Carts and Adventure Golf. The main access to the beach follows a shallow stream (great for sailing boats or paddling) or you can hit the sands by following paths through the dunes. There's plenty of space at Holywell Bay, even at high tide. One of the highlights of the beach, however, is only accessible at low tide when you can walk to a sea cave at the northern end of the bay. Venture inside (with a torch and an eye on the tide) and you'll find a terrace of rock pools filled by water seeping through multicoloured rocks – a 'holy well' renowned for its healing qualities.

Perranporth

At low tide, Perran Bay is fringed by three miles of surf-scoured beach, from dune-backed **Penhale Sands** and **Perran Sands** in the north to the lively resort town of Perranporth where the main street is crammed with beach shops, cafés and amusement arcades. Stranded at low water, a small island known as Chapel Rock (in front of the main beach) has a natural sea pool that will appeal to littl'uns in search of a calmer alternative to Perranporth's surf. There are also rock pools and caves at the base of nearby cliffs.

Trevaunance Cove

A small cove hemmed in by cliffs at St Agnes, Trevaunance is pebbly at high tide, but reveals sand and rock pools as the water recedes. Surfing is good, and there's a small car park near the Breakers Beach Café.

Chapel Porth

Sharing over a mile of sand with Porthtowan at low tide, Chapel Porth shrinks to a small, secluded cove at high water. The cliff tops are littered with tin mining ruins, including the chimney stack of Wheal Coates.

Porthtowan

A popular surfing beach with easy access and good facilities, Porthtowan has a surf school, board hire, a well-stocked beach shop and the trendy Blue Beach Bar (see page 92). The beach is backed by a small area of dunes, behind which you'll find a sandy playground. Check out the rock pools either side of the bay.

Portreath

An interesting beach with a harbour at one end (built to serve the mining industry in the 18th century) and wild cliffs riddled with caves at the other, Portreath is a mixture of sand and shingle with rock pools and a natural swimming pool by the pier. Park by the beach where you'll find cafés and a surf shop.

Hayle Sands

Hayle Sands is the collective name for the beaches stretching three miles from Godrevy Point to the Hayle Estuary. Approaching from the east, the B3301 skirts dramatic cliffs at Hell's Mouth (see page 73) before dropping down to St Ives Bay. A right turn leads to a National Trust car park and the excellent Godrevy Café (see page 92). Stretching away to the south are the unblemished, surf-strafed sands of **Gwithian Towans** and **Hayle Towans** (also accessible across dunes and from various holiday parks further south). Continue past Godrevy Café towards the lighthouse and the coastline becomes rockier and more varied, with secluded coves that are wonderful for swimming, snorkelling and kayaking in calm conditions. And, as is so often the case with Cornish beaches, it just gets better and better as the tide goes out.

Guiding light – Godrevy.

Out & about Northwest Cornwall

Action stations

Boat trips
Padstow boat trips: see page 58.

Newquay boat trips
South Quay, Newquay, T01637-878886, newquay-harbour.com.
May-Sep daily 1000-1800. £6.
One- or two-hour cruises aboard the 12-passenger *Kernow Belle*, *Tamarisk* or *Island Maid*, with a chance to spot seals and catch mackerel. Speedboat trips are also available.

Cycling
Coast to Coast Trail
Linking historic mining harbours on the north coast (Portreath) and south coast (Devoran), this 11-mile route follows the old Portreath tramroad (worked by horses as early as 1812) and the Redruth and Chasewater Railway line, built in the 1820s to transport copper ore from Gwennap to Devoran. Weaving through ancient woodland and heathland, the scenic trail is largely off-road and surprisingly level. You can also embellish your ride with various loops on the newly extended network of Mineral Tramways. See below for routes and cycle hire companies.

Mineral Tramways
Whether you choose to cycle, walk or ride a horse, this network of trails, centred around Camborne and Redruth, provides mainly level, traffic-free access to one of Cornwall's historic mining regions. There are 30 miles of track in total – several linking with the Coast to Coast Trail (see above). Options include the 7½-mile Great Flat Lode Trail, the 2½-mile Tehidy Trail (through Tehidy Country Park) and the 5½-mile Portreath Branchline Trail (a useful link between Portreath and the Great Flat Lode Trail).

Bike Chain Bissoe Bike Hire
Old Conns Work, Bissoe, TR4 8QZ, T01872-870341, cornwallcyclehire.com. Year round daily from 0930. Adult bike £13-15/day, child's bike £8-12/day, tag-a-long £10/day. Located towards the southern end of the Coast to Coast Trail, Bissoe Bike Hire has a café and good range of bikes.

Cornwall Cycle Trails
Elm Farm Cycle Centre, Cambrose, Portreath, TR16 5UF, T01209-891498, cornwallcycletrails.com. Year round daily from 1000. Bikes from £15, child trailers and tag-a-longs £5. The main cycle hire centre for the Coast to Coast Trail and Mineral Tramways, Elm Farm offers guided rides and children's activity packs, as well as a picnic area, farm shop and children's play area.

Cycling: dirt track
The Track
Parc Erissey Industrial Estate, New Portreath Rd, Redruth TR16 4HW, T01209-211073, the-track.co.uk.

Daily during school hols 1100-1800. Dirt bike track with ramps and jumps for all ages and abilities.

Go karting
St Eval Kart Circuit
St Eval, Wadebridge, PL27 7UN, T01637-860160, cornwallkarting.com. Sat 0930-dusk, Mon-Fri call for details. Infant £1/2 mins, Cadet kart £8/10 mins, Junior kart £10/10 minutes, Thunderkart £15/10 mins.
Unleash the Sebastian Vettel in your three-year-old at this supremely child-friendly go-karting circuit with a 1.3-km all-weather track. Electric karts are suitable for kids aged three to six. Cadet Karts (for seven- to 11-year-olds) can top 20 mph, while Junior Karts (12- to 15-year-olds) push the needle to a thrilling 35 mph. Big boys (and girls), meanwhile, can play at being Stig in 70-mph Thunderkarts (16+).

Horse riding
Chiverton Riding Centre
Silverwell, TR4 8JQ, T01872-560471. Daily 0800-2200, call for details. Pony Club-approved school near St Agnes, with indoor and

outdoor facilities, and a lot going on for children, such as introduction to ponies courses and stable and grooming days.

Cornish Riding Holidays

Wheal Buller Riding School, Buller Hill, Redruth, TR16 6SS, T01209-211852, cornishridingholidays.co.uk. Year round, call for details of lessons. This family-run horse-riding centre has lessons available most days (minimum age four). Rides and hacks, also daily, strike out along the Mineral Tramways and Coast to Coast trails. Pony-mad children can join week-long riding holidays.

Reen Manor Riding Stables

Reen, Perranporth, TR6 0AJ, T01872-573064, reenmanorstables.com. Year round, £15/30-min ride, £25/hr ride, £50/2-hr beach ride.
From beginners' lessons to exhilarating hacks across three miles of sandy beach, Reen Manor caters for all abilities. Thirty-minute rides are for under-10s on lead reins.

Kitesurfing
Mobius Kite School

Perranporth, T01637-831383, mobiusonline.co.uk. £65/2½-hr intro session, £100/1-day BKSA/IKO beginner course (minimum age 12). Learn the exhilarating sport of kitesurfing at Perranporth, Hayle, Marazion or Pentewan. Powerkiting, kite buggying and land boarding are also available.

Multi activity
Lusty Glaze Adventure Centre

Lusty Glaze Rd, Newquay, TR7 3AE, T01637-872444, lustyglaze.co.uk. Junior Baywatch (2 hrs) £20 child (8-14), Baywatch Babes (2 hrs) £20 child (3-8); call for rates and minimum ages for coasteering, zip wire, Snakes & Ladders cliff assault course and Rat Run tunnel challenge; for surfing and bodyboarding, see page 82.
Newquay's privately owned Lusty Glaze Beach is an enticing spider's web of zip wires, abseiling ropes and obstacle courses, luring adrenaline junkies from miles around. It also offers surfing, kitesurfing, coasteering and mountain biking, but it's the centre's highly acclaimed Junior Baywatch lifeguard programme that will appeal most to families. Children are taught how to be surf-savvy, learning not only how to avoid riptides and rocks, but also basic techniques of surf rescue. They'll also get to grips with the RNLI Beach Lifeguard flag system. It's a fun way to spend a couple of hours on the beach. There's a version for younger kids called Baywatch Babes which focusses more on safe rock-pooling.

Quad biking
The ATV centre

Blackwater, TR4 8HJ, T01872-560753, atv-centre.com. Easter-Sep daily 1000-1800, Oct-Easter 1000-1700. Minimum age 6. From £20/20 mins. Three dirt-track circuits with coaches on hand for novices.

Surfing
See pages 82-83.

Tree climbing
Mighty Oak Tree Company

Nanswhyden, nr Newquay, T07890-698651, mighty-oak.co.uk. Introductory climbs for families (minimum age 4), call for rates. Rekindle a childhood passion with a rope- and harness-assisted arboreal adventure.

Water sports
Stithians Lake

Menherion, Redruth, TR16 6NW, T01209-860301, swlakestrust.org.uk. Mon-Thu, Sat 0900-1700. Taster sessions (2 hrs) call for rates; RYA Junior Stage 1-4 sailing course (2 days) £135; RYA Youth Stage 1-2 windsurfing course (2 days) £130; BCU 1 Star kayaking courses (1 day) £65. Minimum age 8 for all courses. Wet 'n' Active days £50. Hire rates: sailing dinghies from £15/hr, windsurf £15/hr, Canadian canoe £18/hr, kayak £10/hr, surf ski £10/hr, rowing boat £15/hr. Camping £13-16/pitch.
Water sports with no added salt, Stithians Lake is the perfect venue for learning how to sail, windsurf or kayak. You can enrol on a RYA-accredited course or try out three different activities at a Wet 'n' Active Days for children aged eight and above. Taster sessions are also available for your chosen activity.

Wildlife safaris
Feadon Farm Wildlife Centre

Gwel an Mor, see page 10.

Surf schools

Blue Wings Surf School
Tower Rd, Newquay,
TR7 1LZ, T01637-874445,
bluewingssurfschool.co.uk.
£20/2-hr lesson, £35/day (2 lessons).

Breakers Surf School
Breakers Beach Café, Trevaunance
Cove, St Agnes, T07725-842196,
surf-lessons.co.uk. £27/2-hr lesson,
£45/day, 5-day course £100.

Dolphin Surf School
Eliot Gardens, Newquay, TR7 2QT,
T01637-873707, surfschool.co.uk.
£30/2-hr lesson, £50/day (2 lessons),
2-day course £80, 3-day course £100.

The Escape Surf School
Fore St, Newquay, TR7 1HD, T07810-
805624, escapesurfschool.co.uk.
£30/2-hr lesson, £50/day (2 lessons),
surf and coasteering £70.

Extreme Academy
On The Beach, Watergate Bay,
TR8 4AA, T01637-860840,
extremeacademy.co.uk.
£30/2-hr lesson; £20 improver surf
lesson; private surf lesson £160 for
groups of 2-4 people; surf-and-hire
(morning lesson, then keep your kit
for rest of day) £47. Introduction
courses to kitesurfing, traction kite,
waveski, hand planing and stand-
up paddleboarding £20-100.

Fistral Beach Surf School
Newquay, TR7 1HN, T07739-
536122, fistralsurfschool.co.uk.
£35/2-hr lesson, £50/day
(2 lessons), half-day junior
surfing £25, family surf £160/
day, indoor surfing lesson £100,
private surf lesson £150; stand-up
paddleboarding lessons from £40.

Gwithian Academy of Surfing
Godrevy House, Prosper Hill,
Gwithian, TR27 5BW, T01736-
755493, surfacademy.co.uk.
Surf shop next to Sandsifter Café.
£30/2-hr lesson, £55/day
(2 lessons), 2-day course £85.

Harlyn Surf School
St Merryn, PL28 8SB, T01841-
533076, harlynsurfschool.co.uk.
£40/2-hr lesson; kids (5-8) £25/1-hr
lesson, family package £130/2-hr
lesson, surf 'n' hire from £60/day,
private lesson from £50; stand-up
paddleboarding, coasteering and
kayaking from £40; lifeguard/
instructor courses from £260.

High Five Surf School
Esplanade, Newquay, TR7 1QA,
T01637-874432, reefsurfschool.com.
£25/2-hr lesson, £35/day (2 lessons).

King Surf
Betty's Surf Shop, Mawgan Porth,
T01637-860091, kingsurf.co.uk.
£30/2½-hr lesson, £55/day (2 lessons).

Lusty Glaze Adventure Centre
Lusty Glaze Beach, Newquay
TR7 3AE, T01637-872444,
lustyglaze.co.uk.
£37/2½-hr lesson; private lesson
£70/hr; bodyboarding £37/2½-hr
lesson; surf and massage £60.

National Surfing Centre
Fistral Beach, Newquay,
TR7 1HY, T01637-850737,
nationalsurfingcentre.com.
from £25/2½-hr lesson (4 or more
people), private lesson from £65.

Newquay Surfing School
Newquay, T07592-736820,
newquaysurfingschool.com.
£30/2-hr lesson, £45/day (2 lessons);
coasteering £40/half-day.

Offshore Surf School
Newquay, T0771-624 8705,
offshoresurfschool.com.
£30/2-hr lesson, £45/day (2 lessons),
private lesson £65; coasteering £40/
half-day, surf and coasteer £55.

Porthtowan Surf School
Porthtowan, TR4 8AA, T01326-
212144, falmouthsurfschool.co.uk.
£25/2-hr lesson, £40/day
(2 lessons), Grommet days £15
child (8-13). See advert and also
Falmouth Surf School on page 193.

Quicksilver Surf School
Newquay, TR7 1PS, T01637-851800,
quiksilversurfschoolnewquay.com.
£25/2½-hr lesson , £45/day
(2 lessons); coasteering £40/half-day.

Shore Surf School
46 Mount Pleasant, Hayle, TR27 4LE,
T01736-755556, shoresurf.com.
£30/2½-hr lesson, £50/day
(2 lessons), private lesson from £35.
Offers 'Door to the shore' service
including transfers and lunch £70.

The Winter Brothers Surf School
Headland Hotel, Fistral Beach,
Newquay, T01637-879696.
£25/2hr lesson,
£40/day (2 lessons).

Over the top – learning
to surf with the Extreme
Academy at Watergate Bay.

LEARN TO SURF

GROMMET COURSE £15

`Big days out`

Blue Reef Aquarium

Towan Beach, Newquay, TR7 1DU, T01637-878134, bluereefaquarium.co.uk. Daily from 1000. £9.75 adult, £7.50 child (3-12), £32.50 family. Check online for offers. Sharks lurk just metres away from the bucket-and-spade brigade at Newquay's Towan Beach, but don't worry – they're all behind glass at this stunning aquarium which features a Tropical Shark Lagoon and huge reef display with walk-through tunnel. Other highlights include seahorses, cuttlefish and giant Pacific octopus – try to see them during one of the interesting feeding-time talks.

Crealy Great Adventure Park

Tredinnick, Wadebridge, PL27 7RA, T01841-540276, crealy.co.uk. Apr-Oct (plus school holidays) daily 1000-1800. Check website for rates. Located in lovely countryside south of Padstow, this mildly wild adventure park is largely a glorified playground with slides, zip wires, sand pits and climbing nets. There's a handful of thrill rides, including a swinging pirate ship, a log flume and twin racing waterslide. The Beast (minimum height 105 cm) is hyped as Crealy's 'big one' – a stomach-churning 15-m-tall tower-drop that actually elicits fewer squeals than the waterslide. It's Crealy's tameness, however, that makes it so appealing – kids run free from one play area to the next and queues rarely reach Disney proportions. The Water Walkerz (giant floating orbs that you zip your child inside) cost extra – a bit cheeky when you've already forked out over £50 for a family ticket. Crealy is still good value though – particularly when you factor in the farm animals, shire horse rides, indoor play areas and the Swamp Busters Eco Adventure (a streamside nature trail). Seasonal highlights include a summer sunflower maze and Easter egg hunt. Check the website for news of new rides.

Dairyland Farm World

Nr Newquay, TR8 5AA, T01872-510246, dairylandfarmworld.com. Daily 1000-1700. Check website for rates. Under-3s free. Milk Clarabelle with her realistic udders, pat a pet and ride in a Lamborghini (that's a type of tractor by the way). Dairyland is a gold-top, full-fat farm park with vast indoor and outdoor adventure play areas offering everything from drop slides and soft play to pony rides and nature trails.

Slide rules – the all-action Crealy Adventure Park.

Holywell Bay Fun Park

Holywell Bay, TR8 5PW, T01637-830095, holywellbayfunpark.co.uk. Apr-Nov, dates and times vary. Free entry and parking, pay as you play, plus all-day wristbands. Holywell Bay Fun Park is free to enter, but don't expect a cheap day out once the kids get wind of the array of pay-as-you-play attactions – go karts, crazy golf, bumper boats, trampolines and gold panning to name a few.

Lappa Valley Railway

St Newlyn East, TR8 5LX, T01872-510317, lappavalley.co.uk. Apr-Nov from 1030. Check website for rates. This narrow gauge steam train chuffs along to the old tin-mining site at East Wheel Rose, where you will find the mine's renovated engine house, a café,

Hit or miss?

Treasure Park
Tolgus Mill, Redruth, TR16 4HN, T01209-203280, treasureparks. com. Year round Mon-Sat 0930-1730; Sun 1000-1630. Free entry. Some might argue that the biggest gems in North Cornwall are its beaches, but there's no denying the rainy-day appeal of Treasure Park. Located on the road to Portreath, it's awash with gold and jewellery. Kids can pan for gold, scoop for gems, paint a treasure pot, explore the history of Cornish mining at Tolgus Tin and experience a haunted 4D mine ride. There's also a picnic area and café, as well as The Bear Works and crazy golf.

Left, from top: Shire horse at Crealy; feeding rainbow lorikeets at Paradise Park; meeting meerkats at Newquay Zoo.

☻ **Free** play

Does the weather forecast look bleak? Some attractions, like Crealy, offer a week of free return visits when you purchase a single admission ticket so you can make good use of their indoor play areas when the weather turns against you.

crazy golf, canoeing lake, brick-path maze, play castle and two additional miniature railways.

Newquay Zoo
Trenance Gardens, Newquay, TR7 2LZ, T01637-873342, newquayzoo.org.uk. Daily 1000-1700. £12.65 adult, £9.90 child (3-15), £36.30 family.
A three-acre African Savannah sees wildebeest and warthog rubbing shoulders with ostrich and zebra at this excellent

zoo. Other highlights include the Madagascan Walkthrough (home to vasa parots and crowned lemurs) and Tropical House with its poison dart frogs. Junior Keeper days are available for eight- to 14-year-olds, while daily feeds and talks take place at the macaques (1100), meerkats (1230), big cats (1430) and penguins (1545).

Paradise Park
Trelissick Rd, Hayle, TR27 4HB, T01736-751020, paradisepark.org.uk. Daily from 1000. Check website for rates. Home to the World Parrot Trust, Paradise Park boasts huge freeflight aviaries where you can handfeed lorikeets with nectar. Parrots hog the limelight at this excellent park, but you will also see penguins, owls,

eagles and local rarities like the chough. Non-feathered friends include otters, red squirrels and red pandas. On rainy days let your own wild things loose in the all-weather Jungle Barn with its giant slides, soft play and special toddler zone. Outside there's a new Paradise Island Adventure play area.

Out & about Northwest Cornwall

More family favourites

Blue Hills
Wheal Kitty, St Agnes, TR5 0YW, T01872-553341, bluehillstin.com. Apr-Oct Mon-Sat 1000-1600. £5.50 adult, £3 child.
At Cornwall's only tin producer you can follow the entire process, from extraction, crushing and smelting to pouring ingots and casting finished products.

Cornish Birds of Prey Centre
Meadowside Farm, Winnards Perch, St Columb Major, TR9 6DH, T01637-880544, cornishbirdsofprey.co.uk. Apr-Oct daily 1000-1700. £7 adult, £5.50 child (3-13), £22 family.
Eyeball hawks, owls, falcons, vultures and eagles and watch them fly at 1200, 1400 and 1600. Falconry experiences (minimum age 14) are also available.

East Pool Mine
Pool, nr Redruth, TR15 3NP, T01209-315027, nationaltrust.org.uk. Easter-Nov, Mon, Wed-Fri, Sun 1100-1700; Jul-Aug also Sat. £6.50 adult, £3.20 child (5-17), £16.20 family.
Climb three flights of stairs to reach the top of Taylor's Engine – a mighty beam engine once used to pump water from the mines. You can also walk under a 35-m-tall chimney stack and visit the discovery centre, where a short film provides a gritty and, for children, quite complicated introduction to Cornish mining. Other sites (like Geevor, see page 112) are more child-friendly.

Screech Owl Sanctuary
Goss Moor, nr Indian Queens, TR9 6HP, T01726-860182, screechowlsanctuary.co.uk. Feb-Nov daily 1000-1700 (1800 spring and summer), flying displays 1100, 1300 and 1600. £9.50 adult, £7.50 child (3-15), £29 family.
A right hoot, this superb little sanctuary is home to over 140 owls and hawks from 50 species. As well as guided tours and falconry displays, a hand-tame area allows you to touch and stroke the birds. Find out about the owl hospital and Siberian eagle owl breeding project.

Springfields Fun Park
St Columb, TR9 6HU, T01637-881224, springfieldsponycentre.co.uk. Easter-Oct. £7.95 adult, £6.95 child (3-16), £26.95 family.
Springfields promises a fun day out with pony and train rides, duck racing, bottle-feeding lambs and bunny cuddling. There's also an all-weather fun barn with slides and soft play.

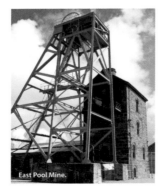
East Pool Mine.

Rain check

Cinemas
Plaza
Lemon St, Truro, T0871-200 3304.
Regal
Fore St, Redruth, T01209-216278.

Indoor play & amusements
Atlantic Lanes Bowling Centre
Trevarrian Holiday Park, Mawgan Porth, TR8 4AQ, T01637-860381. atlantic-lanes.co.uk.

Bombadinga's
Wilson Way, Pool, Redruth, TR15 3RX T01209-219555, bombadingas.co.uk. Daily 1000-1800. Café and pirate-themed soft play.

The Bull Pen
Dairyland Farm World, see page 84 for contact details. Daily from 1000. Soft play and ball pool for littl'uns; huge adventure zone for older children with climbing nets, slides etc.

Country Skittles
Townshend, Hayle, TR27 6ER, T01736-850209, countryskittles.com. School holidays Mon-Sat 1200-2300, Sun 1200-2230. Nine-pin skittle alleys.

Jungle Barn
Paradise Park, see page 85 for contact details. Daily from 1000. Soft play, drop slides, ball pool, toddlers' area and café, all with a jungle theme.

Indoor swimming pools
Carnbrea Leisure Centre
Redruth, TR15 3QS, T01209-714766, carnbrealeisurecentre.co.uk.

Oasis
Hendra Holiday Park, Newquay, TR8 4NY, T01637-870711, oasis-hendra.co.uk. Daily 1000-1800. From £6.15 adult, £4.99 child (5-14), £2.99 child (3-4), £20 family. Heated indoor and outdoor pools with water slides (including 265-ft super flume), river rapid ride and toddlers' area.

Waterworld
Trenance Leisure Park, Newquay, TR7 2LZ, T01637-853829, newquaywaterworld.co.uk. Daily from 1000. £6.40 adult, £4.80 child, £3.90 parent and baby. Tropical fun pool, water flumes, play hut and erupting volcano. Next to Newquay Zoo.

Sleeping Northwest Cornwall

Pick of the pitches

Bedruthan Steps Camping
Bedruthan Steps, T01637-860943, bedruthanstepscamping.co.uk. Aug. From £7.50 adult, £4 child.
Ⓐ Ⓞ Ⓒ Ⓔ

The coast path borders this picture-perfect clifftop site overlooking the famous 'stepping stones' of the giant Bedruthan. Just turn up and pick a spot on the five-acre field. Facilities are limited to toilets, showers and a small kiosk selling local food and snacks.

Berryfields Farm Campsite
Berryfields, Porthcothan Bay, PL28 8PW, T01841-520178. Call for rates.
Ⓐ Ⓔ Ⓞ Ⓖ Ⓢ Ⓒ Ⓞ Ⓦ Ⓔ Ⓢ

Originally a strawberry farm, this peaceful site (with 65 pitches for tents and caravans) has an excellent café with some of the best Cornish cream teas you'll taste anywhere. Located close to Porthcothan beach, the campsite also has a gift shop, games room and crazy golf.

Gwithian Farm Campsite
Gwithian, TR27 5BX, T01736-753127, gwithianfarm.co.uk. Apr-Sep. £15-30/pitch (2 people), plus £5 extra adult, £2 extra child, £1 dog.
Ⓐ Ⓔ Ⓞ Ⓖ Ⓢ Ⓒ Ⓞ Ⓦ Ⓔ Ⓢ

You can almost smell the surf at this friendly campsite 10 minutes' walk from Gwithian's golden sands. After a day on the beach, the family shower room is a welcome change from the limb-crunching cubicles you find at many sites. Kids will enjoy befriending the resident chickens and guinea pigs – not to mention the ice cream vendor and fish and chip van that visit the site. A fresh fish van also turns up and there's a good pub opposite.

Tollgate Farm
Perranporth, TR6 0AD, T01872-572130, tollgatefarm.co.uk. £5-7.50 adult, £2.50-4 child (6-14), £5.50-8 tent; pods £40-50/night
Ⓐ Ⓔ Ⓞ Ⓖ Ⓢ Ⓒ Ⓞ Ⓦ Ⓢ

Tollgate Farm has a large play area and a paddock where kids can feed pigs, goats and guinea pigs. The nearest beach is a 20-minute walk through dunes to Perran Bay. Wooden ecopods (sleeping five) are available.

Treago Farm Holidays
Crantock, TR8 5QS, T01637-830277, treagofarm.co.uk. Year round (shop May-Sep). £7.50-10 adult, £4-5 child.
Ⓐ Ⓔ Ⓞ Ⓖ Ⓣ Ⓒ Ⓞ Ⓒ Ⓢ

Tucked into a sheltered valley just inland from Porth Joke and Crantock, this idyllic site has the best of both worlds – peaceful, unspoilt countryside and easy access (along footpaths) to stunning beaches. Old farm buildings house a cosy bar, games room and shop.

Also recommended
Beacon Cottage Farm
Ⓐ Ⓔ Ⓞ Ⓖ Ⓒ Ⓞ Ⓞ Ⓦ Ⓔ

St Agnes, TR5 0NU, T01872-552347, beaconcottagefarmholidays.co.uk. Apr-Sep. £17-23/pitch (2 adults), plus £4.70 extra adult, £3.20 extra child. Small secluded site on working farm, close to the sea.

Cottage Farm Park
Treworgans, Cubert, TR8 5HH, T01637-831083, cottagefarmpark. co.uk. Apr-Sep. £12-17/pitch (2 adults), plus £6-8.50 extra adult, £4-5 extra child, £1.50 dog.
Ⓐ Ⓔ Ⓖ Ⓒ Ⓞ Ⓦ Ⓔ

Peaceful site, a 20-minute walk to the beach at Holywell Bay.

Silverbow Park
Perranwell, TR4 9NX, T01872-572347, chycor.co.uk/parks/silverbow. Apr-Sep. £16-29/pitch (2 adults), plus £3-6 extra adult, £2.50-4.50 extra child (2-12).
Ⓐ Ⓔ Ⓞ Ⓖ Ⓢ Ⓒ Ⓞ

Quiet, immaculate site close to Perranporth; landscaped gardens and heated pool.

Bedruthan Steps Camping.

Sleeping Northwest Cornwall

Bassets Acre

Portreath, TR16 4JU,
T01209-842367, bassetsacre.co.uk.
Four-bed apartment £370-1550/wk.
Six apartments (sleeping up to
seven) in a Georgian house with
heated indoor pool, play area
and sub-tropical gardens.

The Harlyn Inn

Harlyn Bay, PL28 8SB, T01841-520207,
harlyn-inn.co.uk. Standard cottage
(sleeping 6) £250-1100/wk.
Idyllic location on Harlyn Bay.
Quality B&B and smart new
three-bedroom self-catering
cottages. The pub's restaurant
welcomes families and there's
even a beach shop next door.

Tolcarne Beach Village

Tolcarne Beach, Newquay, TR7 2QN,
T01209-712651, tolcarnebeach.
co.uk. Two-bedroom apartment
£490-1150/wk, surf shack £60-100/nt.
Stylish, bright apartments with
private balconies overlooking
a great family beach. Six surf
shacks, sleeping four in bunk
beds, are also available.

Trengove Farm Cottages

Cot Road, Illogan, TR16 4PU, T01209-
843008, trengovefarm.co.uk. Two-
bedroom cottage from £280-880/wk.
Seven character cottages on a
working farm near Portreath.

YHA Treyarnon Bay

Treyarnon, PL28 8JR, T0845-371
9664, yha.org.uk. Rooms from £20.
Superb location perched above
Treyarnon Bay. Seventy-bed
hostel with family rooms, an
excellent café and a handy
drying room for soggy wetsuits.

YHA Treyarnon Bay.

Cottage agents

See also page 199.

Around Kernow Holidays
T01872-571575, ak-hols.co.uk.
Cottages, apartments and chalets
in and around Perranporth.

Blue Chip Holidays
T00844-2731 934,
bluechipholidays.co.uk.
Large portfolio of four- and five-
star properties in the Southwest.

Cornwall Coast Holidays
T0208-4407518,
cornwallcoastholidays.com.
Luxury cottages and apartments
overlooking Fistral Bay, Newquay.

Duchy Holidays
T01872-572971,
duchyholidays.co.uk.
Wide range of properties from
Newquay to Porthtowan.

Park life

If you yearn for a good value,
home-from-home break on
Cornwall's northwest coast you
can't go wrong with a holiday park.
But which one to choose? Leave it
to the kids and they'll probably go
for the one with the best swimming
pool complex. The Oasis at **Hendra
Holiday Park**, for example, has the
full works – flumes, river rapids
ride, water cannon and geyser.
Proximity to a beach is another key
factor. A short stroll from glorious
beaches, **Atlantic Coast Caravan
Park**, **Mother Ivey's Bay Caravan
Park** and **St Ives Bay Holiday Park**
both score highly on the barefoot-
and-carefree front. Other parks
have a more rural setting – **Tehidy**
is perfect for woodland walks and
getting back to nature, while **White
Acres** overlooks a lake.

Not all holiday parks are large
and rowdy. **Sun Haven Valley** keeps
things simple with a playground
and small games room in place of
the usual clubs, bars and organized
entertainment. If it's five-star
facilities you're after, though, opt
for a fully fledged park like **Monkey
Tree**, **Newperran** or **Trevornick**,
where 'extras' can include anything

from free kids' clubs and on-site shops and restaurants to fishing lakes and golf courses.

As far as accommodation is concerned, the des-res of most holiday parks is the static caravan, typically with two or three bedrooms, lounge, kitchen, shower/bathroom and a good spattering of mod cons such as flatscreen TV, microwave, double glazing and central heating. You might be able to upgrade to one with a deck, ideal for those summer evening barbecues. Many parks also offer more spacious chalets and timber lodges or allocate space for you to hook up your own caravan or pitch a tent.

Finally, look for parks with green credentials. **Trevella**, for example, has its own nature reserve and has received the Gold David Bellamy Conservation Award for 10 years in a row.

Atlantic Coast Caravan Park scores highly on the barefoot-and-carefree front.

Holiday parks

Atlantic Coast Caravan Park
Upton Towans, TR27 5BL, T01736-752071, atlanticcoastpark.co.uk.

Carnevas Holiday Park
St Merryn, PL28 8PN, T01841-520230, carnevasholidaypark.com.

Crantock Beach Holiday Park
Crantock, TR8 5RH, T0844-335 3450, parkdeanholidays.co.uk.

Harlyn Sands Holiday Park
Trevose Head, PL28 8SQ, T01841-520720, harlynsands.co.uk.

Hendra Holiday Park
Newquay, TR8 4NY, T01637-875778, hendra-holidays.com.

Holywell Bay Holiday Park
Holywell Bay, TR8 5PR, T0844-335 3450, parkdeanholidays.co.uk.

Monkey Tree Holiday Park
Rejerrah, TR8 5QR, T01872-572032, monkeytreeholidaypark.co.uk.

Mother Ivey's Bay Caravan Park
Trevose Head, PL28 8SL, T01841-520990, motheriveysbay.com.

Newperran Holiday Park
Rejerrah, TR8 5QJ, T01872-572407, newperran.co.uk.

Newquay Holiday Park
Newquay, TR8 4HS, T0844-335 3450, parkdeanholidays.co.uk.

The Park at Mawgan Porth
Mawgan Porth, TR8 4BD, T01637-860322, mawganporth.co.uk.

Perran Sands Holiday Park
Perranporth, TR6 0AQ, T0871-230276, haven.com.

Perran Springs Holiday Park
Goonhavern, Truro, TR4 9QG, T01872-540568, perransprings.co.uk.

Porth Beach Tourist Park
Porth, TR7 3NH, T01637-876531, porthbeach.co.uk.

Riverside Holiday Park
Lane, Newquay, TR8 4PE, T01637-873617, riversideholidaypark.co.uk.

St Ives Bay Holiday Park
Upton Towans, TR27 5BH, T0800-317713, stivesbay.co.uk.

Sun Haven Valley Holiday Park
Mawgan Porth, TR8 4BQ, T0800-634 6744, sunhavenvalley.com.

Tehidy Holiday Park
Illogan, Redruth, TR16 4JQ, T01209-216489, tehidy.co.uk.

Treloy Touring Park
Newquay, TR8 4JN, T01637-872063, treloy.co.uk.

Trenance Holiday Park
Newquay, TR7 2JY, T01637-873447, trenanceholidaypark.co.uk.

Trencreek Holiday Park
Newquay, TR8 4NS, T01637-874210, trencreekholidaypark.co.uk.

Trevella Park
Crantock, TR8 5EU, T01637-830308, trevella.co.uk.

Trevornick Holiday Park
Holywell Bay, TR8 5PW, T0843-453 5531, trevornick.co.uk.

Treworgans Holiday Park
Cubert, Newquay, TR8 5HH, T01637-830200, treworgansholidaypark.co.uk.

Treyarnon Bay Caravan Park
Treyarnon Bay, PL28 8JR, T01841-52068, treyarnonbay.co.uk.

Watergate Bay Touring Park
Watergate Bay, TR8 4AD, T01637-860387, watergatebaytouringpark.co.uk.

White Acres Holiday Park
Newquay, TR8 4LW, T0844-335 3450, parkdeanholidays.co.uk.

Sleeping Northwest Cornwall

Splashing out

Bedruthan Steps Hotel

Mawgan Porth, TR8 4BU,
T01637-860860, bedruthan.com.
Check website for rates.

Don't feel intimidated by the smart, contemporary style of this cliff-top hotel – it's as child-friendly as they come. In fact, with its indoor and outdoor play areas, daily entertainment, heated pools, OFSTED-registered clubs and special mealtimes, children could be forgiven for thinking that it was made exclusively for them. In a way it was. But grown-ups get a fair share of goodies too. There's the sumptuous spa and an award-winning restaurant (for adults only), as well as exemplary childcare for those moments when you crave 'me time'. The tastefully decorated bedrooms – from spacious family rooms to apartments – often have spectacular sea views.

Rosehill Lodges

Porthtowan, TR4 8AR, T01209-891920, rosehilllodges.com. Two-bed lodge (sleeping 4) £578-1812/wk.

A five-minute walk from Porthtowan and nuzzled in woodland, these classy timber lodges have private hot tubs, glass-covered decks, log burners and outdoor heated drench showers – just the job for rinsing off children and wetsuits after a day on the beach. Each lodge is also equipped with handy extras

like buckets and spades, softball tennis and badminton sets. And they're green too, thanks to solar panels and grass roofs.

Sands Resort Hotel

Watergate Rd, Porth, TR7 3LX,
T01637-872864, sandsresort.co.uk.
B&B from around £50 adult, free and discounted prices for children.

A genuinely family-friendly hotel, Sands does more than most to make parents and children feel welcome and well catered for. Most of the rooms are suites, with separate children's sleeping areas. There are sports facilities, play areas and children's clubs for all ages; the Surf Shack has wetsuits and boards, while two beach adventure centres are just minutes away. Little ones get pre-dinner entertainment; grown-ups get a health spa.

Watergate Bay Hotel

Watergate Bay, Newquay, T01637-860543, watergatebay.co.uk.
Check website for rates.

Behind the quite traditional Victorian-looking façade of this hotel lies Cornwall's ultimate base for surf and chic. Watergate Bay Hotel is right on the beach, with its own watersports centre and no less than four places to eat, including the Hotel Brasserie and Jamie Oliver's Fifteen (see page 93). The hotel has playrooms, an indoor/outdoor swimming pool, supervised Kids' Zone, children's activities and evening entertainment, plus a

baby-listening service. Bright, contemporary family suites feature a king-size bedroom and bunk room for children. Plasma televisions and DVD players come as standard – for those rare moments when you can tear yourself away from the ocean views. Interconnecting rooms, some with balconies overlooking the bay, are also available. Outside there's a lovely terrace with steps to the beach.

Also recommended
Crantock Bay Hotel

West Pentire, TR8 5SE, T01637-830229, crantockbayhotel.co.uk.
Hotel gardens lead to coast path and sandy beach.

The Esplanade Hotel

Fistral Bay, Newquay TR7 1PS, T01637-873333, newquay-hotels.co.uk.
Just 50 m from beach; indoor and outdoor pools, games room, great food and surf centre.

Gwel an Mor

Portreath. See page 11.

The Headland

Fistral Bay, Newquay TR7 1EW,
T01637-872211, headlandhotel.co.uk.
Breathtaking views; village of self-catering cottages.

Retallack Resort & Spa

St Columb Major, T01637-882500, retallackresort.co.uk.
Luxurious self catering lodges and cottages, health club, spa and FlowRider Cornwall.

Eating Northwest Cornwall

Local goodies

Callestick Farm

Callestick, Truro, TR4 9LL, T01872-573126, callestickfarm.co.uk. Summer Mon-Sat 0930-1730, Sun 1100-1700; winter Wed-Sat.

You've probably slurped it at countless places across Cornwall – now visit the farm to find out how Callestick ice cream is made. There's a viewing gallery above the farm's ice cream factory where you can watch – with the help of an explanatory DVD – the entire process from Friesian milk to frozen tub. As well as sampling the sweet sensation at the dairy parlour, you can indulge in other local foods at the farm's café and deli. A typical summer menu will have savoury specials like tomato, basil and cream cheese tart or Cornish brie, bacon and cranberry sauce baguettes. Farm animals are another big attraction at Callestick, with chickens, pigs, calves, sheep dogs and the resident shire horse all vying for attention. Utimately, though, there's only one thing on the minds

of most visitors to this small, friendly farm – which of the 26-plus flavours of Callestick ice cream to sample. Purists will probably plump for clotted cream vanilla, while those with more daring palates can choose from butterscotch and pecan, lemon curd, crunchy toffee or white chocolate and raspberries.

⏱ Ice spy

Download a treasure hunt from Callestick's website (callestickfarm. co.uk), solve eight clues at the farm (there are questions for both older and younger children) and you can claim a free ice cream cone.

Healey's Cornish Cyder Farm

Penhallow, TR4 9LW, T01872-573356, healeyscyderfarm.co.uk. Year round, daily from 0900. Free admission.

No-one's suggesting you initiate the kids to Cornish Scrumpy or Rattler (that's your holiday treat). Instead, they'll get a kick out of the tractor rides, meeting farm animals and completing the quiz on a tour through the Cyder Farm's press house, bottlery, jam kitchen and museum. There's also a suitably fruity farm shop and restaurant.

Trevaskis Farm

Conner Downs, Hayle, TR27 5JQ, T01209-714009, trevaskisfarm.co.uk. Summer daily 0900-1800; winter, daily 0900-1700; organic kitchen garden May-Oct; restaurant Mon-Sat breakfast 0830-1030, lunch

from 1200, afternoon teas 1500-1700, evening meals from 1800, Sun roasts 1200-1800.

There are no less than 70 crops on this 28-acre pick-your-own farm – from strawberries, raspberries and plums to peas, beans and pumpkins. Armed with baskets, kids can plan a soft-fruit safari, bolting for poly-tunnels, if it rains, and gleaning juicy snippets of information from interpretation boards on how each variety has been grown. There are even recipe suggestions and cooking tips but, if you can't wait to taste the fruits of your labours, head for the restaurant, which serves delicious homemade apple pie and clotted cream, plus a full range of snacks and meals. The children's menu (dishes £5.95-6.25) includes home-made sausages and lasagne, while Sunday roasts (with pork and gammon from the farm's rare-breed Cornish lop pigs) range from £6.95 for a child's serving to £10.45 for an adult's portion. There's also a fabulous farm shop with baker, butcher, fishmonger and deli.

Market days

Cambourne Produce Market
Trelowarren St, Friday 0900-1500.

Perranporth Country Market
Memorial Hall, Friday 1000-1200.

Stithians Produce Market
Church Road, Saturday 0930-1230.

Truro Farmers' Market
Lemon Quay, Saturday 0900-1600.

Eating Northwest Cornwall

Quick & simple

The Beach Hut

Watergate Bay, TR8 4AA, T01637-
860877, watergatebay.co.uk.
Breakfast Mon-Fri 1000-1130, Sat-Sun
0930-1100; lunch Sun-Thu 1200-1600;
lunch and dinner Fri-Sat 1200-2100.
This busy, friendly café has
picture-window views of the
beach and serves breakfast,
lunch and dinner. For a pre-surf
energy boost, kids will demolish
the sweet waffles with crispy
bacon and maple syrup (£6.75)
on the breakfast menu. For
lunch, try the fried calamari or
Cornish crab soup (around £7).
Mains on the children's menu
cost from £4 and include an
excellent pasta, homemade
burger and fish and chips. For
grown-ups (and hungry kids)
there's moules marinières
(£8.50/half-kilo), plus mains
such as Cornish steaks, burgers
and daily fish specials (starting
at around £9). If you have
room for pudding, squeeze in
Will's Crème Brûlée (£5) or an
Extreme Ice Cream with cream,
marshmallows and chocolate
(£4.50). For an afternoon snack,

Fish & chips

Try the **Jolly Fryer** (Beach Rd,
Porthtowan) for fish and chips on
the beach. **Morrish's** (Bucketts
Hill, Redruth) has a secret batter
recipe handed down over three
generations, while **Pickwick** (St
Pirans Road, Perranporth) uses the
freshest fish and local potatoes
cooked in beef dripping.

---

the Beach Hut's hot chocolate
and warm chocolate fudge
brownie are legendary.

Blue Beach Bar & Brasserie

Beach Rd, Porthtowan, TR4 8AD,
T01209-890329, blue-bar.co.uk.
Brunch daily 1000-1145; lunch daily
1200-1500; 'avo' daily from 1500;
dinner daily 1800-2100.
Blue has a fantastic beach
location that's perfect for sunset
gazing. The chips 'n' dips (£7.25)
makes a great snack but, for
something more substantial,
try one of the burgers (from
£10.50), stonebaked pizzas (from
£8) or a special from the board.
The kids' menu has scampi and
chips for £5, as well as pasta and
bangers and mash.

Bodhi's Beach Café & Bistro

South Fistral Beach, Newquay,
TR7 1QA, T01637-850793,
bodhisfistral.co.uk. Daily from 1000,
food served until 1500 (Mon-Thu),
2100 (Fri-Sat), 1530 (Sun).
This cool café serves great food,
and you'll be blown away by its
location – perched right above
the beach. The lunch menu has
sandwiches and panninis from
around £6, plus soups, nachos,
burgers and anti pasti, while the
evening menu is beefed up with
steaks, mussels and other mains
from the specials boards.

Carnewas Tearoom

Nr Bedruthan, St Eval, PL27 7UW,
T01637-860563, nationaltrust.org.
uk. Feb-May and Oct-Dec daily 1100-

1600; May-Sep daily 1030-1700.
You can't go wrong with a
National Trust tea room after a
bracing cliff-top walk and this
one is smack in the middle of
some of North Cornwall's most
stunning coastal scenery.

Godrevy Café

Godrevy Towans, Gwithian, TR27
5ED, T01736-757999, godrevycafe.
co.uk. Daily 1000-1700, plus
evenings in summer.
A bright and breezy cabin,
simple, tasty food and a
great location in the dunes at
Godrevy's National Trust car
park (with views across St Ives
Bay) – it's small wonder that this
café is so popular. The breakfast
menu includes Full English,
as well as Belgian waffles,
poached eggs and smoked
salmon. For light bites choose
from a range of sandwiches,
wraps and salads. Daily specials
include vegetarian, meat and
fish options. The finger food
plate on the kids menu is a
great idea, and there's also soup,
sandwiches and 'wrapsicles' for
smaller appetites.

Schooners Bistro

Trevaunance Cove, St Agnes, TR5 0RY,
T01872-553149. Tue-Sun from 1000.
Perched above the cove at

St Agnes, Schooners has a grandstand view of the Atlantic, whether you're lounging on the deck in the sunshine or huddled inside while waves burst on the rocks below. For lunch, there's a good range of toasted ciabattas, while dinner mains include local steamed mussels, grilled mackerel fillets and lamb shank.

Venus Café

Tolcarne Beach, Newquay, T01637-876028, lovingthebeach.co.uk. Easter-Sep daily 1000-1700 (Jul-Aug 0900-1800). Watergate Bay, T01637-860297, daily 1000-1700, closed some dates Nov-Jan.

Both of these excellent cafés offer a great range of locally sourced snacks to eat alfresco or on the beach. The take away menu features all-day breakfasts from around £3.50, plus a selection of paninis, burgers and delicious Strawbridge pasties (triple cheese and onion or minted lamb). For kids, there's sausages and chips, spaghetti or burger and fries – all around £5.

Also recommended
The Mermaid Inn

Alexandra Rd, Porth, TR7 3NB, T01637-872954. Mon-Sat from 1100, Sun from 1200.
Good pub grub at Porth beach.

The Watering Hole

Perranporth Beach, TR6 0JL, T01872-572888, the-wateringhole.co.uk. Lively beach bar with a big menu and summer barbecues.

Posh nosh

Fifteen Cornwall

Watergate Bay, TR8 4AA, T01637-861000, fifteencornwall.co.uk. Daily 0830-0930, 1200-1430, 1815-2115. Buzzing at lunchtime with surf-tussled children, Jamie Oliver's pukka beach restaurant is very popular with families and you'd be wise to book. Bright, lively and trendy (spot Jamie's spray-can signature in magenta paint on one of the walls), Fifteen has friendly service, front-row views of the beach and, of course, fabulous food. Kids are welcome for breakfast and lunch, but there is no children's menu in the evening. A breakfast fry-up for kids costs £5, while lunchtime dishes (Cornish fish pie, pasta etc) start at around £4. In the evening, treat yourself to the Tasting Menu (from £60 for five courses), which uses lamb,

seafood and other local produce in irresistible Italian recipes. It's totally delish.

New Harbour Restaurant

Newquay Harbour, T01637-874062, finns2go.com. Daily from 1200. Superb seafood – from crab sarnies to dressed lobster – served at lunch and dinner.

Rosewarne Manor

Gwinear Rd, Connor Downs, Hayle TR27 5JQ, T01209-610414, rosewarnemanor.co.uk. Wed-Sun 1200-1430, 1800-2100. Award-winning restaurant renowned for its local dishes using fresh seafood, Cornish lamb and steaks. Lunch mains from around £10, two-course dinner menu £24, Sunday carvery from £10.

The Terrace

Gwel an Mor, Portreath. See page 11.

Posh pasta at Fifteen – taglierini vongole (clams).

Contents

96 Map

98 The Far West
100 Fun & free
104 Best beaches
110 Action stations
112 Big days out
114 St Michael's Mount
116 Sleeping
119 Eating

122 St Ives

128 The Lizard
130 Fun & free
132 Best beaches
136 Action stations
138 Big days out
142 Sleeping
145 Eating

148 Isles of Scilly

West Cornwall

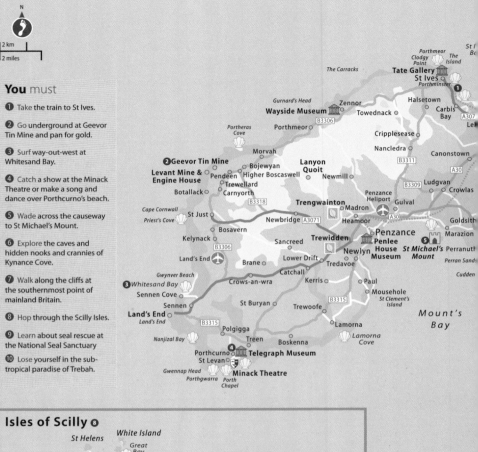

You must

① Take the train to St Ives.

② Go underground at Geevor Tin Mine and pan for gold.

③ Surf way-out-west at Whitesand Bay.

④ Catch a show at the Minack Theatre or make a song and dance over Porthcurno's beach.

⑤ Wade across the causeway to St Michael's Mount.

⑥ Explore the caves and hidden nooks and crannies of Kynance Cove.

⑦ Walk along the cliffs at the southernmost point of mainland Britain.

⑧ Hop through the Scilly Isles.

⑨ Learn about seal rescue at the National Seal Sanctuary.

⑩ Lose yourself in the sub-tropical paradise of Trebah.

Porthmeor
Clodgy The
Point Island
Tate Gallery
St Ives
Porthminster

The Carracks

St I
B

St I

Gurnard's Head Zennor Halsetown
Wayside Museum Towednack Carbis
Bay
A307
B3306 Cripplesease Le

Portheras Porthmeor Nancledra
Cove Canonstown
Morvah B3311
②Geevor Tin Mine A30
Levant Mine & Bojewyan **Lanyon** Newmill Ludgvan
Engine House Pendeen Higher Boscaswell **Quoit** B3309 Crowlas
Trewellard Penzance
Botallack Carnyorth Heliport Gulval
B3318 **Trengwainton** Madron
Cape Cornwall **St Just** Heamoor A30 Goldsith
Priest's Cove Newbridge A3071
Bosavern **Trewidden** **Penzance** Marazion
Kelynack Sancreed **Penlee** St Michael's Perranuth
B3306 **Newlyn** **House** **Mount**
Land's End Brane Lower Drift **Museum** Perran Sand
Catchall Tredavoe
Gwynver Beach Crows-an-wra Kerris Cudden
③Whitesand Bay Paul
Sennen Cove Mousehole
Sennen St Buryan Trewoofe St Clement's
Land's End Island
Land's End B3315 **Mount's**
Polgigga Lamorna **Bay**
Nanjizal Bay Treen Lamorna
Porthcurno **Telegraph Museum** Boskenna Cove
St Levan
Gwennap Head **Minack Theatre**
Porthgwarra Porth
Chapel

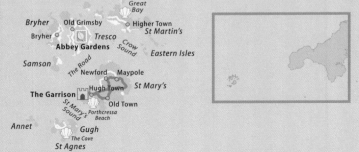

Isles of Scilly ⑧

St Helens White Island
Great
Bay
Bryher Old Grimsby Higher Town
Bryher Tresco St Martin's
Abbey Gardens Crow
Sound Eastern Isles
Samson The Road
Newford Maypole
The Garrison Hugh Town St Mary's
St Mary's Old Town
Annet Sound Porthcressa
Beach
Gugh
The Cove
St Agnes

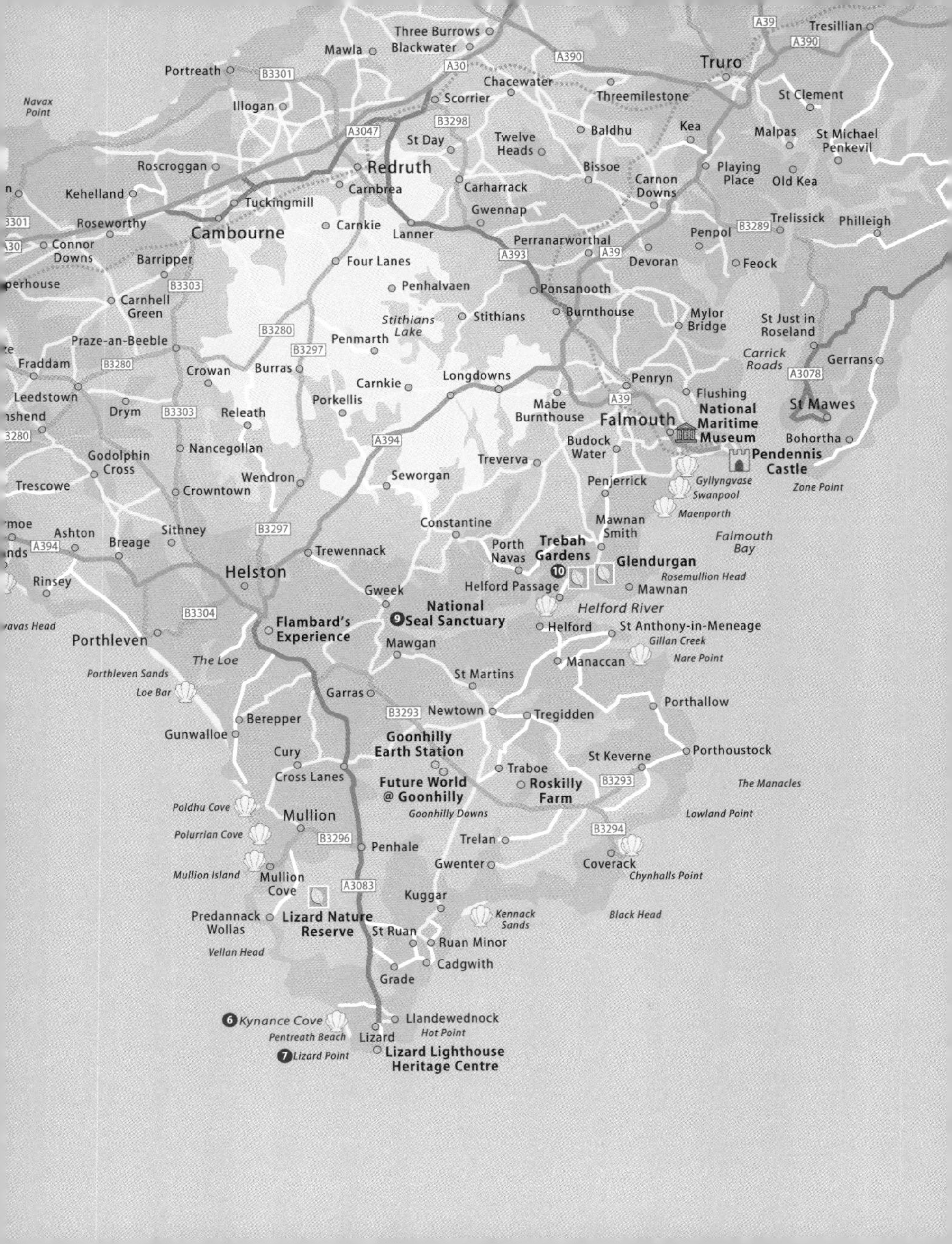

Tresillian

A39

Truro

A390

A390

Three Burrows
Blackwater
Mawla
Chacewater
St Clement
Portreath
B3301
Scorrier
Threemilestone
Malpas
St Michael
Penkevil
Illogan
A30
Baldhu
Kea
St Day
B3298
Twelve
Heads
Bissoe
Playing
Place
Old Kea
Navax
Point
A3047
Roscroggan
RedruthCarnbrea
Carharrack
Carnon
Downs
Kehelland
Roseworthy
Tuckingmill
Carnkie
Gwennap
Penpol
B3289
Trelissick
Philleigh
Cambourne
Lanner
Perranarworthal
A39
Devoran
Feock
Connor
Downs
Barripper
B3303
Four Lanes
A393
Ponsanooth
Mylor
Bridge
St Just in
Roseland
perhouse
Carnhell
Green
Penhalvaen
Stithians
Lake
Burnthouse
Carrick
Roads
Gerrans
A3078
Fraddam
B3280
Praze-an-Beeble
B3280
Crowan
B3297
Penmarth
Stithians
Penryn
Flushing
St Mawes
Leedstown
Burras
Porkellis
Carnkie
Longdowns
A39
Falmouth
National
Maritime
Museum
Bohortha
hshend
B3303
Drym
Releath
Mabe
Burnthouse
Budock
Water
Pendennis
Castle
Zone Point
Godolphin
Cross
Nancegollan
A394
Seworgan
Treverva
Penjerrick
Gyllyngvase
Swanpool
Maenporth
Trescowe
Wendron
Crowntown
Constantine
Mawnan
Smith
Falmouth
Bay
moe
Ashton
Sithney
B3297
Trewennack
Porth
Navas
Trebah
Gardens
Glendurgan
Rosemullion Head
Breage
Gweek
Helford Passage
Mawnan
Rinsey
Helston
Flambard's
Experience
National
Seal Sanctuary
Helford River
St Anthony-in-Meneage
avas Head
B3304
Mawgan
Helford
Gillan Creek
Nare Point
Porthleven
The Loe
St Martins
Manaccan
Porthleven Sands
Loe Bar
Garras
B3293
Newtown
Tregidden
Porthallow
Gunwalloe
Berepper
Goonhilly
Earth Station
Traboe
St Keverne
Porthoustock
Cury
Cross Lanes
Future World
@ Goonhilly
Roskilly
Farm
B3293
The Manacles
Poldhu Cove
Mullion
Goonhilly Downs
Lowland Point
Polurrian Cove
B3296
Penhale
Trelan
B3294
Coverack
Mullion island
Mullion
Cove
A3083
Kuggar
Gwenter
Chynhalls Point
Predannack
Wollas
Lizard Nature
Reserve
St Ruan
Kennack
Sands
Black Head
Vellan Head
Ruan Minor
Cadgwith
Grade
Kynance Cove
Llandewednock
Pentreath Beach
Lizard
Hot Point
Lizard Point
Lizard Lighthouse
Heritage Centre

Main photo: Embracing the surf scene at Whitesand Bay.
Opposite: Geevor Tin Mine and Penzance harbour.

The Far West

The journey to the road's end may be long and tiring. It may be fraught with crawling traffic and toilet stops, but there's something undeniably liberating and otherworldly about arriving in Penzance on the A30. Perhaps it has something to do with those exotically planted roundabouts on the town's outskirts.

Yet, in many ways, **Penzance** is only the beginning – the hub from which a web of minor roads fans out across the Penwith Peninsula to a whole 'island' of holiday opportunities in hidden fishing villages, old mining communities, organic farms, cliff-top retreats and surf spots.

If you're lucky, Penzance is also a departure point for daytrips or longer visits to the **Isles of Scilly** aboard a Skybus aircraft or the plucky little *Scillonian III*. Lying just 28 miles to the southwest, this idyllic archipelago seems to have a toehold in the tropics, with brilliant turquoise seas, powder-white beaches and rampant plantlife.

If you're sticking to the mainland, though, the natural thing is to keep heading west from Penzance on the A30 until it finally fizzles out at **Land's End**. Before you reach the mighty, wave-chewed toe of Britain, however, you can't help but notice all those enticing signs luring you down side lanes to places like **Porthcurno** (with its show-stopping line-up of beach, Minack Theatre and Telegraph Museum) or **Sennen Cove** (surf central and all-round beach beauty).

Closer to Penzance, fishing villages like **Newlyn** and **Mousehole** add weight to postcard stands with their colourful trawlers and cutesy harbourfronts, while **Marazion** is the stepping-off point for **St Michael's Mount** – the crowning glory of the region, if not the entire county.

Further west, towards The Lizard, you'll find rocky nooks and blousy bays like Prussia Cove and Praa Sands. Head inland from Penzance and the B3071 weaves past prehistoric remains to **St Just** – gateway to Cape Cornwall and the starting point for a spectacular coastal drive on the B3306, linking historic mining settlements before reaching **St Ives**. If there's one thing worth driving all the way to the far west of Cornwall for, it's this beautiful harbour town with its dazzling beaches and dynamic arts scene.

Here to there

The Far West chapter of *Cornwall with Kids* covers the Penwith Peninsula (stretching west from St Ives to Cape Cornwall, south to Land's End, then east to Penzance) and Mount's Bay (east from Penzance to Praa Sands). For information on beaches east of Praa Sands, refer to the chapter on The Lizard (see pages 128-147). St Ives is covered in detail on pages 122-127, while the Isles of Scilly section starts on page 148. See also Northwest Cornwall (pages 68-93) for attractions within easy reach of the far west.

Out & about The Far West

Stroll into a good book

Antonia Barber's much-loved children's classic, *The Mousehole Cat* (Walker Books) describes the epic tale of an old fisherman called Tom and his cat, Mowzer, as they set sail into a terrible storm. The gripping yarn get's an extra splash of reality if, afterwards, you stroll around **Mousehole** (pronounced 'Mowzel'), the fishing village near Penzance on which the book is based. A Cornish folktale by Charles Causley, *The Merrymaid of Zennor* (Orchard

Books) has its roots in a small village near St Ives where a church chair bears the carving of a mermaid.

Cue *Jaws* music – but don't worry: basking sharks are harmless.

Spot a basking shark

Basking sharks are becoming an increasingly common sight around Cornwall during summer. Growing to a length of up to 11 m, these gentle, plankton-eating giants can be spotted from clifftops anywhere along the coast. Look for the broad, triangular dorsal fin breaking the surface. With binoculars, you might also be able to spot the white gape of the shark's mouth. If you join a boat trip in search of basking sharks and other wildlife (see page 110), be sure to choose an operator that's signed up to guidelines for minimal disturbance (wisescheme.org).

❝ ❞ For a day away from it all I love nothing more than Prussia Cove, diving off the rocks or snorkelling around the gullies. A day surfing at Sennen Cove is the children's choice, followed by fish and chips from Lewis's in Newlyn – eaten sitting on a bench overlooking Mount's Bay. If we're feeling greedy, a Jelbert's home-made vanilla ice cream with a flake and a dollop of clotted cream goes down a treat! As for walks, one of our favourites is to head east along the coast path from Marazion to Perranuthnoe – it's exhilarating with the sea pounding the rocks below. Great fun on a calm summer's day is the walk along the causeway to St Michael's Mount as the tide starts to come in – see how far, and how wet, you get! Another fun and free pastime, rock-pooling is one of our specialities. My grandparents taught us well and there's no better place than Prussia Cove. Prise a limpet off the rocks, tie a length of cotton around it (and perhaps a tiny stone as a weight), dangle in a pool, then sit and wait. Before long you'll have a bucket full of blennies...

Philippa Penney
Property Manager, Classic Cottages, T01326-555555, classic.co.uk.

Get an early start and watch the fish being landed at Newlyn Harbour, cluttered with its fleet of long-liners and crabbers.

Take a walk on the wild side

Discover how wildlife thrives in the old mining landscape around Geevor and Levant. You can pick up a leaflet or booklet at Geevor Tin Mine's reception describing a two-hour walk that weaves through a fascinating array of habitats. Depending on the season (late spring or summer is best), you'll see Cornish hedges ablaze

with wildflowers, heathland fussed over by stonechats, an insect bank where mining bees burrow into an old spoil heap, coastal grassland flickering with butterflies, cliff-top views of seabirds and, perhaps, basking sharks and dolphins, a reptile slope where adders and lizards enjoy sunbathing and old mine buildings where bats have taken up residence.

Ancient wonders

It requires a bit of tracking down, but delve into the lanes between Madron and Morvah on the Penwith Peninsula and you should spot the Neolithic tomb of **Lanyon Quoit** poking above the hedgerows. There's a small parking layby from where you can walk to the imposing three-legged structure. The capstone alone weighs over 13 tons and stands 2 m above ground – it used to be higher, but one of the 'legs' collapsed during a storm in 1815 and only three were used in the reconstruction. For more prehistoric detective work, head to **Chysauster Ancient Village** (TR20 8XA, T07831-757934, english-heritage.org.uk, Apr-Oct daily from 1000) located just over two miles northwest of Gulval (near Penzance) on the B3311. You have to pay a modest admission fee (£3.60 adult, £2.20 child) to explore the remains of this 2000-year-old Iron Age settlement and its unique stone-walled homesteads known as 'courtyard houses'. Other ancient sites include the **Boscawen-un Stone Circle** (near the village of Drift). You can even stay in a Celtic chief's roundhouse at **Bodrifty** (bodriftyfarm.co.uk) just three fields from the Bodrifty Iron Age Aettlement, and signposted from Newmill beween Penzance and Zennor.

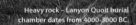

Heavy rock – Lanyon Quoit burial chamber dates from 4000-3000 BC.

Slick treatment is required for this oiled egret.

Visit Mousehole Wild Bird Hospital

Why? It provides a lifeline to sick or injured birds, like this oiled egret, and relies entirely on donations and the support of visitors. There's no admission fee, but anything you spend in the gift shop will go towards caring for birds until they are ready to be returned to the wild or, if that's not possible, providing a long-term home for them at the sanctuary. Residents range from ducks and gulls to lapwings and turnstones. The hospital rose to fame in 1967 when it treated over 8000 oiled sea birds following the *Torrey Canyon* disaster.

Where? Mousehole Wild Bird Hospital, Raginnis Hill, Mousehole, TR19 6SR, T01736-731386, mouseholebirdhospital.org.uk.

How? The hospital is open year round daily 1030-1430.

Get to the point

Distil everything that is magical about a family holiday in Cornwall – from surf, sand and rock pools to wild headlands and cutesy fishing villages – and you could well end up with this wonderful walk to **Land's End.** Following the South West Coast Path, the route starts at Gwynver, descending to a wave-pummelled beach at the northern end of Whitesand Bay. At low tide you can then stroll the best part of a mile along the entire scimitar curve of mainland Britain's most westerly beach, playing chicken with the waves, flying a kite, or simply enjoying the sensation of bare feet sinking into powder-soft sand. Approaching **Sennen Cove,** you'll reach a lifeguard-patrolled zone where it's safe to swim or surf (wetsuits and boards can be hired from the surf shop), but be sure to leave enough time to explore the rock pools near the lifeboat ramp. Continue through the village, stopping at The Blue Lagoon for fish and chips, or Breakers Café for a pasty. Peruse the local crafts in the Round House Gallery, then rejoin the coast path for the steady climb to an old coastguard lookout. There's a superb view across Whitesand Bay from here, but it's to the west that your eyes are drawn – to heather-capped cliffs rearing from a filigree of waves and marching west towards Land's End. Follow the clifftop path, passing the remains of Maen Castle, an Iron Age fort, then celebrate your arrival at the edge of Britain with ice creams at the First and Last House. There's an RSPB Discovery Centre just below the Land's End signpost where, for free, you can use telescopes to scan for dolphins, seals and basking sharks. The walk from Gwynver to Land's End is around two miles. Buses run from Land's End to Sennen Cove and Penzance.

Opposite: Maen Cliffs near Land's End.
This page: shrimping at Sennen Cove; rusty chain
in the harbour; a fisherman returns to shore; distant Gwenver
Beach merges with Whitesand Bay; heather-clad clifftops;
Sennen Cove fishing boats; body boarding at Whitesand Bay.

SENNEN

BECCY

Out & about The Far West

Best beaches

The beaches described here are found anticlockwise, from just west of St Ives to Praa Sands. For St Ives' beaches, see pages 124-127; for beaches on The Lizard, see pages 132-135.

Portheras Cove
Ⓟ ⊜ ❢

A strong contender for wildest beach in the west, Portheras is a sandy cove on a spectacular stretch of otherwise cliffy coast between St Just and St Ives. You can park near Pendeen Lighthouse and walk across to Portheras at low tide, but a more exciting approach is from Chypraze Farm, tucked down a narrow lane off the B3306 between Pendeen and Morvah. Park in the small field by the farm, drop £2 in the box at the farmhouse, then follow the short, fairly steep track towards the sea. At first, all you can see are waves breaking on the rocky, offshore Kenidjacks and the white dome of Pendeen Lighthouse poking above a distant headland. Keep walking (looking out for adders which like to bask on these slopes) and a crescent of sand slowly comes into view. The path enters a gully where you boulder-hop across a tea-coloured stream, then you're confronted by a sign warning of strong currents and fragments of metal from an old shipwreck. Portheras is not

the kind of place for swimming or bare feet. But what a beach! Surf lacing smooth banks of fine golden sand, seals cruising the breakers; brilliant tuquoise sea and jumbled granite boulders that wouldn't look out of place in the Seychelles – Portheras is a beach to sit and stare, enjoy a secluded picnic and play chicken with the waves. Just be very careful, though, as surf can unexpectedly sweep high up the beach, funnelled by a channel carved by the stream.

Priest's Cove (Cape Cornwall)
Ⓕ ⊕ Ⓟ ⊜ ❢

Topped by the chimney of an old mining engine house, Cape Cornwall (the only cape in England and Wales) has a small rocky beach snagged with Atlantic flotsam, from old ropes to worn chunks of driftwood covered in goose barnacles. It's a wonderfully wild and remote place – perfect for walks and picnics in the kind of solitude you rarely find at Land's End.

Whitesand Bay
⊜ Ⓕ Ⓕ ⊜ ⊜ ⊕ ⊕ Ⓟ

Just shy of Land's End, mainland Britain's most westerly beach has child appeal by the bucket load: a mile-long swathe of sand, turquoise sea white-ribbed by breakers and the cutesy fishing village of Sennen Cove with its surf school, fish and chips and lifeboat station. Scrawl your name in house-size letters

Portheras Cove.

What a beach! Surf lacing smooth banks of fine golden sand, seals cruising the breakers; brilliant turquoise sea and jumbled granite boulders that wouldn't look out of place in the Seychelles – Portheras is a beach to sit and stare, enjoy a secluded picnic and play chicken with the waves.

across acres of rippled sand, learn to surf, play beach cricket or frisbee, build a dam to hold back the tide and befriend a shaggy 14-stone Newfoundland called Bilbo – the adorable canine contingent of Sennen Cove's beach lifeguard crew (bilbosays.com). You could also try dipping a net in the rock pools near the lifeboat ramp, spotting seals by the harbour, walking across the bay at low tide to Gwynver Beach (where the surf is usually at its wildest) or striking out in the opposite direction, across the cliffs, to Land's End (see page 102). You'll need to arrive early during high season if you want to bag a space at Sennen Cove's main car park overlooking the beach. This is also where you'll find the Sennen Surfing Centre (see page 111) and Beach restaurant (see page 121). If this car park is full, try the one at the other end of the village, near the Round House Gallery. Otherwise, you'll have to park at the top of the hill and walk down to the beach.

Nanjizal

Follow the coast path a mile south from Land's End to reach this secluded cove – or park at Porthgwarra (see right) and walk north. Either way, you're in for a treat as Nanjizal's turquoise waters and rugged headlands come into view. At low tide there's sand, rock pools

and an enticing offshore sand bar which you can wade out to. Take care if swimming at Nanjizal – the currents and surf can be strong. Don't miss the Song of the Sea – a narrow cleft in the cliffs that leads through shallow pools to the sea.

Porthgwarra

A Cornish smugglers' cove if ever there was one, Porthgwarra even has a 'secret' tunnel leading from the slipway (just don't tell the kids it was excavated by miners to help farmers transport seaweed to their fields for use as fertiliser). A crabbing boat still operates from Porthgwarra, working the inlets along this dramatic and secluded stretch of coast south of Land's End. The cove has sand at low tide and swimming is safe as long as you stay close to shore. Keen rock-poolers should head right from the slipway. A café sells snacks and drinks.

Porth Chapel

This sandy cove has no facilities and requires a steepish walk, starting either at the car park near St Leven's church or by following the coast path from Porthgwarra (15 minutes) or Porthcurno (30 minutes).

Porthcurno

The best family beaches hold

secrets back, revealing them one by one as the tide ebbs and flows – and Porthcurno is a master of suspense. Stunning even by Cornish standards, it nestles beneath the stone ramparts of the cliff-top Minack Theatre, brilliant turquoise waters lapping its sweep of white sand or pounding the cliffs in a magnificent procession of curling, spray-whipped breakers. Then, as the tide drops, the beach slowly creeps along the rocky coast, stranding an enticing string of rock pools and knee-deep lagoons. Tiny coves appear and, if you're lucky, a spit of sand emerges to form the perfect ephemeral wicket for beach cricket – best played as the tide turns again and fielders are sent splashing into the encroaching waves in pursuit of the ball. Porthcurno's most unusual secret is that it was once the site of the first transatlantic submarine cable telegraph station – a museum in the village (see page 113) reveals all. Keep your eyes peeled for basking sharks near Porthcurno – particularly if you venture west along the coast path towards Land's End.

Lamorna Cove

A rocky cove approached along a beautiful wooded valley, Lamorna is sheltered and south facing with good rock-pooling at low tide.

Mousehole

A tiny, sandy cove is exposed at low tide in this picture-postcard, yet unspoilt, fishing village.

Marazion

Better known as the stepping-off point for walking across to St Michael's Mount (see page 114), Marazion is also a fine beach in its own right, with gently sloping sand and fine shingle.

Perran Sands

A wide sandy beach near the village of Perranuthnoe with just a strip of shingle at high tide.

Prussia Cove

Remote and tricky to reach, Piskies Cove and Bessy's Cove are linked by the coast path to Kenneggy Sands; a good spot for adventurous rock-poolers.

Praa Sands

One of Cornwall's most popular family beaches, Praa Sands (pronounced locally as 'Pray Sands') has a mile of golden sand, excellent swimming, great rock pools at the western end and even a dollop of surf when there's a south-coast swell. A spattering of beachfront shops, a café and watersports centre makes Praa a doddle for a relaxed family day out.

Rock-pooling at Porthgwarra.

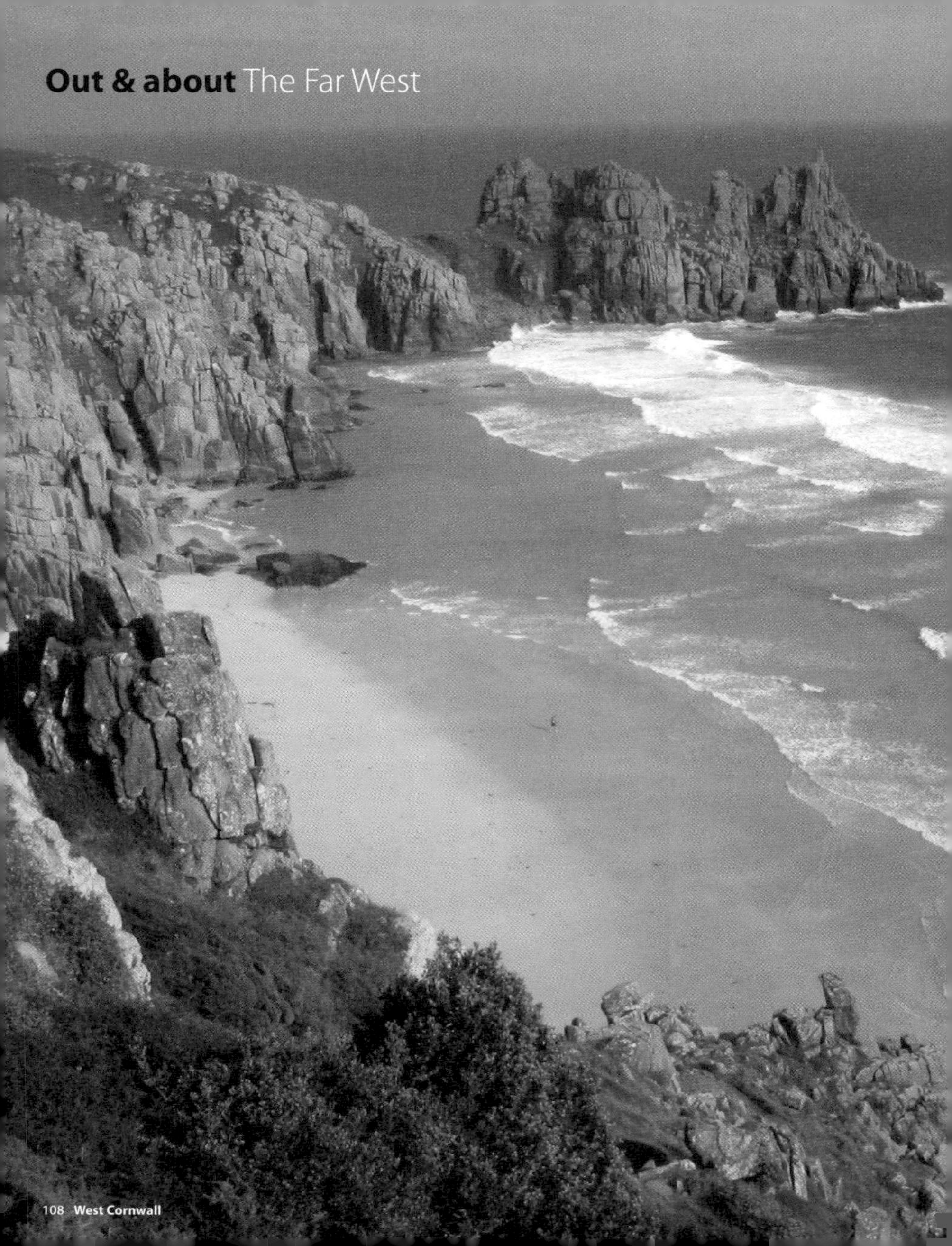

Stunning even by Cornish standards, Porthcurno nestles beneath the stone ramparts of the cliff-top Minack Theatre, brilliant turquoise waters lapping its sweep of white sand or pounding the cliffs in a magnificent procession of curling, spray-whipped breakers.

Out & about The Far West

Action stations

Boat trips
Elemental Tours

Penzance, TR18 2LL, T01736-811200, elementaltours.co.uk. Atlantic Adventure (2 hrs) £33 adult, £24 child (5-15), £95 family; Ocean Safari (3 hrs) £38 adult, £32 child (10-14); Sunset Cruise (2½ hrs, summer only) £25 adult, £15 child; land safaris (4 hrs) £40 adult, £25 child (10-15). Hold on tight for a wave-skipping, wind-in-your-face high-speed RIB ride in search of whales, dolphins, seals, basking sharks and seabirds. Enthusiasts can venture far offshore on three-hour Ocean Safaris, but the shorter Atlantic Adventure is a better bet for young families. It cruises the waters of the Penwith Peninsula, taking in famous landmarks like St Michael's Mount, the Minack Theatre and Land's End. Elemental Tours also offer 4WD land-based safaris, bouncing around remote parts of Penwith

in search of its wildlife, culture and industrial mining heritage.

Marine Discovery Penzance

Shed 5, Albert Pier, Penzance, TR18 2LL, T07749-277110, marinediscovery.co.uk. Mar-Nov. Bay Discovery (1-1½ hrs, minimum age 3) £18 adult, £14 child, £55 family; Ocean Discovery (3 hrs, minimum age 6) £35 adult, £25 child (6-15), £108 family; Discovery Voyage (4 hrs, minimum age 12) £40.
Marine Discovery operate their wildlife watching adventures on the sailing catamaran, *Shearwater II*. The crew know the area intimately and you have an excellent chance of seeing grey seals, harbour porpoises, seabirds, various dolphins, basking sharks (depending on the season), and sometimes even whales. Check out their Facebook page or sightings page on their website for what's been spotted on recent trips. Marine Discovery are the only company in the south west to

run wildlife watching trips on an environmentally friendly sailing boat, which means you are safe in the knowledge that your trip is having as little impact on marine wildlife as possible (they won the Responsible Whale Watch Awards in 2013). You are welcome to help crew the boat if conditions are suitable, and even have a go on the helm. The shorter trips are more suited to those with smaller children. The Ocean Discovery is the most popular and frequent, while the Discovery Voyage is for true wildlife enthusiasts.

Mermaid Pleasure Trips

The White Shed, Ross Bridge, Wharf Rd, Penzance, TR18 4AH, T07901-731201, cornwallboattrips.com. Mackerel fishing (2 hrs) £15 adult, £2 child (under 5). Seal Cove Cruise (2 hrs, summer and school holidays, daily 1300 and 1500) £12 adult, £10 child (5-12), £5 infant (2-4). Shark & Theatre Cruise (3hrs) £18 adult, £15 child (5-12), £5 child (2-4).
Having worked on local ferries and lifeboats, skipper Adrian Thomas knows the seas around Penzance like the back of his hand. He's also lived on St Michael's Mount, so a cruise aboard his boat, *Mermaid II*, is a great opportunity not only to catch mackerel, observe seals and haul in lobster and crab pots, but also to learn about the history and legends of this beautiful stretch of Cornish coast. The 33-ft boat is licensed

Surf's up – Praa Sands.

See life

Warmed by the Gulf Stream, the seas around West Cornwall are positively squirming with life. Join a boat trip and you could find yourself bobbing alongside bottlenose dolphins or racing towards a rendezvouz with a pod of leaping Risso's or common dolphins. Harbour porpoises tend to make more fleeting appearances, while any sighting – no matter how brief – of an orca, minke whale or fin whale is a bonus. Grey seals, meanwhile, are the staple sighting of wildlife cruises – they breed in local sea caves and can often be seen dozing on rocky outcrops. Summer visitors include basking sharks (see page 100), sun fish and leatherback turtles. Keep a lookout for common seabirds like gannets (pictured) and fulmars. Most puffins breed in the Scillies.

to carry 35 passengers for summer cruising and up to 18 for fishing trips. Mermaid also offers wildlife-watching cruises, heading out towards Cudden Point in search of seals, seabirds, whales, dolphins and basking sharks. The Shark & Theatre cruise gives you a great view of the Minack Theatre from the sea, while the clear waters are ideal for spotting basking sharks and other marine life.

Cycling
First & Last Trail
Part of this trail includes a level, mainly traffic-free link between Penzance and Marazion, with views of St Michael's Mount.

The Cycle Centre
New St, Penzance, TR18 2LZ, T01736-351671, cornwallcyclecentre.co.uk.

Mount's Bay Cycle Hire
Station House, Marazion, T01736-363044.

Horse riding
Trevescan Farm Equestrian Ctr
Trevescan Farm, Sennen, TR19 7AQ, T01736-871989, trevescanfarm.co.uk. Livery yard with indoor and floodlit outdoor arenas.

Surfing
Global Boarders Surf School
Marazion, TR17 0EA, T01736-711289, globalboarders.com. £35/2-hr lesson, Surf Experience Days £85 (minimum 2 people).
Operating from Marazion, Global Boarders takes you to the beach with the best surf conditions

that day – transport, two surf sessions and all gear included.

Sennen Surfing Centre
Sennen Cove, TR19 7AD, T01736-871561, sennensurfingcentre.com. £30/2-hr lesson, £25/family course. Located beneath the Beach restaurant (see page 121), this well-established surf school is a short sprint from the waves at Whitesand Bay and offers beginner, improver and advanced coaching.

Smart Surf School
Sennen Cove, T01736-871817, sennensurfschool.com. £28/2-hr lesson, £50/1½-hr private lesson. Small, friendly surf school located on the seafront.

Stonesreef Surfshop
Praa Sands, T01736-762991, stonesreefsurf.co.uk. £25/2-hr lesson, £20 for groups of four or more. More than just a surf shop, Stones can arrange snorkelling and stand-up paddleboarding. Sit-on sea kayaks can also be hired on the beach.

Geevor Tin Mine

Pendeen, TR19 7EW, T01736-788662, geevor.com. Apr-Oct Sun-Fri 0900-1700 (1600 Nov-Mar); mine tours hourly 1000-1600. £10.50 adult, £6.50 child (5-16), £33 family. Geevor Tin Mine really evokes the atmosphere of Cornwall's rich industrial heritage – pick up hard hats at the ticket office and you know you're in for something authentic.

A working mine until 1990, Geevor's tunnels are now open to visitors but first you need to navigate the mine building – a vast metal skeleton of rusted beams, pipes, plankways and colossal stone-grinding cauldrons. Don't worry – the route is clearly marked and quite safe. Every now and then you come across a friendly member of staff who will demonstrate an aspect of the tin-mining process. You'll get to weigh up a nugget of tin ore against a similarly-sized lump of granite; you'll learn about giant stone crushers and watch tin ore being separated from sandy waste on large, juddering sorting tables. It all makes perfect sense to children – a ginormous, smashing, sieving, sorting machine that could almost have been hatched from the mind of Willy Wonka.

Eventually you reach a door where more smiling ex-miners hand out overcoats and direct you to the underground section of the tour – a 300-year-old mine that was only discovered in 1995. Bent double (even a nine-year-old will have to duck in places) you shuffle along dank tunnels, passing narrow shafts and cramped chambers where costumed mannequins reinact the grim realities of mining three centuries ago. One of the figures rather alarmingly comes to life – at least, that's how it seems in the dim light until you realise it's another of Geevor's engaging miners waiting to chat to you about what it was like to work in the modern mine.

Plans are afoot to build a new, bigger underground experience, but for now this is an utterly mesmerising insight into the very heart of Cornwall's World Heritage mining site. Back above ground you can

All mine – panning for gold at Geevor.

pan for fool's gold, explore sheds full of machinery, uncover nuggets of wisdom at the Hard Rock Museum and even have a go at hand drilling.

Land's End

Land's End, Sennen, TR19 7AA, T0871-720 0044, landsend-landmark. co.uk. Easter-Oct, from 1000, Nov-Easter from 1030. £10 adult, £7 child, £25 family all-inclusive, or pay for individual attractions, from £3 adult, £2 child; £5 all-day parking.

As well as the spectacular coastal scenery and clifftop walks at England's southwest extremity, there are plenty of indoor attractions should a soaking westerly send you scuttling for cover. Arthur's Quest is an interactive experience that takes you into the magical realm of Merlin, witches and dragons. A 4D cinema features different films each year, while a rattling 'motion cinema' reinacts an air-sea rescue. There's also The End to End Story – a free exhibition about people who have made the intrepid journey from Land's End to John O'Groats. Outside you can have your photo taken beneath the famous signpost (John of Groats 874 miles, New York 3147 miles). There's also a 'wreckreation' playground and a wildlife observation post manned by RSPB volunteers. Don't miss the 200-year-old Cornish farmstead of Greeb Farm with its animals to pet and feed and craft studios to peruse.

Minack Theatre

Porthcurno, TR19 6JU, T01736-810181, minack.com. Open to visitors Oct-Mar daily 1000-1600; Apr-Oct Mon, Tue, Thu, Sat, Sun 0930-1700, Wed, Fri 0930-1130. £4 adult, £2 child (under 16), free for under-12s. Call or check website for forthcoming productions.

Cornwall's iconic open-air theatre, clinging to the cliffs above Porthcurno, is well worth a visit even if you're not planning on taking in a show (several family-friendly productions are scheduled each season). As well as the triumphant setting, there's an interesting exhibition about the theatre's creator, Rowena Cade, as well as a coffee shop and dazzling sub-tropical rockeries.

More family favourites

Levant Mine & Beam Engine

Trewellard, Pendeen, TR19 7SX, T01736-786156, nationaltrust.org.uk. Mar-Oct days vary (engine is steaming Jul-Sep Tue-Fri and Sun, 1100-1700). £6.50 adult, £3.20 child, £16.20 family.

Still standing proud on the cliff edge, Levant is Cornwall's only working steam-powered beam engine. Underground tours and a short film help to tell its story.

Trewidden Garden

Buryas Bridge, Penzance, TR20 8TT, T01736-351979, trewiddengarden. co.uk. Mar-Sep daily 1030-1730. £6 adult, children free.

Rain check

Cinemas
Savoy
Causewayhead, Penzance, TR18 2SN, T01736-363330.

Indoor swimming pools
Penzance Leisure Centre
St Clare, TR18 3QW, T01736-874744.

Museums
Penlee House Gallery & Museum
Morrab Rd, Penzance, TR18 4HE, T01736-363625, penleehouse.org.uk. £4.50 adult, children free.
Victorian home with impressive collection of paintings and museum artefacts relating to the history and culture of West Cornwall. Children's workshops take place during school holidays and there's also a café, gift shop and play area.

Porthcurno Telegraph Museum
Eastern House, Porthcurno, TR19 6JX, T01736-810966, porthcurno.org.uk. Apr-Oct daily. Major refurbishment in 2014. Call for times and prices.
Fascinating museum all about communications and Porthurno's famous undersea cable. Second World War tunnels to explore, quiz trails, play tables and plenty of hands-on, touch-screen displays.

Wayside Museum
Zennor, TR26 3DA, T01736-796945. Apr-Oct daily from 1030. £3.95 adult, £2.75 child, £12 family.
This evocative time-capsule has themed areas including a watermill, cobbler's shop and blacksmith, as well as artefacts dating from the Bronze Age.

Ten-pin bowling
Grand Casino
Promenade, Penzance, TR18 4HH, T01736-363824.

Riddled with enticing pathways this peaceful, 15-acre garden is particularly impressive during spring when the magnolias are in bloom. Nearby Trengwainton is a peaceful woodland garden.

Don't miss St Michael's Mount

It's a cliché, but getting here really is part of the adventure. Few landmarks in Cornwall are more evocative, or enticing, than St Michael's Mount, especially at low tide when a cobbled causeway emerges from the sea, extending an irresistible invitation to walk across to the rocky islet crowned with its medieval castle and church. Better still, wait for an ebbing tide, roll up your trousers and wade across.

Once on the island, you may be surprised to find a thriving little community (home to 30 islanders), complete with harbour, sub-tropical gardens, shops, café and restaurant.

Collect children's quiz sheets before walking up the steep, but short, path to the castle. If you look carefully, you'll find a cobblestone in the shape of a heart which, according to legend, once beat in the chest of the giant Cormoran – a big bully prone to snacking on the island's cattle until he was lured into a pit and slain by a local lad called Jack (the original giant killer). A more uplifting legend refers to a vision of the Archangel St Michael that appeared to fishermen in the year 495 AD.

The views from the summit of St Michael's Mount are spectacular, while the castle itself is a small but fascinating window on the past, with cannons and suits of armour dating from the War of the Roses and the Civil War, when the fortress was under seige.

The Mount's religious roots go back to the Norman invasion, when the island was granted to the Benedictine Abbey of Mont St Michel in Brittany. There's an exquisite chapel deep inside the castle which has been the family home of the St Aubyn family since the 17th century. Don't miss the elegant rococo-style Blue Drawing Room or the Chevy Chase Room with its 17th-century frieze depicting hunting scenes described in the *Ballad of Chevy Chase*.

Wade to go – barefoot to St Michael's Mount.

At low tide a cobbled causeway emerges from the sea, extending an irresistible invitation to walk across to the rocky islet.

Mount a plan

St Michael's Mount
Marazion, nr Penzance, TR17 0EF,
T01736-710507 or 710265 (tide and ferry
information), stmichaelsmount.co.uk,
nationaltrust.org.uk. Late Mar-Jun Sun-Fri
1030-1700; Jul-Aug Sun-Fri 1030-1730;
Sep-early Nov Sun-Fri 1030-1700, last
admission 45 mins before castle closing time.
£9.60 adult, £4.80 child (5-17), £24 family.

Getting there
On foot At low tide, follow in the footsteps
of pilgrims and giants as you walk across the
causeway to St Michael's Mount. It only takes a few
minutes, but you should wear sensible shoes as
the cobbles are slippery and uneven. Bear in mind
that the climb to the castle is steep and cobbled
and, therefore, unsuitable for pushchairs.
By boat At high tide small motor boats ply back
and forth between the Mount and three landing
points along the shore at Marazion. One-way fares
£2 adult, £1 child.

Sleeping The Far West

Pick of the pitches

Higher Pentreath Farm

Praa Sands, TR20 9TL, T01736-763240, higherpentreathcampsite.co.uk. Easter-Oct. From £12/pitch.

⊙ ⊙ ⊙ ⊙ ⊙

Unzip your tent each morning to an invigorating view over mile-wide Praa Sands. The facilities at this campsite might be quite basic (a converted barn for a toilet and shower block, plus a tiny shop), but its location more than compensates. It takes just five minutes to stroll down the (steep) hill to the beach where there are cafés, pubs and shops.

Kelynack Caravan & Camping Park

Kelynack, St Just, TR19 7RE, T01736-787633, kelynackholidays.co.uk. Mar-Oct. Pitches £7.50 adult, £3.75 child (3-12); static caravans £210-550/wk.

⊙ ⊙ ⊙ ⊙ ⊙ ⊙ ⊙ ⊙

This small, secluded site offers a range of sleeping options, including 45 touring pitches, a cluster of holiday homes and luxury bed and breakfast/self-catering accommodation. A shop sells freshly made rolls, sandwiches and cakes, as well as everyday groceries. Children will find plenty to do at Kelynack. As well as a playground and wood to explore, they'll be forever fussing over the small herd of friendly donkeys and a lone Shetland pony called Pedro. Kelynack is also well located – hop on a bus at the end of the road and you can be in Land's End or St Ives within the hour.

Kenneggy Cove Holiday Park

Higher Kenneggy, Rosudgeon, TR20 9AU, T01736-763453, kenneggycove.co.uk. May-Oct. £17-26/pitch (2 adults), plus £5.50 extra person.

⊙ ⊙ ⊙ ⊙ ⊙ ⊙ ⊙ ⊙

A quiet, well-tended site with 50 touring pitches and seven holiday homes, Kenneggy Cove Holiday Park is just a 12-minute walk from the coast path and Kenneggy Sands, a secluded beach (with sand and rock pools) between Perranuthnoe and Cudden Point.

Noongallas

Gulval, Penzance, TR20 8YR, T01736-366698, noongallas.com. Jul-Aug. £6 adult, £3 child (under 16).

⊙ ⊙

Snug in the depths of the Penwith countryside with views of Mount's Bay, this back-to-nature campsite is one of the very few in Cornwall that permits campfires (don't forget your marshmallows). There's a relaxed, almost festival-like, atmosphere here – families get together for communal barbecues, while children make a bee-line for the nearby woods, building camps and damming the stream. As you might expect, facilities are few and far between (just a small shower and toilet block). However, if you don't mind basic camping, this is the ideal site for a relaxed holiday.

Tower Park Caravans & Camping

St Buryan, TR19 6BZ, T01736-810286, towerparkcamping.co.uk. Mar-Oct. £10-19/pitch (2 adults), plus £5 extra adult, £3.50 extra child (5-15); holiday tents £235-410/wk; static caravans £255-490/wk.

⊙ ⊙ ⊙ ⊙ ⊙ ⊙ ⊙ ⊙ ⊙ ⊙

Handy for both Sennen Cove and Porthcurno, Tower Park is a short walk from the village of St Buryan with its general store and pub. The site is divided into seven level fields of mown grass, sheltered by trees and Cornish hedges. As well as camping pitches and five static caravans (sleeping up to six), Tower Park has six-berth, fully equipped pre-erected tents for hire.

Trevedra Farm

Nr Sennen Cove, TR19 7BE, T01736-871818, trevedrafarm.co.uk. Apr-Oct. £5.50/adult, £3/child (5-15).

⊙ ⊙ ⊙ ⊙ ⊙ ⊙ ⊙ ⊙

Occasionally windy, but with a superb location above Whitesand Bay, Trevedra has direct access to the steep coastal path leading to Gwynver Beach (see pages 102 and 106). Book early to secure a pitch in the field with sea views. Trevedra gets busy during summer, so don't expect total peace and quiet – especially if a group of surfers pitch up next to you. The site is kept immaculately clean by the friendly owners and there is a well-stocked shop and a handy snack van.

Porthcurno and the Minack Theatre.

Treverven Touring Caravan & Camping Park

Treverven Farm, St Buryan, TR19 6DL, T01736-810200, treverventouringpark.co.uk. Apr-Oct. £10-14/pitch (2 adults), plus £4 extra adult, £3 extra child (3-15);

You can see the sea from this lovely, elevated site two miles west of Lamorna Cove. A farm track delves into a wooded valley, thick with ferns and wildflowers and ringing with birdsong in spring and summer, while a traffic-free country lane leads directly to the coast path, 10 minutes' walk away. On-site facilities include a children's play area, nature trail and snack van.

Also recommended
Bone Valley Holiday Park

Heamoor, Penzance, TR20 8UJ, T01736-360313, bonevalleyholidaypark.co.uk. Easter-Oct. Call for rates.

Quiet, sheltered site a short walk from Heamoor with its general store, fish and chip shop, bakers, pub and bus stop.

Secret Garden Carvan & Camping Park

Bosavern House, St Just, TR19 7RD,

T01736-788301, secretbosavern. com. Mar-Oct. £17/pitch (2 adults), plus £3.80 extra person.

Tiny, intimate site with just 12 pitches within the old walled garden of a 17th century house.

Sennen Cove Camping & Caravanning Club Site

Higher Tregiffian Farm, St Buryan, TR19 6JB, T01736-871588, campingandcaravanningclub.co.uk. Mar-Nov. Call for rates.

Immaculate 72-pitch site with modern facilities and children's playfield. Gwynver Beach is a 25-minute walk away.

Trevair Touring Park

South Treveneague, St Hilary, TR20 9BY, T01736-740647, trevairtouringpark.co.uk. Easter-Oct. £2-8/tent, £5 adult, £3 child (3-16), static caravans £200-310/wk.

Peaceful, three-acre site with sub-tropical palms and lush lawns, surrounded by woodland.

Farm favourite

For camping in style, try Boswarthen Farm, near Madron – it's the only Feather Down Farm site in Cornwall. See pages 12-13 for details.

Holiday parks

Mount's Bay Holiday Park
Marazion, TR17 0HQ, T01736-710307, mountsbay-caravanpark.co.uk.
Small family-run park with 18 caravans and a heated outdoor swimming pool just 50 m from the beach at Marazion.

Praa Sands Holiday Park
Praa Sands, TR20 9SH, T01736-762201, haulfrynholidays.co.uk.
Five minutes' walk from the beach, Praa Sands Holiday Park has been redeveloped into a smart new retreat for families and couples. In addition to top-of-the-range caravans, facilities include an indoor heated swimming pool, sauna, fitness room, nine-hole golf course, restaurant and terrace bar with sea views.

River Valley Country Park
Relubbus, TR20 9ER, T0844-8800 144, rivervalley.co.uk.
As well as pitches for touring caravans and tents, River Valley Country Park has holiday homes and luxury lodges (some with hot tubs). The park is located in a quiet valley close to Marazion and Praa Sands and offers breakfast packs on arrival.

Praa Sands Holiday Park.

Sleeping The Far West

Atlantic House

Sennen Cove, T01326-555555, classic.co.uk. £579-1620/wk.
This gorgeous, open-plan New England-style property sleeps seven and is crisp, fresh and uncluttered – exactly how you wished your own home could be. The path to surf-sensation, Whitesand Bay, is steep, but the views more than compensate.

St Aubyn Estates

The Manor Office, Marazion, TR17 0EF T01736-719693, staubynestatesholidays.co.uk. From around £500-1150/wk for a cottage sleeping four.

Cottage agents

See also page 198.

Cornish Riviera Holidays Westcotts Quay, St Ives, TR26 2DY, T01736-797891, cornishrivieraholidays.co.uk. Portfolio of over 70 fishermen's cottages and harbourside flats in the heart of St Ives.

Furthest West Cornish Holidays Treen, TR19 6LQ, T01736-810452, furthestwest.com. Three properties in Sennen Cove and two in Treen, between Porthcurno and Penberth.

Trevarthian Holiday Homes Marazion, TR17 0EG, T01736-710100, trevarthian.co.uk. Beachside self-catering apartments close to the sandy beach and children's playground at Marazion.

Six lovingly restored seaside botholes (sleeping up to eight) in the Porthgwarra area. Faraway Cottage is a gem, just minutes from the coast path and with views over Nanjizal Cove; Cove Cottage is metres from the water's edge at Porthgwarra, while Bosistow Farmhouse has panoramic sea views and is ideal for larger families.

Queens Hotel

The Promenade, Penzance, TR18 4HG, T01736-362371, queens-hotel.com. B&B from £66 adult, £15 child.
Handy if you need to spend a night in Penzance prior to sailing to the Isles of Scilly, this Victorian seafront hotel has family rooms and a children's menu.

Rosudgeon Farm

Prussia Cove, T01702-475075, rosudgeonfarm.com. £495-870/wk.
A 15-minute walk from Prussia Cove, this fine farmhouse with its three crisply converted barns (sleeping up to six) is set around a courtyard, with wonderful coastal views and opportunities for cliff-top walks.

Wesley's Barn

Bosavern Farm, St Just, T01736-787007, cornwallwestcottage.co.uk. £370-800/wk.
An immaculate granite barn conversion near St Just, split into two properties, each with two bedrooms, an open-plan living room, kitchen and dining area, plus private garden.

Wesley's Barn.

YHA Penzance

Castle Horneck, Penzance, TR20 8TF, T0845-371 9653, yha.org.uk. Rooms from £20.
Recently refurbished, this smart hostel occupies a Georgian manor house on the outskirts on Penzance and has family rooms, a café, self-catering kitchen and landscaped woodland gardens.

Tregenna Castle Estate

St Ives, TR26 2DE, T01736-795254, tregenna-castle.co.uk. Check online for special offers.
Standing proud above St Ives, this 72-acre estate has a luxury hotel, 70 self-catering cottages and apartments and a collection of wooden lodges (each with jacuzzi and sauna). Leisure facilites include an 18-hole golf course, two heated swimming pools, tennis courts, croquet and a spa. Tregenna also boasts one of Cornwall's best kids' programmes, with a packed schedule of treasure hunts, discos, craft modelling, cooking, wildlife activities and soft play.

See also **The Cove**, page 121.

Eating The Far West

Local goodies

Bill & Flo's
Trevarrack, nr Lelant, TR26 3EZ,
T01736-798885.
Home-grown veg and salad,
plus local meats, cheese, honey,
cider and apple juice.

Chegwidden Farm Shop
St Levan, TR19 6LP, T01736-810516,
chegwiddenfarm.com.
Delicious rare-breed sausages,
bacon and burgers, along
with a good selection of fresh
vegetables, cheeses and other
local produce. The farm also
offers accommodation at The
Granary and Old Farm House.

Higher Trenowin Farm Shop
Nancledra, TR20 8BE, T01736-
362439, highertrenowin.co.uk. Wed-
Sat 0900-1730, Sun 0900-1300.
A family-run farm between
St Ives and Penzance, Higher
Trenowin Farm runs a single
suckler beef herd and stocks
its farm shop with free-range
hen and quail eggs, seasonal
vegetables, herbs and salads,
cakes, jams, preserves and local
ice cream from Zennor.

Trevathan Farm Shop
St Endellion, PL29 3TT, T01208-
880164, trevathanfarm.com.
Daily from 0900.
Pick your own fruit and veg or
find it in the farm shop, together
with farm-fresh beef, lamb and
eggs, plus lots of other Cornish
goodies – jams, chutneys,

Fishy business
The **Pilchard Works** at Newlyn
(pilchardworks.co.uk) uses only
line-caught fish – look out for their
distinctive tins of pilchards and
mackerel, decorated with Newlyn
School paintings.

honey, cheeses, fudge and
clotted cream. Children can
pamper the fluffies in the pets'
corner, while grown-ups peruse
the country wines, Cornish beer
and scrumpy. Afterwards, treat
them to Treleavens ice cream or
go the whole hog and sit down
to a traditional Sunday roast or
cream tea in the restaurant.

Trevelyan Farm Shop
Rosudgeon, TR20 9PP,
T01736-710410.
Organic farm shop selling a
good range of meat, dairy,
vegetables and fruit products,
plus preserves, bread and cakes.

Dating from the 13th century, the pasty
became established as the staple diet of
miners across Cornwall. A portable
and durable convenience food, its
crimped crust was used as a handle
which was later discarded due to
the high levels of arsenic in many
Cornish tin mines.

Market days

Lamorna Produce Market
Village Hall, Friday 0900-1300.

Penzance Country Market
St Johns Hall, Alverton Street,
Thursday 0830-1230.

Penzance Farmers' Market
St John's Hall, Alverton Street,
Friday 0900-1400.

Sennen Farmers' Market
Sennen Community Centre,
Tuesday 0900-1200.

St Erth Farmers' Market
Methodist Church, Saturday
1000-1200.

St Ives Farmers Market
The Guildgall, Thursday
0900-1400.

Ice cream
Milking the legend of the Zennor
Merrymaid (see page 100) **Moomaid
of Zennor** (moomaidofzennor.com)
creates sumptuous ice cream and
sorbet using milk and cream from
the dairy herd at Tremedda Farm.
There's a Moomaid parlour on the
Wharf, St Ives, and Porthtowan.

Perfect pasties
The **Genuine Cornish Pasty Association** is a group of more than 50 pasty
makers in Cornwall, baking around 90 million pasties each year – check online
for a list of members (cornishpastyassociation.co.uk). They know exactly what
makes a proper Cornish pasty. For starters, it has to be a 'D' shape, crimped on
one side – never the top. The filling should be chunky with no less than 12.5%
roughly cut chunks of beef, plus swede or turnip, potato and onion, with a
light pepper seasoning. Glazed with milk or egg, the pastry casing should be
golden with no splits. And, finally, it should always be made in Cornwall.

Eating The Far West

Quick & simple

Old Success Inn
Sennen Cove, TR19 7DG, T01736-871232, oldsuccess.co.uk. Food served 1200-1400, 1800-2100.
A pub alternative to the nearby Beach restaurant (right), this 17th-century fisherman's inn is a local watering hole with a good range of Cornish bitters and ciders, a cosy bar and old pictures of the Sennen lifeboat. There's also a pool table and photos of big waves – no doubt to appease the surf crowd – but this busy pub is also a good bet for families. The menu features light bites such as fish goujons (£6.95), sandwiches (from £5.25) and jacket potatoes (from £4.95). Mains include Cornish pasty and salad (£7.95), fish pie (£10.95), catch of the day (£8.95) and wholetail scampi (£8.95), while the kids' menu is equally 'safe' with fish and chips, sausage and mash or pasta from £4.75. There's a carvery on Sundays from 1200 – and you can even order a hamper to take to the Minack Theatre.

Poolside Indulgence
Jubilee Pool, Wharf Rd, Penzance, TR18 4HH, T0777-999 8590, poolside-indulgence.co.uk. Daily from 1000.
Just imagine a long summer's evening, fresh tasty food, a poolside table and lights twinkling across the bay... This irresistible little café is as close to

the Mediterranean as Penzance gets – and the menu reflects just that. Overlooking Jubilee Pool, one of the best preserved lidos in the country, and beyond to St Michael's Mount, Poolside Indulgence serves freshly made salads, seafood platters, sandwiches, pastas and burgers. For a tasty snack, try the Share Plate (£10.95) where you can nibble at sun-dried tomatoes, olives, anchovies, cheese, chorizo and bread.

Renaissance Café
Wharfside Shopping Centre, Market Jew St, Penzance, TR18 2GB, T01736-366277, renaissancepenzance.co.uk. Mon-Sat 0930-23.30, Sun 1000-1130.
With views across the harbour to St Michael's Mount, the Renaissance serves some of the town's best pizza (from £7.95), plus a good range of seafood, steaks, burgers and salads.

Sandbar
Praa Sands, TR20 9TQ, T01736-763516, sandbarpraasands.co.uk. Mon-Fri from 1100, Sat-Sun from 1000.
Smack bang on the golden, surf-raked beach of Praa Sands, the Sandbar has an oceanfront view to rival any of the beach cafés on the North Cornwall coast. Lively and popular, it serves a good range of snacks and beach bites, pizzas, salads, decent home-made burgers and locally caught fish. There's also a Sunday lunchtime carvery (from £7.50).

Poolside Indulgence overlooks the lido.

Also recommended
The Cook Book
St Just, TR19 7JZ, T01736-787266, thecookbookstjust.co.uk.
Home-made cakes, cream teas, soups and salads – with a second-hand book store upstairs. Also in St Just, the Warren's bakery has excellent pasties.

Count House Café
Geevor Tin Mine, Pendeen, TR19 7EW, T01736-788662. Free entry.
Simple, tasty food and picture-window views of the Atlantic. Few places serve a better pasty in a more spectacular location.

Fish & chips
Captain's (Daniel Pl, Penzance) has been established for over 50 years. Also try **Lewis's** (The Strand, Newlyn), **Jeremy's** (Market Sq, St Just), **Beck's** (Longstone Hill Carbis Bay), **The Kingfisher** (Wharf Rd, St Ives) and **The Blue Lagoon** on the seafront at Sennen Cove.

The Gurnard's Head

Nr Zennor, St Ives, TR26 3DE, T01736-796928, gurnardshead.co.uk.
A perfect pitstop if you've been out stomping the cliff paths between St Ives and St Just, the 'Gurn' has a relaxed atmosphere, fine views and good simple food, using fresh local ingredients.

Posh nosh

Beach

Sennen Cove, TR19 7BT, T01736-871191, thebeachrestaurant.com.
Mon-Sat 1000-1630, 1845-2045; Sun 1000-1730.
Located right above Whitesand Bay, the Beach restaurant practically dabbles its toes in the Atlantic. There's a surf shop underneath it, so no excuses for not working up an appetite for lunchtime bites such as crab soup (£12.25), steak ciabatta (£10.50) or soup of the day (£5.95) – best enjoyed on the large terrace with views of the beach and distant Cape Cornwall. More substantial lunchtime mains (from around £12) include seafood pie and Cornish roast beef.

The children's menu features pasta (£5.25) and fish, sausage or chicken and chips (£6.50). For dinner, expect to pay around £14-19 for a main course. There are always a couple of meat dishes on the menu, but it's seafood that the Beach really excels at – whether it's seared scallops, seafood linguine or a Newlyn hake chowder. Much of it is fresh off the restaurant's boat, *Rosebud*.

The Cove

Lamorna, TR19 6XH, T01736-731411, thecovecornwall.com. Brunch 1000-1200, light bites and afternoon tea 1430-1800 , dinner 1900-2200.
With just 16 stylish self-catering apartments, this exclusive hotel peeps through the trees at Lamorna Cove. Open to non-residents, The Cove's terrace bar is a gorgeous spot to enjoy a cream tea or a light snack, such as a plate of mezze or charcuterie (from £7.50). Lunch and dinner (taken on either the terrace or in the restaurant) feature seafood dishes ranging from steamed mussels and crab salad to catch of the day and roast monkfish. You can also expect to find one or two tempting meat dishes using

local lamb or beef. Lunchtime meals start at around £7, while dinner mains cost from about £14. Children's meals (all around £7.50) are home-made and organic – choose from pasta, chicken, bangers and mash or fish and chips.

The Land's End Restaurant

The Land's End Hotel, Lands End, TR19 7AA , T01736-871844, landsendhotel.co.uk. Daily 1200-1500, 1830-2100.
Open to non-residents of the Land's End Hotel, the restaurant is located in the conservatory, where window seats bag stunning views of the sea. Sandwiches and paninis are available at the bar, while the very reasonable lunchtime Evergreen Menu (two courses £6.95, three courses £8.95) features soup, salad, pâté or melon for starters and steak pie, poached salmon, roast dinner or a vegetarian dish for main courses. The evening à la carte menu, meanwhile, has a classic selection of starters (mussels, baked mushrooms etc), followed by an equally traditional range of mains, featuring fish, steak and chicken. Expect to pay from around £15 to £20 for two courses.

View towards Sennen Cove from the Beach restaurant.

Let's go to...

St Ives

How do you sell a day out at a modern art gallery to children? You could mention that the Tate St Ives is renowned for its child-friendliness and has family activities that sometimes spill onto Porthmeor Beach. You could add that St Ives is the epicentre of Cornwall's thriving art scene and that a visit to the Tate embodies the region's creativity. Or you could simply slip in the gallery as part of a fun-filled day trip that starts with a train ride on the St Ives Bay Line, an hour or two on Porthminster Beach, followed by a spot of crabbing along the harbourfront as you amble towards the Tate.

Get your bearings

St Ives has everything you could possibly want in a Cornish seaside town – from bustling harbour and beautiful beaches to great food and fine art. Small wonder it's heaving with tourists during the high season. The trick for a stress-free visit is to leave your car behind and explore on foot.

The 12-minute train ride from St Erth on the **St Ives Bay Line** (T08457-000125, firstgreatwestern. co.uk) provides dreamy views across the bay towards Godrevy Point and birdwatching as you trundle past the Hayle Estuary. The train stops at Porthminster Beach, just south of the harbour, but you could also get off at Carbis Bay and stroll into town along the coast path (about 20 minutes).

St Ives Tourist Information Centre (The Guildhall, Street-an-Pol, TR26 2DS, T0905-252 2250, stivestic.co.uk) is located close to the main shopping area behind the harbour. Follow The Wharf around the harbour to Smeatons Pier or cross over the narrow peninsula separating the harbour from Porthmeor Beach.

View towards St Ives harbour, with Godrevy lighthouse in the distance.

Let's go to... St Ives

Hit the beach

A slightly quieter alternative to the busy town beaches in St Ives, **Carbis Bay** is a dune-backed, Blue-Flag beauty, covering acres of sand with just the right consistency for sandcastles. The swimming here is generally sheltered and safe.

Another Blue Flag contender, **Porthminster** is a stunning beach with fine golden sand gently shelving into a sheltered corner of St Ives Bay. Popular with families, it boasts safe swimming, fabulous cafés (see opposite), mini golf, beach huts and an almost Mediterranean vibe, thanks to its sparkling waters and exotic palms.

Tucked up along the seafront right in the thick of things, **Harbour Beach** is a great place to paddle, dig and muck about in shallow, calm waters – although you do have to watch out for boats coming and going. Young families also love **Porthgwidden**, the smallest of the town beaches at St Ives, east-facing and sheltered between the harbour and The Island.

On the west side of the town, just below the Tate Gallery, **Porthmeor Beach** reaps some hefty Atlantic swells and is one of the region's most popular surf spots. Lessons are available from the **St Ives Surf School** (T01736-793938, stivessurfschool.co.uk). There are also rock pools either end of the lifeguard-patrolled bay.

Take to the water

Self-drive motor boats can be hired along the harbourfront during summer. For organized boat trips, **St Ives Pleasure Boat Association** (T0777-300 8000, stivesboats.co.uk) operates fishing trips in St Ives Bay from £15 adult and £10 child, as well as cruises out to Seal Island (£10 adult, £8 child) – a 90-minute jaunt westward to see a colony of Atlantic grey seals. For sailing times, check out the noticeboards near the lifeboat station.

Visit the gallery

You may catch your children casting wistful glances at Porthmeor Beach, but you can't

Barbara Hepworth Museum.   Carbis Bay.

leave town without at least a stab at some contemporary art appreciation in the **Tate St Ives** (T01736-796226, tate.org.uk/stives, daily from 1000, check times before visiting as the gallery began a three-year expansion programme in 2013; around £8 adult or £11 if combined with the Barbara Hepworth Museum, free for under 18s).

This curvaceous vision of clean-cut modernism presiding over Porthmeor's Bohemian surf scene is actually quite family friendly. Activity packs, talks, events and a team of helpful staff aim to make everything fun and accessible to children. And, even if your visit doesn't coincide with a family activity, kids can pick up free I-Spy sheets and set off on a search for abstract shapes and patterns. A family trail guide, meanwhile, will help parents make sense of the exhibits and frame pertinent questions to bemused children. In the studio, kids can get creative on the Tate's website, with activites linked to the current exhibition.

A family trail at the nearby **Barbara Hepworth Museum & Sculpture Garden** on Barnoon Hill (see Tate St Ives for contact details) provides an intriguing journey through a verdant garden 'sprouting' abstract works of art.

All sounds too high-brow? The **St Ives Museum** (Wheal Dream, TR26 1PR, T01736-796005, Easter-Oct Mon-Sat from 1000, £2 adult, 50p child) has a more down-to-earth collection of fishing nicknacks and the like. And, if you just want somewhere indoors for the kids to burn off energy, make tracks for the **Play Zone** (Carbis Bay, TR26 3HW, T01736-799499, daily from 1000).

Porthmeor Beach.

Canvas & cottages

The beaches and galleries of St Ives are just a short stroll from **Ayr Holiday Park** (T01736-795855, ayrholidaypark.co.uk, Apr-Sep, £7.50-20/pitch, plus £5-8 adult, £3-4 child) – a popular cliff-top campsite and touring park with excellent facilities and chest-swelling views across the bay.

St Ives Cottages (T0800-328 8051, stivescottages.co.uk) has a small collection of character properties, many with that all-important parking space and some right on the harbourfront.

Located off the B3306 between Zennor and St Ives, **Trevalgan Holiday Farm** (St Ives, TR26 3BJ, T01736-796529, trevalgan.co.uk) has four cottages sleeping up to six, plus a wealth of facilities to keep families happy – from play barn to pets corner.

Lavish living near Porthmeor Beach, **Sail Lofts** (T01736-799175, thesaillofts.co.uk) has two-, three- and four-bedroom open-plan boutique apartments with luxurious interiors – and also offers indulgent treatments at its Ocean Spa. See also **Tregenna Castle Estate**, page 118.

Grab a bite

A sunny, beachside café with a zesty menu, fusing local seafood with imaginative Asian and Italian recipes, **Porthminster Beach Café** (St Ives, TR26 2EB, T01736-795352, porthminstercafe.co.uk, daily during spring and summer from 0900, closed Mon during winter) is the hottest reservation in town. Haddock and chips will set you back £12.95. Nestled beneath the grassy slopes of the Island on the other side of St Ives, the sister property, **Porthgwidden Café** (T01736-796791, porthgwiddencafe.co.uk, daily from 0900) serves equally delicious food.

Among the plethora of restaurants and cafés along the harbourfront, **The Hub** (Wharf Rd, T01736-799099) and **The Wave** (St Andrews St, T01736-796661) are both highly recommended. Try **The Italian** (Fore St, T01736-798235) for excellent pasta and stone baked pizza (including takeaway) from £7.95.

Get all arty

Seek inspiration in Cornwall's myriad galleries, then equip your kids with a sketch pad, pencils and paints for an art session at a colourful fishing harbour like St Ives. On the beach, make collages from strandline finds, fashion silly faces from shells and seaweed and build sandcastles modelled on St Michael's Mount. If you're stuck for ideas, there's an excellent giftshop in the Tate St Ives, brimming with books, postcards and art kits guaranteed to get the creative juices flowing.

Let's go to... St Ives

The golden sands of Porthminster
Beach stretching towards St Ives.

Main photo: Kynance Cove – the gem in the Lizard's glittering crown. Opposite: On the trail at Trebah Gardens, stream jumping at Kennack Sands.

The Lizard

You won't find much in the way of big, blousy beaches on the Lizard. Instead, its crinkle-cut coast is riddled with the kind of coves, creeks and fishing hamlets that have smugglers' den written all over them. The Lizard is a land of adventure, helped in no small part by several of Cornwall's top attractions.

Adrenaline addicts can binge on the rides at **Flambards**, budding botanists can explore the leafy trails of **Trebah Gardens**, while close encounters with marine mammals await visitors to the **Cornish Seal Sanctuary**.

All three big days out are within easy reach of **Helston**, a small market town at the gateway to the Lizard. Apart from a rather splendid playground next to the boating lake, there's little to waylay holidaying families in this modest town. Most visitors slingshot through its roundabouts and continue south on the A3083, a seriously exciting road that hugs the perimeter fence of **RNAS Culdrose** (look out for helicopters) before dropping like a stone towards the village of **Lizard** and its iconic headland.

Rising like an exclamation mark at mainland Britain's most southerly point, Lizard Lighthouse has a fascinating new heritage centre and is the starting point for some of Cornwall's finest cliff walks – the sea chewing over the coastline, stiff-winged fulmars riding the ocean breeze and, if you're lucky, a Royal Navy ship sidling out into the Atlantic.

Backtrack slightly and you can delve off the A3083 to **Kynance Cove** (everyone's favourite Lizard pin-up), **Cadgwith** (a fairytale fishing village) and **Mullion** – gateway to a string of sandy inlets and the stoic little harbour at **Mullion Cove**.

Back at RNAS Culdrose, the B3293 branches eastwards and, soon after, a sideshoot wriggles up to **Gweek** where the contented honks of the sanctuary's seals echo across the mudflats of the **Helford Estuary**. Lose yourself in the knot of lanes around this idyllic waterway and, hopefully, you'll find yourself unravelling at hidden gems like **Helford Passage** or **Mawnan** – a stone's throw from magical Trebah Gardens.

Stick to the B3293 and you'll scale **Goonhilly Downs**, where Arthur and his fellow satellite dishes sprout from the Lizard like white mushrooms. Roskilly's ice cream calls nearby as the road continues east to **Coverack** and south to **Kennack Sands** – that rarity on the Lizard: a big golden beach.

Here to there

The Lizard chapter of *Cornwall with Kids* covers the peninsula south from Porthleven and Helston to Lizard Point and east to the Helford River – including attractions on the north bank like the gardens of Trebah and Glendurgan. See pages 190-193 for Falmouth and its beaches (including Maenporth). For Praa Sands, Penzance and other highlights west of Porthleven, see The Far West chapter (pages 94-121). Truro, linked to Falmouth and Helston via the A394, is covered on pages 194-195.

Porthleven – Helford River

Fun & free

Take a walk on the wild side

Stretching almost four miles from Porthleven to Gunwalloe, Loe Bar is a shingle and flint ridge separating the sea from a freshwater lake called The Loe. It was formed during storms in the 12th century, blocking the Cober Valley and preventing merchant ships from sailing up the estuary to Helston. You can access the Bar from a small car park about halfway along, or by walking two miles along the coast path from Porthleven. The beach shelves steeply and fierce currents strafe the coast (many ships have been wrecked here). Take a picnic and a kite and enjoy this lonely, wild stretch of coast, but don't be tempted to swim. Birdwatchers will enjoy strolling the woodland paths around Loe Pool.

Watch the choppers

King of spin, RNAS Culdrose is one of Europe's largest helicopter bases with squadrons specializing in anti-submarine warfare and surveillance. Most people are more familiar with its red and grey search-and-rescue Sea Kings, which can often be seen whirring overhead on training missions or dealing with emergencies. You can get a closer look by visiting the air station's free-to-enter Public Viewing Area. The Merlin Café & Gift Shop (Apr-Oct Mon-Fri from 1000) is also located here, along with the departure point for coach tours (T01326-565085).

Unravel a crab line from the harbour walls of fishing villages like Porthleven and Coverack.

❝❞ I've lived in Cornwall for over 20 years – both of my children were born here. Dollar Cove, near Gunwalloe, is our favourite beach as it has spectacular rock formations and holds many happy memories. At low tide, Castle Beach in Falmouth is fantastic for rock-pooling. Falmouth also has the best fish and chips at Harbour Lights, as well as plenty of things to do on a rainy day, like the maritime museum and Ships & Castles' swimming pool with its river run and slide. For walks, the coast path from Kynance Cove to Lizard Point is stunning.

Nicola Wharton
Garden Team, Trebah Gardens, Mawnan Smith, T01326-252200, trebah-garden.co.uk.

Visit Cadgwith Cove

Why? It's not exactly the kind of beach you're going to stake out with a windbreak for the day, but Cadgwith Cove is still not to be missed. It's a proper little Cornish fishing village, with trawlers and fishing paraphernalia scattered over a shingle beach, thatched cottages and a tiny tin-roofed church clinging to a hillside, and gardens crammed with flowers and flotsam sculptures. The Cornish accents here are as thick as the milkshakes served at Minnie Moon down by the pilot gig boathouse. Above the café, the Crow's Nest gallery has vibrant paintings of the village. Boat trips can be arranged (T01326-290716) and there's a cosy pub with folk music on Tuesday and Friday nights. Don't forget to check out the fishing contest results chalked up by the beach.

Where? Cadgwith (cadgwith.com) is located on the southeast tip of the Lizard.

Walk the Lizard

Located at latitude 49°57'N and longitude 5°12'W, Lizard Point is the most southerly point of the British mainland – a wave-gnawed headland with fierce tidal races and ship-snagging reefs. Walk from the National Trust car park down to the point and you'll see maps in the Lizard Point Gift Shop scrawled with shipwrecks (about 400 vessels have floundered here, including the *Royal Ann* which ran onto Stag Rock in 1720 with the loss of 207 lives).

Built by Trinity House in 1752, the Lizard Lighthouse originally had two towers lit by coal fires. It went electric in 1878 and is now fully automated, with flashes every three seconds that are visible for 25 miles out to sea. A new heritage centre at the lighthouse (see page 139) shines a light on the area's history.

Some of Britain's oldest rocks can be found at the Lizard, including serpentine – pop into PL Casley & Son's stonemason hut at the Point to see some beautiful examples. You might meet the grandson of artist William Casley, renowned for his evocative seascapes of the area.

You'll feel like you are walking into a masterpiece when you set out, east or west, along the coast path from Lizard Point. Eastwards, the trail leads past the sandy cove at Housel Bay and the Coastwatch Lookout at Bass Point before reaching Kilcobben Cove where, in 2012, the RNLI opened a new lifeboat station (thelizardlifeboat.co.uk) at the base of 140-ft cliffs. The Lizard's original lifeboat house can still be seen at Polpeor Cove, just to the west of Lizard Point. Continue westwards from here for a spectacular, two-mile walk to Kynance Cove, passing wild Pentreath Beach. With luck, you'll spot a pair of the rare crow-like choughs that nest along this stunning stretch of coast.

From top left: The Lizard National Nature Reserve is home to a wealth of flora and fauna – from thrift to choughs; the old lifeboat house at Polpeor Cove; Lizard Lighthouse; a handful of snails, and the cliff-top approach to Kynance Cove.

West Cornwall 131

Out & about The Lizard

Best beaches

The beaches described here are found west to east, from Porthleven to the Helford River.

Gunwalloe Church Cove

South of Loe Bar (see page 130), the Lizard's coastline rucks up into cliffs, nicked in places by small coves and fishing harbours. Gunwalloe Church is the first of these little havens – a sandy, dune-backed cove with a car park and seasonal café. Good surf rumbles into Gunwalloe on a strong southwesterly and, although lifeguards are on duty during summer months, you should always beware of strong undercurrents and steeply shelving sand. The cove gets its name from the 15th-century church of St Winwaloe, constantly battling against storm-shifted sands at the northern end of the beach. Some of the woodwork inside the church is said to be from the wreck of a Portuguese carrack (sunk here in 1527). Coins from this and other shipwrecks are still found on the beach, so keep your eyes peeled (see Treasure Hunting, page 137).

Poldhu Cove

One of the Lizard's most popular sandy coves, Poldhu lies a short distance to the north of Mullion. A road loops around the back of the cove with a car park providing easy, level access to both the beach and a funky little café perched in the dunes (see page 146). Like Gunwalloe, left, Poldhu gets decent surf when conditions are right – just stay well clear of the rocks either side of the cove. Children enjoy playing in the shallow stream that flows over the beach – it's littered with small flat pebbles that are perfect for stacking into weirs. If it's not really beach weather, Poldhu is still worth a visit. Walk onto the grassy cliff-top and you will find the remains of the Marconi Wireless Station, where Italian, Guglielmo Marconi, sent a wireless message (three dots for 'S' in morse code) across the Atlantic Ocean on 12 December 1901. A few building foundations and the anchor points for aerial masts are all that remain to mark this defining moment – the birth of modern telecommunications. It's a far cry from today's world of Wi-Fi – you might need to help your children make the connection.

Mullion Cove

Although the tiny harbour beach here only appears at low tide, this is a wonderful base for cliff walks and exploring. When it comes to Cornish fishing hamlets, Mullion Cove is as close to picture-book perfection as you'll find. Granite piers embrace a harbour tucked into serpentine cliffs, where whitewashed cottages huddle out of the wind. The cobbled slipway is still strewn with fishing boats and lobster pots, but it was in the 18th century that Mullion Cove thrived as a pilchard fishery (supplemented, no doubt, by smuggling). The harbour master's house used to be a pilchard cellar, while opposite the café are the remains of a Second World War anti-tank wall. Stake out the harbour walls for crabbing (you might be lucky enough to catch a glimpse of a seal or basking shark) and wait for low tide to scramble through the cave that leads from the harbour beach to a neighbouring cove. Offshore you can see uninhabited Mullion Island, a nature reserve with the Lizard's only breeding colonies of kittiwakes, razorbills and guillemots – ask at the harbour about boat trips.

Kynance Cove

The rough diamond in the Lizard's crown, Kynance is the stuff of childhood fantasy. The moment you first glimpse this wild beach on the half-mile walk down from the National Trust car park, countless beach adventures surge to mind – from delving in caves and rock pools to exploring the serpentine stacks and pinnacles that rear above this extraordinarily beautiful cove.

Facilities are limited to a single beach café (see page 146), but it's the remoteness and solitude of Kynance that makes it so compelling. Aim to get there at least three hours before low tide, when sugary sand envelops the bases of the rock formations. Take care when swimming, as strong currents strafe the cove.

Kennack Sands

A sheltered bay of sand and fine shingle on the eastern side of the Lizard Peninsula, Kennack Sands has a lovely café with a small sun terrace overlooking the beach (the hot waffles with ice cream are the perfect energy boost after a bodyboarding session). The beach is gently shelving and has good, level access, but can get quite crowded in summer due to the close proximity of holiday parks. There's a challenging stream to dam and some interesting rocky outcrops to explore, while organized activities include horse riding and scuba diving.

Coverack

Low tide reveals plenty of sand at Coverack, an unspoilt fishing village that faces west and enjoys the best of any late afternoon sunshine. The harbour wall is a good spot for crabbing. There's a fleet of about 40 boats here, some of which offer mackerel fishing trips.

Top: Cliff-top view of Mullion Cove. Above left: Helford Passage. Above right: Kynance Cove.

Gillan Creek

Snaking between wooded banks, this pretty creek has stony beaches – many requiring a 15- to 20-minute walk to reach. A lovely, peaceful area for picnics and skimming stones.

Helford Passage

Little more than a narrow strip of gritty sand and shingle, Helford Passage enjoys an idyllic location on the northern shore of the Helford River. Crowded with sailing dinghies and motor boats, it feels like the setting for a *Swallows and Amazon*-style adventure on the Helford Estuary – and that's precisely what you'll get if you hire a self-drive boat from Helford River Boats (see page 136) which also operates a ferry to Helford on the south shore. Walk up the hill to the left of the beach at Helford Passage for a prime picnic spot overlooking the estuary, or treat yourself to a meal at the excellent Ferryboat Inn (see page 146), right in the heart of the cluster of whitewashed cottages.

A Cornish beach all to yourself in the height of summer? Get hold of a detailed map and a tide chart, pack a picnic and stride out for deserted coves, like Gew-Graze (or Soapy Cove) shown here. Only exposed for a few hours during the lowest tides, it can be reached by following the coast path north from Kynance Cove.

Boat trips

Danda & Starfish

Porthleven Angling Centre, Harbour Head, Porthleven, TR13 9JY, T01326-561885. Fishing trips and coastal cruises, call for rates.

Operating from the picturesque harbour at Porthleven, the 27-ft *Danda* and 31-ft *Starfish* ply the coast in search of mackerel, garfish and pollack. Boat trips are also available from local operators in fishing villages further south on the Lizard, such as Cadgwith and Coverack.

Helford River Boats

Helford Passage, T01326-250770, helford-river-boats.co.uk. Apr-Oct. Six-person motor boats £40/hr, £60/2 hrs, £150/day, £700/wk; four-person rowing boats £20/hr, £30/2 hrs, £70/day, £250/wk; paddleboards and kayaks from £10/hr, £20/2 hrs, £60/day, £200/wk. Guided river trips from £60.

You can peek at it from the thickly wooded shoreline, but in order to really soak up the special atmosphere of the Helford River, you need to get afloat and explore the myriad creeks. Various craft are available for hire from the kiosk by the jetty. No experience is needed and all boats come with life jackets, maps and fuel.

Ferry to Helford

Linking north and south shores of the Helford River, the Helford Passage to Helford Ferry operates from early April to late October, daily 0930-1700 and until 2130 (Tue, Wed) during July and August, return fares £6 adult, £3 child (under 14).

Horse riding

Bosvathick Riding Stables

Bosvathick Farm, Constantine, TR11 5RD, T01326-340367, bosvathickridingstables.co.uk. Tue-Sun. Adult rides £18/hr, children's lesson £13/30 mins (minimum age 4 on lead reins).

Set on a 92-acre farm just to the north of the Helford River, this friendly, family-run yard has an indoor arena for rainy days.

Newton Riding Stables

Newton Farm, Mullion, TR12 7JF, T01326-240388, newton-equestrian. co.uk. Lessons £16/hr, hacks from £16/hr, beginner's sessions (half-hr lesson plus half-hr hack) £18.

This approved Pony Club Centre offers exhilarating beach rides, as well as more sedate countryside hacks for the less experienced.

Poltesco Valley Stables

Treal Farm, Ruan Minor, T01326-240591, poltescovalleystables.com. Lessons £9/30 mins, hacks from £10/30 mins, 1-hr beach ride £15.

Located just a mile from Kennack Sands, Poltesco Valley Stables organizes beach rides at 0900 and 1800 during the summer (you need to be able to canter). For the ultimate rush, combine this with a moorland hack or, if you're new to riding,

Sea horses at Kennack Sands.

opt for the more gentle farm ride where there is the option for children under 12 with little or no experience to be led on reins by a ride escort.

Multi activity

Lizard Adventure

Hellarcher Farm, Penmenner Rd, TR11 7NN, T01326-290894, lizardadventure.co.uk. Coasteering, climbing, kayaking half day £45 adult, £35 child (8-15), full day £85 adult, £65 child; bush craft half day £30 person; guided walks from £20. The Lizard's rugged shoreline is perfect for coasteering, rock climbing or exploring by sea kayak – and this highly experienced adventure operator offers all three activities. Sea kayaking usually operates out of Mullion Harbour where it's not unusual to spot seals. Lizard Adventure can also kit you out for kayak fishing or arrange a guided walk, learning about the wildlife and history of the area.

Scuba diving

Kennack Diving

Sea Acres Holiday Park, Kennack Sands, TR12 7LT, T07816-903260, kennackdiving.co.uk. Bubblemaker 'try a dive' pool session (minimum age 8) £15, pool session and sea dive (minimum age 12) £50; Junior Open Water Diver (ages 12-14) or Open Water Diver (minimum age 15) £300. This PADI dive centre offers a full training programme, including introductory courses for children in an indoor heated swimming pool and an Open ater Diver qualification for children as young as 12, consisting of five pool sessions, some basic theory and four sea dives.

Windsurfing

Coverack Windsurfing Centre

Cliff Cottage, Coverack, TR12 6SY, T01326-280939, coverack.co.uk. Call for rates and details of courses. This RYA training centre caters for all levels of windsurfer, from novice to advanced.

Treasure hunting

Dig a sandcastle or comb the strandline at Gunwalloe Church Cove (see page 132) and you might just strike it rich. According to folklore, the pirate John Avery (aka Long Ben) stashed his booty here. And that's not all. In 1527, the 300-ton Portuguese carrack *San Antonio* floundered on rocks near the cove and spilled her cargo of copper and silver ingots. A Spanish galleon met the same fate in 1785, adding two tons of gold and silver coins to Davy Jones's Locker. Despite search efforts, neither cargo has been recovered. Coins, however, are sometimes found on the beach.

Cornish Seal Sanctuary

Gweek, TR12 6UG, T01326-221361, sealsanctuary.co.uk. Daily from 1000. Online tickets from around £10 general admission, £35 family. Home to sea lions, fur seals and otters, this is primarily a rehabilitation centre for common and grey seals rescued around Cornwall's coast. The Seal Rescue Hospital provides a fascinating glimpse into the whole process, from rescue to release, and enables children to see pups at various stages of recuperation. The hospital is usually at its busiest during autumn and winter (the pupping period when young are at their most vulnerable). By the time the summer holidays arrive, most, if not all, of the patients have been treated and released back to the wild (or the sanctuary's convalescence pool). It can be disappointing for children to see the empty hospital pens, but they can still take part in mock medical examinations using a lifelike seal model, complete with head marker tag, blanket and feeding tube. There are also plenty of other exhibits to keep them entranced at this gentle, slow-paced attraction on the banks of the Helford estuary.

Several pools (many with underwater viewing chambers) are home to resident seals, sea lions and Humboldt penguins. Feeding times and talks are displayed at the entrance.

There's also a quiz trail and a woodland nature walk that leads to an enclosure inhabited by Starsky and Hutch – two frisky and inquisitive Asian short-clawed otters.

At the Rockpool Experience you can hold a crab and touch a starfish. A children's play area is nearby, while the grassy

Life's a beach

Rescued as a seal pup in the early 1970s after being thrown against rocks during a winter storm, Fatima's head injuries were so severe that it was feared she might not survive. Unable to return to the wild, she has spent a long, happy life at the Seal Sanctuary and, although her eyesight is deteriorating with age, she still enjoys her sprats and conger eel chunks.

Fatima at the Cornish Seal Sanctuary.

Balloon Race and Victorian Village at Flambards.

Lizard Lighthouse.

bank above the seal pools makes a lovely spot for a picnic overlooking the estuary. Don't forget your pocket money – the sanctuary's gift shops sell cuddly seals in all shapes and sizes, and every penny you spend helps to fund the vital work of the seal rescue team.

The Flambards Experience

Helston, TR13 0QA, T01326-573404, flambards.co.uk. Apr-Oct daily from 1030, but check whether exhibitions *and* rides are open. Around £18 adult, £12.50 child (95 cm to 15 years). Limited opening Nov-Mar. With its Hornet rollercoaster and stomach-lurching Skyraker 001 and Thunderbolt rides, Flambards is an adrenaline blast for older kids, while littl'uns can get a buzz from gentle alternatives like the Animal Express. The closest Cornwall gets to a full-blown theme park, Flambards is not as rural or pretty as Crealy, the county's

other big fun park (see page 84). Where Flambards really scores, however, is sheer variety.

Kids will stampede towards the big rides, but rein them in for the outstanding Victorian Village. This indoor attraction recreates Victorian life with walk-through streets, shops and houses crafted in exquisite and original detail, without the merest whiff of MDF.

Kids will stare in wonder (or total disbelief) at the toy shop, which has nothing more high-tech than wooden jigsaw puzzles and rocking horses. There's also a baker, butcher, tobacconist, dairy, pub, school, milliner, boot shop, barber, grocer – each one populated by lifelike characters.

Flambards' Britain in the Blitz Experience is equally spellbinding. Vera Lyn's dulcet tones give way to the whine of air-raid sirens followed by the ominous drone of German

bombers overhead; then the shells start exploding and you're transported back to Second World War London – a war-torn world of burning houses, rations and evacuees.

Other undercover exhibits at Flambards include the War Gallery and Aviation Experience, which has a fullscale flightdeck of Concorde. You won't have time to see everything in a single day. Not when there's also a F1 kart track, crazy golf, the Really Wild Experience (animal show) and the Hands On Science Experience. Flambards is also home to One-2-Eleven – a large indoor soft-play barn (see page 141 for details)

Future World @ Goonhilly

This is being redeveloped into a new space-themed visitor centre featuring a planetarium and planetary surface for robotics exploration. Visit goonhilly.org/ goonhilly-visitor-centre for updates.

Lizard Lighthouse

Lizard Point, T01326-290202, trinityhouse.co.uk. Check online for opening times. Heritage Centre and grounds £2.50 adult, £1.50 child; Heritage Centre and lighthouse tour £7 adult, £4 child.

An excellent visitor centre has transformed the engine room at Lizard Lighthouse into a beacon of interactive, audio-visual wizardry. As well as learning about the history of mainland Britain's southernmost lighthouse, you can get hands-on by sounding a foghorn, tracking ships in one of the world's busiest sea lanes, sending messages using morse code, semaphore and signal flags, writing an entry in the weather log book and even building your own model lighthouse. There are fascinating displays on shipwrecks and the history of sea rescue with riveting yarns from lighthouse keepers and their families. To top it all, you can also climb the lighthouse, from where there are spectacular views along the Lizard's gnarled coastline.

Trebah Gardens

Mawnan Smith, TR11 5JZ, T01326-252200, trebahgarden.co.uk. Daily from 1000, last admission 1600. Check website for rates. Free entry during winter for RHS members. This beautiful ravine garden leads to a small, secluded beach on the Helford River and,

in addition to being a leafy sub-tropical paradise, is quite possibly the most child-friendly of Cornwall's gardens.

Nature trails and quiz sheets are available for various age groups, while Tarzan's Camp provides arboreal adventure thrills for the over-fives, with climbing nets, rope swings and a zip wire tucked away in a shady grove of fir trees. Another play area, Fort Stuart, provides a gentler play option for toddlers.

Even without these extras, however, Trebah is virgin jungle for mini-Tarzans and Janes. Side paths lure you from the main beach track to ponds, streams, and shady tunnels beneath tree ferns. Kids can tiptoe through a Brazilian swamp beneath a canopy of giant gunnera leaves, which block out the sky with their 2-m-wide leaves, or probe a mysterious bamboo maze known as the Bamboozle. At the height of summer, Hydrangea

Valley is like something out of Willy Wonka's chocolate factory with blue and pink flower balls scattered everywhere, like an explosion of strawberry and blueberry bonbons – all reflected in Mallard Pond where huge rainbow trout cruise the shallows. Another diversion leads to Koi Pool, a hidden retreat with more whopping great fish and a waterfall.

There are maps to guide you around the garden, but it's more fun following your instincts and seeing where they lead you. A dead-end? A hidden pool? A mossy monster lurking in Dinky's Puddle? Eventually, though, you will reach Polgwidden Cove, an estuary beach of skimming-stone-shingle with a small café selling drinks and ice creams. It's a fine spot for a picnic, gazing out to sea where cargo ships are often moored, waiting to enter Falmouth harbour. It was all a

Galloping through the gunnera at Trebah.

very different place on 1 June 1944, when 7500 American troops embarked here for the D-Day landings at Omaha Beach in Normandy. Trebah now exudes peace and tranquillity. Take your time exploring its hidden secrets, but don't leave it too late to visit the superb Planters Café (see page 145) and gift shop.

Glendurgan

Mawnan Smith, TR11 5JZ, T01326-252020, nationaltrust.org.uk. Feb-Oct Tue-Sat (plus Mon in Aug) 1030-1730. £6.40 adult, £3.20 child (5-17), £16 family.

Like Trebah (above), Glendurgan is a slice of sub-tropical paradise with plenty to keep children occupied. As well as racing through the fiendish laurel maze, there's a giant rope swing and a beach with sand, pebbles and rock pools.

Poldark Mine

Wendron, TR13 0ES, T01326-573173, poldark-mine.co.uk. Jul-Aug daily 1000-1730, Sep-Nov and Apr-Jul Sun-Fri 1000-1730. £8 adult, £5 child, £20 family, including guided mine tour (last mine tour 1600).

Fascinating tours of an 18th-century tin mine, plus beam engine, museum, panning area, craft activities and play area.

Rain check

Cinemas
Flora
Wendron St, Helston, TR13 8PT, T01326-569977.
Phoenix
Berkeley Vale, Falmouth, TR11 3PL, T01326-313072.

Craft centres
Chocolate Factory & Craft Centre
Mullion, TR12 7HB, T01326-241311, the-chocolatefactory.co.uk. Trenance Chocolate, craft shops, coffee shop.

Indoor play & amusements
One-2-Eleven
From 0900 week days, 1000 weekends. Play barn at Flambards (see page 139) with rope walkways, slides etc, plus toddler arena and a café, animal hospital, supermarket and garage for role play. Flambards' Victorian Village and other indoor attractions are also great for a rainy day.

Indoor swimming pools
Helston Sports Centre
Church Hill, TR13 8YQ, T01326-563320.
Ships & Castles Leisure Centre
Castle Drive, Falmouth, TR11 4NG, T01326-212129, shipsandcastles.co.uk. Rapid river ride, 70-m flume and ridewave machine.

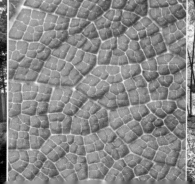

Garden of delights – Trebah's treasures include (left to right) hydrangeas reflected in Mallard Pond, daisies from South Africa, tree ferns from New Zealand, the Tarzan's Camp play area, giant gunnera leaves and the Bamboozle.

Sleeping The Lizard

Boscrege Caravan & Camping Park

Ashton, nr Helston, TR13 9TG, T01736-762231, caravanparkcornwall.com. Mar-Nov. £13-20/pitch (4 people), static caravans £165-795.

A short drive from Praa Sands (see page 107), this quiet, spacious and well-run site is within easy reach of the Lizard's attractions and has a nature trail and games room.

Chycarne Holiday Park

Kuggar, Ruan Minor, TR12 7LX, T01326-290200, chycarne.co.uk. Apr-Oct. Camping £1.25-5.25/pitch, plus £3-5.75 adult, £1.50-4 child (3-16), static caravans and chalets £250-495/wk.

Kennack Sands is just a few minutes' walk from this low-key holiday park with its sheltered, tree-lined camping field, modern shower block, playground and shop. Four- and six-berth holiday caravans and chalets are also available.

Franchis Holidays

Mullion, TR12 7AZ, T01326-240301, franchis.co.uk. Apr-Oct. £11-18/pitch (2 adults), plus £1.50-2 extra person (free for children under 3), static caravans and chalets £245-485/wk.

A couple of miles' drive from Mullion, this peaceful site is a mixture of mown lawns and mature trees, with tent pitches and a few caravans and chalets backing onto woodland. A great location for wildlife and walking.

Gwendreath Holiday Park

Ruan Minor, TR12 7LZ, T01326-290666, tomandlinda.co.uk. May-Sep. £238-499/wk.

Although there's no camping here, this tiny park (with just 17 four-berth holiday caravans) is a great choice for young families. In addition to a play area for under-fives and a field for older children to kick a ball around, a short woodland walk leads to Kennack Sands (see page 133), with its safe swimming and handy beach café.

Little Trevothan Caravan & Camping Park

Trevothan, nr Coverack, TR12 6SD, T01326-280260, littletrevothan.co.uk. Mar-Oct. £13-16/pitch (2 adults), plus £3 extra adult, £2.50 extra child (up to 16), static caravans £220-550/wk.

A secluded 10-acre site with plenty of open space and a playground for children to run around in, Little Trevothan is close to Coverack with its beach, harbour and watersports. Two- and three-bedroom caravans are available.

Lower Polladras Touring Park

Carleen, Breage, TR13 9NX, T01736-762220, lower-polladras.co.uk. Apr-

Several campsites and holiday parks are close to Kennack Sands on the Lizard's southeast coast.

Dec. £11-17/pitch (2 adults), plus £2-3 extra adult, £1.50-2 extra child (3-16), static caravans £240-595/wk.

Located north of Helston, Lower Polladras is ideally placed for exploring West Cornwall. A small site with just 39 touring pitches and a group of three very smart, contemporary-styled caravans (sleeping four), it's also the proud recipient of a Gold David Bellamy Conservation Award – recognition of its environmental policy and nature walk.

Skyburriowe Farm

Garras, nr Helston, TR12 6LR, T01326-221646, skyburriowefarm.co.uk. Easter-Oct. £10-18/pitch (2 adults), plus £1 extra person, B&B from £30.

A delightful, family-run dairy farm, Skyburriowe has shifted the cows off two fields to create a spacious campsite bordered

Holiday parks

Mullion Holiday Park
Nr Mullion, TR12 7LJ, T0844-335 3450, parkdeanholidays.co.uk. Located on the main A3083 between Helston and Lizard Point, this fun-packed park is close to top attractions and stunning beaches like Kynance Cove. Facilities include indoor and outdoor swimming pools, play areas, go-karts, children's clubs (for tots to teens), evening entertainment, a bar and grill, nature trail and crazy golf.

Retanna Holiday Park
Edgcumbe, TR13 0EJ, T01326 340643, retanna.co.uk. Peaceful caravan park between Helston and Falmouth.

Sea Acres
Kennack Sands, TR12 7LT, T0844-335 3450, parkdeanholidays.co.uk. More relaxed than its sister park near Mullion (see above), Sea Acres is just up the lane from Kennack Sands and has an indoor pool, nature trail, play area and pitch 'n' putt. It's also the base for Kennack Diving (see page 137).

Seaview Holiday Park
Gwendreath, Kennack Sands, TR12 7LZ, T01326-290635, seaviewcaravanpark.com. Small park with 17 caravans, seven chalets, a cottage and an indoor pool. Great views and a short walk to the beach.

Silver Sands Holiday Park
Gwendreath, Kennack Sands, TR12 7LZ, T01326-290631, silversandsholidaypark.co.uk. Well-run tent and caravan park with conservation award. Short stroll to Kennack Sands.

by trees and hedges that are bursting with wildlife. A smart toilet block features a family shower room. If camping doesn't appeal but you still fancy a rural bolthole, the 120-year-old farmhouse offers B&B (in a double, twin and family bedroom) as well as self-catering in a barn conversion which sleeps four and provides glimpses of the sea.

Budget break

Premier Inn
Clodgey Lane, Helston, TR13 8FZ, T0871-527 8512, premierinn.com. Rooms from £50, check online for special offers and meal deals. OK, so you won't find a Premier Inn in a prime beachfront position with lots of leisure facilities – their town-outskirts locations are handy rather than handsome. However, for a budget hotel, Helston's Premier Inn is excellent value for money – under-16s can stay and eat breakfast for free. Family rooms have a double bed and two comfy pull-out beds, along with bright, immaculate bathrooms, air conditioning, Freeview TV and tea- and coffee-making facilities. Kids receive an inflight-style goodie bag and there are some great deals at Table Table – the hotel's bar and restaurant – where you can tuck into Sunday roasts, gourmet burgers, salads and steaks, as well as a good range of pub grub, from ham, egg and chips to pies, scampi and lasagne. There are other Premier Inns at Bodmin, Hayle, Liskeard, Newquay, St Austell and Truro.

Sleeping The Lizard

Lizard Lighthouse Cottages

Cornish Cottages, T 01326-240333, cornishcottagesonline.com. Cottages (sleeping 4-8) Around £340-1200/wk. Never mind the foghorn (which has a range of three miles) – the Nanny State Alert at these six newly refurbished ex-lighthouse keepers' cottages rings loud and clear! Granted, this is not somewhere to let children roam at will, but no one can deny the thrill of living in the shadow of Cornwall's most famous lighthouse, walking straight from your front door onto the cliff tops. Surrounding a large courtyard, the cottages are well equipped with all mod cons.

Heath Farm Cottages

Ponsongath, nr Coverack, TR12 6SQ, T 01326-280521, heath-farm-holidays.co.uk. £280-820/wk. These six beautifully restored cottages are arranged around a courtyard and have the added child appeal of copious farm animals, fresh eggs to collect and a woodland to explore.

Mudgeon Vean

St Martin, TR12 6DB, T 01326-231341, mudgeonvean.co.uk. Call for rates. Snug in a rolling patchwork of fields and ancient woodland, this gorgeous 18th-century farm has three cottages for hire. Home to chickens, ducks, pigs, and pygmy goats, the farm also has a wild side, best explored on the Woodland Walk.

Also recommended
Polurrian Hotel

Mullion, TR12 7EN, T 01326-240421, polurrianhotel.com. Call for rates. Cliff-top luxury, with swimming pool, spa and a footpath to a sandy beach. Choose from family suites, interconnecting rooms and a two-bedroom cottage.

Trelowarren Estate

Mawgan, TR12 6AF, T 01326- 221224, trelowarren.com. See also page 147. Collection of 18 fine properties on a 1000-acre estate with pool, craft centre, restaurant and walks down to the Helford River.

Cottage agents

See also page 199.

St Anthony Holidays
T 01326-231357, stanthony.co.uk. Self-catering cottages (sleeping up to eight) in a beautiful waterside hamlet on the Helford River. See advert opposite.

Cadgwith Cove Cottages
T 01326-290162, cadgwithcovecottages.co.uk. Thatched-cottage heaven in the idyllic fishing village that inspired a million jigsaw puzzles.

Porthleven Holiday Cottages
T 01326-563404, porthlevenholidays.co.uk. Collection of over 20 cottages (sleeping up to eight) around the unspoilt harbour in Porthleven.

Get afloat from St. Anthony — Helford River

Hassle free low key boating and child friendly creekside holiday homes

St. Anthony Holidays, Manaccan, Helston, Cornwall TR12 6JW

01326 231357   info@StAnthony.co.uk   www.StAnthony.co.uk

Eating The Lizard

Minnie Moon
Cadgwith, TR12 7JX, T01326-290539,
minniemoon.co.uk. Easter-Nov.
Landed, cooked and prepared
daily, Minnie Moon's succulent
crab finds its way into delicious
(and good value) baguettes
or you can buy whole dressed
crab and lobster. Thick creamy
milkshakes are also a treat.

Sweet sensations from the Lizard
Peninsula include **Heatherbell
Honey** (cornwallhoney.com) and
Helford Creek Apple Juice
(helfordcreek.co.uk), freshly
pressed at Mudgeon Vean Farm
(see opposite).

Planters Café
Trebah Gardens (see page 140).
Daily 1000-1530. Free entry.
A champion of local producers,
this fabulous café is famous for
its freshly made flans, salads and
soups, and also offers traditional
Sunday roasts, picnic boxes and
healthy children's meals.

Roskilly's
Tregellast Barton Farm, St Keverne,
TR12 6NX, T01326-280479,
roskillys.co.uk. Farm open daily;
restaurant 1000-1800 (summer; later
during holidays), from 1100 (winter).
Free entry.
Roskilly's ice cream comes in
flavours ranging from clotted
cream vanilla to hoky poky and
can be bought by the scoop
or tub at the farm shop. Take

Pull the udder one – of course
we make Cornwall's best ice cream.

your pick at the Ice Cream
Parlour where you can also get
gooey with cream- and sauce-
drenched sundaes, or whizz
up your own milkshake. Other
home-made treats, like fudge,
jams, marmalades, mustards and
chutneys, are also for sale.

Roskilly's cows are milked
twice a day at 0500 and 1630:
125-odd Jerseys and Guernseys
filing into the barn, which has
a viewing gallery with displays
on countryside wildlife and why
milk is good for you. The milking
process is clinical and efficient,
with cows barely visible beneath
a tangle of hoses, cooling sprays
and machinery. You can see
cows with their calves to the
side of the collecting yard.

Roskilly's original milking
parlour has been converted into
the Croust House Restaurant,
which serves pizzas, pasties,

salads, pies, cakes, teas and the
farm's very own apple juice.
Evening barbecues are held
during summer.

Don't forget to leave time
for a mosey around the Bull
Pen Gallery which showcases
local artists' work, including
driftwood furniture, stained
glass, ceramics and traditional
children's toys. There are also
some beautiful walks from the
farm, leading to water meadows
and withy woods (trail leaflets
are available).

Roskilly's offers self-catering
accommodation in cottages
near the farm.

Market days
Falmouth Farmers' Market
The Moor, Tuesday 0900-1400.

Helston Farmers' Market
Boating Lake, first Saturday of
every month, 0930-1330.

Eating The Lizard

Ferryboat Inn
Helford Passage, TR11 5LB, T01326-250625. Daily from 1100.
Always busy, this beachfront pub overlooking the Helford Estuary combines traditional pub fare (scampi, steak etc) with more imaginative dishes, often featuring local seafood. Expect to pay around £7 for a fishcake starter, £12 for haddock, chips and mushy peas, £20 for an 8oz steak and around £6 for desserts like apple crumble and custard.

Kynance Cove Beach Café
Kynance Cove, TR12 7PF, T01326-290436, kynancecovecafe.co.uk.
Dating from the 1920s, this whitewashed café presides over the quintessential Cornish cove (see page 132). Sandwiches, baguettes, jacket potatoes, ploughmans, pasties and a tasty range of salads are all on the menu – just make sure you leave room for the home-made caramel and apple cake; it's one of a mouthwatering selection of sweets that all come with a dollop of Rodda's Clotted Cream

Lay down your chips – it's a safe bet that the Polpeor Café has the best view in Cornwall.

or Kelly's Ice Cream. The café has a small shop selling beach gear and, if you book far enough in advance, there's a cosy cottage for hire next door (from £370 per week), with just enough room for a lucky family of four.

Poldhu Beach Café
Poldhu Cove, TR12 7JB, T01326-240530, poldhu.net. Easter-Sep plus school holidays. Daily from 0930.
Tucked into the dunes at Poldhu Cove, this is a proper little 'barefoot and bacon baps' type of beach café. Don't expect much in the way of fresh salads or sandwiches – it's calories that count here. A Full English cooked breakfast costs from around £6, while the Ultimate Hot Chocolate (with cream, marshmallows and chocolate sauce) is around £3.

Polpeor Café
Lizard Point, TR12 7NU, T01326-290939. Daily from 1000.
All too often a superb location goes hand in hand with mediocre food and indifferent service – but not here at Britain's most southerly café, right on the cliffs at Lizard Point. The owners of this newly refurbished café are not only friendly, but the food is delicious and good value (with healthy-sized children's dishes). If the weather allows, eat outside on the west-facing terrace so you can bask in the glory of a Lizard sunset, sheltered behind a hedge that's not too high to obscure the views. You can't go wrong with the luxury fish pie (£10) with local crab and prawns, followed by Granny's Apple Cake and clotted cream. Cooked

---

Fish & chips
Try **Thurley's** (Meneage St, Helston), **Roland's Happy Plaice** (Shute Lane, Porthleven) and **The Galleon** (Nancemellyon Rd, Mullion). Or, if you're north of the Helford River, make for the **Harbour Lights** in Falmouth (see page 193).

breakfasts (served until 1230), sandwiches, omelettes, salads, jacket potatoes and cream teas are also on offer. Remember to use the toilet in the National Trust car park before walking down to Lizard Point – there isn't one at the café.

Also recommended
Kennack Sands Beach Café
Kennack Sands, TR12 7LX
T01326-291246.
Handy café opposite the beach car park, serving cream teas, jacket spuds, all-day breakfasts etc. Turbo's Café, next door, serves good pasties and waffles, and has a small terrace overlooking Kennack Sands.

Munchies
Mullion, TR12 7BZ, T01326-241132.
Everything you need for a picnic, from freshly made sandwiches and pasties to salads, quiche, pasta bowls and cakes.

Porthmellin Café
Mullion Cove, TR12 7ES
T01326-240941.
Harbourside café serving crab sarnies, pasties, cream teas and all day breakfasts.

The Wave
The Cove, Coverack, TR12 6SX,
T01326-281526, coverack.org.uk.
Cosy café with seasonal menu and views across Coverack Bay.

Posh nosh

Halzephron Inn
Gunwalloe, TR12 7QB, T01326-240406, halzephron-inn.co.uk.
Daily 1200-1400, 1830-2100.
Cornwall Dining Pub of the Year in 2001 and 2005, the Halzephron Inn is just up the lane from Gunwalloe Fishing Cove and the coast path that skirts the wide expanse of Porthleven Sands, south to Halzephron Cove and the rocky Pedngwinian headland. No excuses, then, for not building up an appetite for a meal at this 500-year-old pub. Bag an outdoor picnic table for lunch with panoramic views across Mount's Bay. Starters (from around £6) usually include soup of the day and local seafood in the form of fishcakes, chowders or salads, while mains (starting at around £10) feature fish, steaks and casseroles. The junior menu (from £5.95) has a typical quartet of scampi, fish, sausages or burger.

The Housel Bay Hotel
Housel Bay, TR12 7PG, T01326-290417, houselbay.com. Call for times.
Perched above a sandy cove just to the east of Lizard Point, this small, romantic hotel has a fine restaurant with menus oozing local flavour and freshness. The bar menu includes steaks, burgers, fish and chips and a range of gourmet sandwiches, while dinner mains feature local meat and fish. Expect to pay around £18 for a main course, choosing from mouthwatering dishes like rack of lamb and line-caught sea bass. Two-course Sunday lunches cost from £17.

New Yard Restaurant
Trelowarren, Mawgan, TR12 6AF, T01326-221595, newyardrestaurant.co.uk. Call for times.
Occupying a converted 18th-century carriage house, this excellent restaurant sources fish and shellfish caught by local dayboats, game from the Trelowarren Estate and herbs, vegetables, meat and poultry from local farmers. Two-course set lunches cost £20, while dinner mains start at around £13 and often include superb seafood, steaks or vegetarian dishes cooked in the restaurant's wood-fired oven. Pizzas are also available from £7.50.

Isles of Scilly

Cornwall plays its trump card with these wonderful islands. Just saying the three words 'Isles of Scilly' is enough to make the most jaded traveller go all tingly. The archipelago is only 28 miles southwest of Land's End, but that's far enough to give them an exotic, mysterious feel. And when you arrive – whether it's just for the day or at the start of a two-week island sojourn – you'll wonder whether the Scillies do in fact dabble their toes in the tropics. Abbey Gardens on Tresco is like the Eden Project with the roof off, while the surrounding shallow seas are dazzling turquoise and teeming with sponges and sea fans. All this is nurtured by the Gulf Stream and one of the UK's mildest and sunniest climates. The flip-side, of course, is that anything the Atlantic decides to hurl at Britain reaches the Isles of Scilly first. Witnessing the sea flex its muscles – surf blooming on the headlands above Hell Bay on Bryher – is all part of the adventure. Scilly in the extreme, but unforgettable nonetheless.

Get your bearings

First you need to get there. There are two options for reaching the Isles of Scilly: plane or boat (see page 197 for details). Flying is certainly quicker (15 minutes from Land's End as opposed to a 2½-hour voyage), but somehow it just feels right to sail to the Scillies. Besides, if you're camping – and the islands have some superb sites – you'll need the *Scillonian III* to transport all your gear. Setting off from Penzance, the 600-passenger ship also affords great views of the southern Penwith coastline and Land's End (try to get an outside seat on the starboard side), as well as potential sightings of dolphins.

Arriving at St Mary's, the largest of five inhabited islands, the *Scillonian III* glides into the harbour at Hugh Town – the hub of island life – and disgorges passengers, luggage and cargo onto the quayside. You'll see smaller boats fussing around her, like worker bees attending their queen. These are the islands' water taxis, a fleet of 10 vessels belonging to the **St Mary's Boatmen's Association** (T01720-423999, scillyboating.co.uk).

A noticeboard on the jetty is chalked up with the day's departures. You can buy tickets from the quay kiosk (daily 0930-1015, 1330-1400, later during high season, returns £8.40 adult, £4.20 child) or the **Tourist Information Centre** (Schiller Shelter, Porthcressa, TR21 0JW, T01720-424031, simplyscilly.co.uk). The friendly staff will also clue you up on anything from tide times to bus tours on the **Island Rover** (T01720-422131, islandrover. co.uk, Mon-Sat, 1015 and 1330, £8).

As well as the tourist office, Hugh Town has a post office, supermarket, chemist and baker, plus various gift shops, galleries, pubs, restaurants and cafés. On the far side of the green, a sports shop sells masks, snorkels and other outdoor gear, while the hardware store stocks basic camping supplies.

Cornwall plays its trump card with these wonderful islands. Just saying the three words 'Isles of Scilly' is enough to make the most jaded traveller go all tingly.

The **Isles of Scilly Museum** (T01720-422337, Church St, Easter-Sep, Mon-Fri 1000-1630, Sat 1000-1200) has exhibits charting the islands' history, from prehistoric times to the present, as well as shipwreck artefacts and a shell collection.

The **Isles of Scilly Wildlife Trust** (T01720-422153, ios-wildlifetrust.org.uk, Mar-Oct, Mon-Wed and Fri-Sat 0930-1630, Thu 0930-1200) has a tiny visitor centre on the quay with aquariums, a touch table, colouring sheets and details of activities, such as rock-pool rambles and nature trails. Next door, **The Pilchard Pit** is a handy spot to pick up sandwiches, pasties, paninis, drinks and ice creams.

Camping on the edge – Troytown Farm on St Agnes is wild, windy and wonderful.

Let's go to... Isles of Scilly

Pitch your tent

The *Scillonian III* may charge an extra £20 or so for carrying large amounts of camping gear, but that's a small price to pay for pitching your tent and playing the castaway on the Isles of Scilly.

On St Mary's you can set up camp at the Garrison, a ring of fortifications on the headland near Hugh Town. **Garrison Holidays Campsite** (The Garrison, St Mary's, TR21 0LS, T01720-422670, garrisonholidays.com, May-Oct, pitches from £9 per person, readi-tents from £110/3 nights) is sheltered by pine trees and blackberry-laden hedges. Each pitch has a wooden picnic table, and there are clean washrooms and a well-stocked shop. It only takes 10 minutes or so to walk down into Hugh Town, passing the local football field and a ship-themed adventure playground.

Snug in a valley with views of the harbour and neighbouring island of Tresco, **Bryher Campsite** (Bryher, TR23 0PR, T01720-422559, bryhercampsite. co.uk, Apr-Sep, £10.25 per person, plus £20 luggage transfer) is a fabulous spot for those who relish remote camping. The site is not without its home comforts, however. As well as an excellent toilet block and free showers, the cosy Fraggle Rock Bar (see page 154) is just a short walk away.

St Martin's Campsite (Oaklands Farm, Middletown, St Martin's, TR25 0QN, T01720-422888, stmartinscampsite.co.uk, Mar-Oct, £9.50-11.50 per person, plus £10 luggage transfer) is tucked behind hedges in fields once used in the Scillies' famous flower industry. You can virtually roll out of your sleeping bag onto a sandy beach from where there are panoramic views of the archipelago. Facilities include toilets, coin-operated showers and a barn stocked with eggs

Islands at a glance

St Mary's Hugh Town (see page 149) is pinched between the Town Beach and the sandy bay of Porthcressa. The Garrison stands proud on a nearby headland, while the south and east coasts are crinkle-cut with idyllic bays, such as Pelistry and Porth Minick. Towards the north, you'll find the Iron Age village of Halangy, while inland there are nature trails at Lower Moors and Higher Moors.

Tresco At low tide you'll land at Carn Near Quay on the southern tip of Tresco, from where it's a short walk to Abbey Gardens (see page 154). Bear right for beachcombing at Pentle Bay or continue past the gardens and Great Pool (a magnet to birds) to New Grimsby with its bike hire, grocery store, post office, art gallery, pub and smart rental accommodation.

St Martin's From Lower Town (with its pub and luxury hotel), the island's single track straddles the island, threading between flower fields and drystone walls – stunning sandy beaches left and right – to Higher Town where you will find craft galleries, cafés, gift shops and even a vineyard. Down at the jetty, St Martin's Dive School (see page 159) organizes guided snorkelling trips.

Bryher Smallest of the five inhabited islands, the coastline of Bryher ranges from the white sands of Rushy Bay and the calm waters of Green Bay (ideal for kayaking) to rugged Shipman Head where Hell Bay is lashed by storm-driven waves. The island has a post office and grocery store, café, campsite, B&Bs, self-catering cottages, a hotel and England's most westerly pub.

St Agnes The 'wild west' of the Scilly Isles, St Agnes has a spectacular campsite overlooking the Western Rocks. Boats slip into the sheltered anchorage at Porth Conger where a short stroll takes you past the Turk's Head pub to The Bar – a causeway between St Agnes and Gugh that reveals an idyllic sandy cove at low tide (see page 156). Walk across St Agnes to find a lighthouse, cafés and farms selling local produce.

Uninhabited islands
Abandoned in 1855, **Samson**, with its twin hills, is the largest of the uninhabited islands and has wonderful sand flats to explore at low tide. The **Western Rocks** and **Eastern Isles** are a spray-whipped haven for grey seals, while seabirds rule the roost on **Annet** (closed to visitors during the summer nesting season).

All in a day's holiday on St Mary's (from top left) – Scilly urchins for sale, detail of a ferryboat's wheel, Hugh Town harbour, setting sail for Tresco, a handful of periwinkles and top shells from the beach at Porthloo, walking to Hugh Town through the gateway to the Garrison, the *Scillonian III* offloading at the quayside.

Let's go to... Isles of Scilly

and seasonal vegetables. Nearby Highertown has a general store and bakery (see page 154).

If you fancy huddling down on the edge of the Atlantic, ducking the spray, watching glorious sunsets and generally getting away from it all, look no further than **Troytown Farm Campsite** (Troytown Farm, St Agnes, TR22 0PL, T01720-422360, troytown.co.uk, Mar-Oct, £5-8.75 per person, plus £2-8 charge for tents during summer holidays, bell tents for hire from £300/wk, £3 luggage transfer). With views of the Bishop Rock Lighthouse and Western Rocks, this spectacular site is tucked into fields above a beach of large cobbles and sand. The farm makes its own ice cream and also keeps campers happy with fresh milk, yoghurt, clotted cream and jacket potatoes (cooked in the farmhouse Aga). Facilities are excellent too, with modern toilets and washrooms.

Cottages & hotels

There's a wide range of cottages and guesthouses on the Isles of Scilly – the tourist board's website (simplyscilly.co.uk) has a search facility. Hotels on St Mary's include the **Star Castle Hotel** (The Garrison, TR21 0TA, T01720-422317, star-castle. co.uk) which has family-friendly garden suites, an indoor swimming pool and tennis court.

If you want to splash out, the **Flying Boat Cottages** (Tresco, TR24 0QQ, T01720-422849, tresco.co.uk, from £1475-5000/wk) consists of 12 luxury beachfront houses (sleeping up to 10) with satellite television and membership of an exclusive holiday club with its own restaurant, bar, indoor pool, spa and tennis courts. Tresco's traditional holiday cottages (same contact details as above) are no less desirable, and cost from around £630-1615 per week for a four-bed bolthole.

Also run by the Tresco Estate, **Hell Bay Hotel** (Bryher, TR23 0PR, T01720-422947, hellbay.co.uk) has rooms from £135 per person, including dinner and bed and breakfast (children between two and 12 pay £55 for high tea and bed and breakfast).

A granite hotel with lovely gardens overlooking

WELCOME TO
TROYTOWN FARM
Carry on For Campsit
Coast Path + Ice Crea

Let's go to... Isles of Scilly

the quay, **St Martin's on the Isle** (St Martin's, TR25 0QW, T01720-422090, stmartinshotel.co.uk) offers bed and breakfast from £135 per person (£25 for children sharing with two adults). The hotel has a fine restaurant, as well as an indoor pool.

For a traditional B&B in a great location, try **Greenlaws** (Old Town, St Mary's, T01720 422045, scillyguesthouse.com, £40 per person).

Visit the gardens

Built around the ruins of a 12th-century priory, **Abbey Garden** (Tresco, T01720-424105, tresco. co.uk, daily 1000-1600, £12 adult, free for children under 16) seems to sprout from another world. Exploring the sub-tropical oasis, with its terraces and interconnecting pathways and steps, children can embark a global plant safari. The garden is arranged in geographical zones, so challenge them to find New Zealand tree ferns, orange Namaqua daisies from South Africa, weird succulents from the Canary Islands, bamboo from Asia and banksias from the Australian Outback. There are manmade treasures to find as well. See if you can track down the Shell House with its amazing mosaic, or the statues of Gaia, Neptune and *The Tresco Children*. Just to the right of the garden entrance, the Valhalla Museum, with its extraordinary collection of shipwreck figureheads, is also worth a look. The gardens have a shop, an exhibition about the history of the site and a café with a pleasant outdoor eating area. The food is fine, but you might want to save yourself for Tresco Stores in nearby New Grimsby where the deli counter is groaning with goodies.

Grab a bite

On St Mary's, try **Dibble & Grub** (The Old Fire Station, Porthcressa, T01720-423719) for café snacks right by the beach. A half-hour stroll from Hugh Town, **Juliet's Garden Restaurant** (Porthloo, T01720-422228, julietsgardenresturant.

co.uk) has views across the harbour and serves a tempting array of light lunches, home-made cakes and evening meals. The local crab salads (around £15) are delicious, while generously filled sandwiches (from £4.60) come with a healthy pile of salad. For a sweet treat, try the old-fashioned ginger bread. The restaurant also has an evening menu with some excellent local seafood dishes.

On Tresco, the **New Inn** (New Grimsby, T01720-423006, tresco.co.uk) has a tasty lunch menu with sandwiches, burgers, fishcakes, fish and chips etc, as well as a traditonal roast on Sunday. You can also just pop in for Treleaven ice cream or a wicked hot chocolate. With views towards St Martin's and the Eastern Isles, **Ruin Beach Café** (Old Grimsby, T01720-424849) offers a Mediterranean inspired menu with a selection of pasta and salad dishes, as well as pizzas. You can also pick up freshly-baked bread here from 1000.

A must if you're on St Martin's, the **Bakery** (Highertown, T01720-423444, stmartinsbakery.co.uk) rustles up sublime bread, cakes, pasties and pizza – often embellished with its own locally caught and smoked Atlantic salmon. Also on St Martin's, **Little Arthur's Café** (Highertown, T01720-422457, littlearthurcafe.com) serves home-made food, using local seafood and organic vegetables. A quirky little place with a cosy conservatory half consumed by a grapevine, it has stunning views over the Eastern Isles.

On St Agnes, you must try the ice cream at **Troytown Farm** (see page 152). Just up the lane, **Coastguards Café** (T01720-422197) serves yummy cream teas, while **The Turk's Head** (T01720-422434) is renowned for its pasties.

Close to the campsite, Bryher's **Fraggle Rock Bar Café** (T01720-422222) is a wonderful spot to relax with a coffee or fruit drink, with views across Kitchen Porth towards Tresco. If you're feeling peckish, it also serves impressive crab doubledecker sandwiches.

Island oasis – Tresco's Abbey Gardens are a paradise for plants, including agapanthus (top left), South African daisies (middle) and succulents (bottom left). Sculptures, including the Tresco Children (opposite), water features and a Shell House dot the gardens and there's a maze of pathways to explore, some leading to the remains of the 12th-century priory (bottom middle).

Beach beauties

The beauty of the Scilly Isles is that you can land on an island and then simply wander off to find your own secluded beach where you may well be making the first and only sets of footprints in the sand. However, two particularly gorgeous beaches worth spending a day on can be found on St Martin's and St Agnes.

Great Bay on St Martin's is like a slice of the Bahamas slipped beneath heather-flushed hills on the island's north coast. The sand has the texture of fine granulated sugar; granite boulders form dramatic bookends to the beach and the water is so clear that snorkellers get goggled-eyed with excitement. Comb the strandline for tiny periwinkle shells and don't forget to bring a picnic – there are no facilities whatsoever.

If anything, **The Cove** on St Agnes is even better. Located on the south side of The Bar that links St Agnes to the smaller islet of Gugh (pronounced Goo), it has squeaky-clean sand, glittering with fine grains of mica. At low tide, long whip-like strands of seaweed are drizzled like honey over the rocks – shallow pools trapped between them crying out for a shrimping expedition. Sheltered from westerly winds that can batter the Atlantic shore of St Agnes, The Cove also has sheltered swimming, and there's always the added excitement of the tide coming in and submerging the sand bar (just make sure you're on the right side of it come high water).

Great Bay, St Martin's.

Let's go to... Isles of Scilly

From top to bottom: aerial view showing St Martin's, Teal and St Helen's; close encounter with a grey seal in the Eastern Isles; Island Sea Safaris RIB in Hugh Town's harbour.

Action stations

Beachcombing Glass beads from a Venetian wreck are sometimes washed into the cove at Beady Pool, St Agnes.

Birdwatching An RSPB volunteer is often on board the *Scillonian III* to help point out seabirds like Manx shearwater and storm petrel. Take a boat trip to the Annet Bird Sanctuary near St Agnes to see breeding puffins and common terns; Samson and Gugh have nesting gulls and kittiwakes, while the Western Rocks are home to shags, storm petrels and great black-backed gulls. The islands are an important stopover for migrant birds during spring and autumn – join a wildlife tour in autumn to see sanderling, ringed plover and little egret.

Boat trips The **Boatmen's Association** (see page 148) runs two or three 90-minute circular trips each day (usually departing at 1015 or 1400, £13 adult, £6.50 child). The Eastern Isles cruise visits a colony of grey seals and lands at St Martin's; the Norrard Rocks trip noses around rugged islets near Samson (also good for seals) before landing at Tresco or Bryher, while the Annet cruise takes in the bird sanctuary (only available until late July). Two-hour trips (£16 adult, £8 child) venture to the Bishop Rock Lighthouse and Western Rocks, visiting shipwreck sites and colonies of seals and seabirds before landing at St Agnes. There's a Shearwater Special (Mon, Thu), accompanied by wildlife expert Will Wagstaff (see below), visiting Annet in search of Manx shearwaters. Serious birdwatchers should also consider the pelagic trips. Other island boat operators include **Bryher Boats** (T01720-422886, bryherboats.co.uk), **St Agnes Boating** (T01720-422704, stagnesboating.co.uk) and **St Martin's Boating** (T01720-422814).

For day trips visiting two or three islands, contact **Blue Hunter** (T01720-423377), **Calypso** (T01720-422187) or **Crusader** (T07748-243122, crusaderboating.co.uk) – all running 12-passenger launches. For glass-bottom boat trips, hop aboard the **Sea Quest** (T01720-422511). For boat trips with added 'oomph', **Island Sea Safaris** (T01720-422732, islandseasafaris.co.uk) operates a feisty 8-m RIB called *Firebrand* which has an onboard underwater camera for spying on marine life. Three trips are offered: the two-hour Shipwrecks, Seals & Seabirds (£32 adult, £25 child under 12) does what it says on the tin; the one-hour Island Taster (£23) includes a visit to a seal colony, while the Evening Gig Race (£18) trails the Friday-evening island gig race.

Craft making The magical light and scenery of the Scilly Isles has inspired numerous artists and there are galleries and craft shops dotted all over the islands. To have a go yourself, wander over to the **Phoenix Craft Workshops** (Porthmellon, St Mary's, T01720-422962, phoenixcrafts. co.uk, Mon-Fri 1000-1700, Sat 1000-1230) where adults and children can get arty making enamel jewellery, prints and seaside mobiles.

Cycling Bikes are an ideal way to explore St Mary's – an easy five-mile circuit of quiet roads taking in fabulous coastal views and secluded beaches. You can hire them from **St Mary's Bike Hire** (The Strand, Hugh Town, T0779-663 8509, scillybikehire.co.uk, Mon-Sat 0900-1700, from £6 half day, £10 full day, tag-a-longs from £8). Bikes can also be hired on Tresco.

Horse riding Saddle up at **St Mary's Riding Centre** (Maypole, St Mary's, TR21 0NU, T01720-423855, horsesonscilly.co.uk) where 30-minute lead-rein rides (£20) are ideal for children or first-timers. Group lessons cost from £25, while hacks cost £25-50 and, depending on your level of experience, take to the bridleways, beaches and farm tracks around the east coast.

Rock-pool rambles Two of the best spots are Cove Vean on St Agnes and Porthloo on St Mary's. Check at the **Isles of Scilly Wildlife Trust Visitor Centre** (see page 149) for details of organized rock-pool rambles.

Sailing There are two watersports centres in the Isles of Scilly – **The Sailing Centre** (Porthmellon, St Mary's, T01720-422060, sailingscilly.com) and **Ravensporth Sailing Base** (Tresco, T01720-424919, Jul-Aug only). Windsurfing and dinghy sailing lessons cost from around £40 per hour or you can hire windsurfers (£15/hr), sit-on kayaks (singles £12/hr, doubles £15/hr) and sailing dinghies (from £20/hr).

Snorkelling You can hire wetsuits, masks, fins and snorkels from **Island Sea Safaris**, **Ravensporth Sailing Base** and **The Sailing Centre** (see above). **St Martin's Dive School** (Higher Town, St Martin's, TR25 0QL, T01720-422848, scillydiving.com) organizes three-hour snorkelling-with-seals safaris (£40, minimum age 8) and introductory scuba dives (£49, minimum age 14) which descend to around 2 m off a sheltered beach.

Wildlife watching Will Wagstaff is your man. No one knows the bird life of the Scilly Isles better. Contact **Island Wildlife Tours** (Sally Port, St Mary's, TR21 0JE, T01720-422212, half-day tours £6) for details of guided walks.

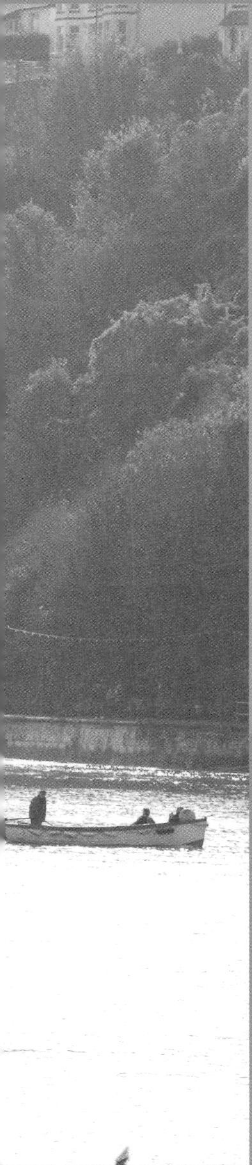

Contents

162 Map

164 Southeast Cornwall
166 Fun & free
168 Best beaches
170 Action stations
173 Big days out
178 Eden Project
180 Sleeping
184 Eating

186 The Roseland

190 Falmouth

194 Truro

South Cornwall

Park Head
Penrose
Tredinnick
St Ervan
Rumford
St Jidgey
Burlawn
Washaway
Hellar
Bodmin
Forest
St Eval
B3274
Nantallon
St Lawrence
Bodm
A389
Trenance
Berryl's Point
Trevarrian
St Mawgan
Rosenannon
Ruthernbridge
Talskiddy
Withiel
Lanivet
Trebyan
Watergate
Bay
B3276
Tregurrian
A39
St Wenn
Tregonetha
Newquay
St Columb
Major
Belowda
Victoria
Lockengate
Sweethol
Redmoor
Towan Head
Fistral
Bay
St Columb
Minor
A3059
Trebudannon
A391
Bilberry
Newquay
Bay
Mountjoy
Trevarren
A30
Tregoss
Roche
Bugle
Lanlivery
Pentire
Kelsey Head
West Pentire
A392
Lane
Kestle Mill
St Columb
Road
Indian Queens
Trezaise
Luxulyan
Penhale
Point
Holywell
Crantock
Carines
A3075
Fraddon
B3279
Hensbarrow
Downs
Whitemoor
Stenalees
Penwithick
Trethurgy
Penp
Eden
Project
Cubert
St Newlyn
East
A3058
St Dennis
Nanpean
5
St Blaz
Penhale
Ligger Sands
or
Perran
Bay
Mount
Rejerrah
Summercourt
B3275
Treviscoe
Trethosa
B3279
China Clay
Country
Park
Trewoon
B3274
St Tywardre
Perranporth
Newlyn
Downs
Mitchell
Foxhole
High
Street
St Austell
Par
Par
Sands
Bolingey
Goonhavern
Carland
Cross
Trelassick
A3058
St Stephen
Coombe
St Mewan
Charlestown
Carlyon Bay
Porthpean
B3285
Trevellas
Mithian
Perranzabuloe
Zelah
Trispen
Ladock
Hewas
Water
Sticker
Polgooth
Shipwreck
& Heritage Centre
B3284
Goonbell
Callestick
New Mills
Grampound
B3273
Porthpean
St Austell Ba
Three Burrows
Blackwater
A30
Allet
Shortlanesend
Probus
A390
Tortoise
Garden
7
Trenarren
Pentewan
A390
Kenwyn
Tresillian
Tresawle
Trewithen
Gardens
B3287
Lost Gardens
of Heligan
Mevagissey Beach
Mevagissey Bay
Threemilestone
Royal
Cornwall
Museum
Truro
Merther
St Ewe
4
Kestle
3
Mevagissey
Sealife Aquarium
B3298
Baldhu
Kea
Truro
Cathedral
St Clement
Tregony
Polmassick
Mevagissey
Museum
Mevagissey
Portmellon
St Day
Bissoe
Playing
Place
Old Kea
Malpas
St Michael
Penkevil
Trevarrick
St Michael
Caerhays
Gorran Churchtown
Chapel Point
Carharrack
Carnon
Downs
King Harry
Ferry
Treworga
A3078
Portholland
East & West
Portholland
Boswinger
Gorran Haven
Gwennap
Trelissick
Treworlas
Veryan
Caerhays
Penare
Vault Beach
Perranarworthal
Penpol
Feock
Trelissick
Gardens
Philleigh
Trewithian
Carne
Portloe
Veryan
Bay
Hemmick
Beach
Dodman Point
Ponsanooth
Burnthouse
A39
Mylor
Bridge
St Just in
Roseland
Pendower
Beach
Gerrans
Bay
Nare Head
The Roseland
Stithians
Longdowns
A394
Mabe
Burnthouse
Penryn
Flushing
A39
National
Maritime
Museum
Carrick
Roads
Gerrans
2
Portscatho
Greeb Point
Budock
Water
Falmouth
1
Pendennis
Castle
St Mawes Castle
St Mawes
Bohortha
Towan Beach
Penjerrick
Gyllyngvase
Swanpool
St Anthony
Falmouth
Bay
Constantine
Trebah
Gardens
Mawnan
Smith
Maenporth
Rosemullion Head
Helford
Passage
Mawnan
Helford
Helford River
St Anthony-in-Meneage
Manaccan
Nare Point

You must

❶ Steer a course to the amazing National Maritime Museum.

❷ Find a beach all to yourself on the Roseland Peninsula.

❸ Catch a crab off the harbour wall in Mevagissey or Looe.

❹ Lose yourself in the beautiful Lost Gardens of Heligan.

❺ Explore the steamy tropics at the iconic Eden Project.

❻ Learn to sail or windsurf from the beach at Polkerris.

❼ Ride the ferry between Mevagissey and Fowey, keeping a lookout for dolphins.

❽ Paddle a kayak to lovely Lerryn on the Fowey Estuary.

❾ Marvel at the treasure house of Cotehele.

❿ Plan a picnic in Mount Edgcumbe Country Park.

English Channel

N

2 km

2 miles

Main photo: Little nipper – another one for the bucket. Opposite: Digging at Talland Bay; the harbour at Polperro.

Southeast Cornwall

A rolling landscape of dairy farms dimpled with market towns, where hills nuzzle wooded creeks and fishing villages huddle around narrow harbours, the southeast is the soft underbelly of Cornwall – a gentle contrast to the drama-queen north with its showy beaches, surf and adrenaline sports.

But there's nothing flabby about the southeast. It might have more than its fair share of cream tea shops, but you can easily burn off the calories by kayaking, cycling, hiking and even surfing when there's a southwesterly swell.

Lying at the hub of the region, the china clay mining centre of **St Austell** snags the A390 as it meanders across southern Cornwall, passing the county's ancient seat of power at **Lostwithiel** before reaching the present-day capital of **Truro**. Cornwall's only city has a fine cathedral and museum, but it's the **Eden Project** near St Austell that gets the vote for Cornwall's most popular attraction. Over one million people make the pilgrimage to Eden each year – a green giant among lesser, though no less fascinating, sites nearby, such as the Shipwreck & Heritage Centre at the historic port of **Charlestown**.

South of St Austell, **Mevagissey**'s harbour is gridlocked with colourful trawlers and stalked by hordes of excited crab-hunters. Seek refuge from the ankle nippers in the nearby **Lost Gardens of Heligan**, or explore sandy beaches north and south of Mevagissey at **Pentewan** and **Gorran Haven**.

The coastline becomes wilder as you venture west onto the unspoilt Roseland Peninsula, a rural backwater that has sleepy **St Mawes** within waving distance of funky **Falmouth** – haven to yachties and home of the **National Maritime Museum**.

East of St Austell, fashionable **Fowey** (pronounced 'Foy') is another place where people love messing about on the water: sailing, pottering around in motor boats or kayaking to peaceful hamlets on the Fowey Estuary like **Lerryn**. Cross the estuary from Fowey to **Polruan** and the coast takes a rugged turn: cliffs marching eastwards, with narrow clefts leading to cutesy **Polperro** and the more substantial harbour town of **Looe**. Beyond lies the surf-strafed sweep of **Whitsand Bay** and the 'forgotten corner' of the **Rame Peninsula**, where historic **Mount Edgcumbe** presides over the Tamar Estuary. Plymouth is just a ferry ride (or bridge crossing) away, but steer yourself northwards and you'll find the Cornish treasure of **Cotehele House**.

Here to there

The Southeast Cornwall chapter covers the south coast, west from the Rame Peninsula to Dodman Point, just beyond Gorran Haven. Points west of this are covered by sections on The Roseland (see pages 186-189) and Falmouth (see pages 190-193). The Southeast Cornwall chapter extends north to include highlights in the Lower Tamar Valley, such as Cotehele House. Lostwithiel, the Fowey Estuary and attractions near St Austell, like the Eden Project, are also covered. For Truro, see pages 194-195.

Rame Head – Gorran Haven

Out & about Southeast Cornwall

Fun & free

Linger in Looe

Cornwall's southeast coast reaps a bumper catch of quaint fishing villages, and Looe is one of the best for a family day out that will barely cost you a penny. Park in **West Looe** beside the harbour, then walk across the bridge (admiring the beautiful views up the estuary) into **East Looe**. Fore Street has a good baker, so now is the time to stock up on picnic supplies if you need to. Nip down a side street to the quay and find a quiet spot for some crabbing. With a bit of luck you might be able to watch fishermen unloading

their catch from brightly painted trawlers. Keep an eye out for grey seals – Looe Harbour is one of the best places in Cornwall to see them. If it's low tide, there's a tiny shingle cove next to the slipway, but you're better off walking towards Banjo Pier where Looe's main sandy beach stretches along the seafront (see page 169). This is also where you will find the lifeboat station. When you've finished your beach session, backtrack to the quayside, where a passenger ferry will take you back across the harbour to West Looe. From here, walk along Marine Drive for superb views across the harbour, continuing around the headland

East Looe

to find a rocky shore that's good for rock-pooling at low tide. Looming offshore, **Looe Island** can be visited on boat trips (see page 170).

Remember the Rame

Roam free in the magnificent 865-acre **Mount Edgcumbe Country Park** on the Rame Peninsula – Cornwall's so-called 'Forgotten Corner'. There's an admission charge for the historic house (see page 176), but the

Did you see that splash? The tranquil tidal creeks of the Fowey Estuary are home to otters and kingfishers, so keep alert for signs of movement along the riverbank.

Visit Mevagissey

Why? Because not only is the crabbing around the harbour some of the best in Cornwall, but there's also a free museum and aquarium. The Mevagissey Sealife Aquarium is in a small building on the right-hand side of the harbour. There's barely enough space inside to swing a batfish, and it will only take you ten minutes or so to peruse the half-dozen tanks, but it's a great opportunity to see local fish (accompanied, you may well find, by bracing classical music). See if you can spot the conger eel in its pipe, Shelley the UK's largest oyster, dogfish and their egg cases, mullet, gurnard, triggerfish and flatfish. The aquarium also claims to have the biggest lobster in Cornwall, but Dai the Claw at Padstow's National Lobster Hatchery (see page 57) might have something to say about that. On the left-hand side of the harbour is the fascinating little Mevagissey Museum. Even the building itself is interesting: it was once used as a repair shop for smugglers' ships. Inside, you'll find all sorts of historical artefacts, but perhaps the most eye-catching exhibits are the wonderful black-and-white photos depicting life in Mevagissey during the 19th century.

Contact Mevagissey Sealife Aquarium, New Pier, T01726-843305; Mevagissey Museum, East Wharf, T01726-843568, Easter-Oct from 1100.

park costs nothing to visit and is open year round, daily from 0800. Dating from the 1500s, it's the earliest landscaped park in Cornwall and features ancient ruins, a Coastwatch station, free-running deer, formal Italian gardens and views across the sound towards Plymouth.

Catch a crab

Fowey, Looe, Mevagissey, Polperro... the crabbing in these south Cornwall fishing villages is legendary. Crab lines and buckets are sold everywhere, or you could make your own crabbing kit for nothing (see page 26).

Tackle the Tamar

A lofty lump of granite rearing above the Tamar Valley near Callington, 334-m-high **Kit Hill** (cornwall.gov.uk) has stunning views towards Bodmin Moor and Dartmoor, south to Plymouth Sound and (on a clear day) north to Bude. Grab your kite and a picnic and set off on the two-mile circular walk. The area is rich in history, with 19th-century mining remains (including the summit chimney stack) and a Neolithic long barrow dating from 3000 BC. Your kite, meanwhile, will probably share air space with buzzards and kestrels. Adders enjoy basking on sunny slopes and furry moth caterpillars can be seen on the heather during summer months.

Top: Pebble tower– how high can you go? Above: Is this the perfect skimmer?

What? No sand?!

No sulks or tantrums please. There's nothing wrong with a pebbly beach. In fact, you can have just as much fun on one of Cornwall's stony coves (and there are several on the southeast coast) as you can on a golden-sand one. For starters, there's stone-skimming. You'll need smooth, flat pebbles that fit comfortably between thumb and forefinger – crouch down, let loose with a flick of the wrist and see how many times you can make them skip across the sea (anything above seven is impressive). Pebble towers are also fun – see how many stones you can stack on top of each other, or use it as target practice (in an empty corner of the beach). If you're feeling arty, collect pebbles that all have a white vein running through them and arrange them side-by-side to create a 'rivulet' of quartz flowing across the beach.

Out & about Southeast Cornwall

Best beaches

The beaches here are found west to east, from Dodman Point to the Rame Peninsula. For Roseland beaches, see page 188.

Gorran Haven

Sheltered by a harbour wall, this sandy beach has safe swimming and is popular with families. Get your shrimping nets, crab lines, bait and inflatable dolphins at the Beachcomber.

Pentewan

This half-mile strip of sand is kept spotless by staff from the Pentewan Sands Holiday Park (see page 181) that backs much of the beach. The swimming is good and you can hire kayaks from Pentewan Watersports (T01726-844777).

Porthpean

A popular sandy cove with rock pools at low tide.

Charlestown

The pebble cove near the harbour is a good place for kids to burn off energy after all the cabinet perusal in the shipwreck museum (see page 173).

Carlyon Bay

This long sandy beach is in the throes of a controversial development plan to build a £250 million leisure resort. Get the latest news at carlyonbeach.com.

Par Sands

A dune-backed beach with lots of sand and shallow water at low tide, easy access and a nearby café, Par Sands is a favourite with young families.

Polkerris

A small crescent of sand, partly sheltered by a stone quay, Polkerris combines an idyllic Cornish cove with excellent watersports at the Polkerris Beach Company (see page 171).

Readymoney Cove

A 20-minute walk from Fowey, Readymoney is a shingle and sand beach surrounded by woody cliffs and overlooked by the ruins of St Catherine's Castle.

Lantic Bay

Hemmed in by the 122-m hulk of Pencarrow Head, Lantic Bay is reached by a steep climb down

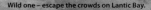

Wild one – escape the crowds on Lantic Bay.

from the cliff tops. There are no facilities and swimming can be dangerous due to rip currents – but this is still a hidden gem for escaping the crowds, watching the waves whomp against the rocks, or combing the strandline.

Talland Bay

🏄 🌊 🏖️ 🅿️ 🦀

Talland Bay is a sheltered cove with low headlands of mauve rock. Sand and rock pools are exposed at low tide and you can park right behind the beach, next to the Talland Bay Beach Café (see page 185).

East Looe Beach

🏄 🌊 🐟 🏖️ 🌊 🏖️ 🅿️

With facilities close by, East Looe's sandy seafront beach is always a safe bet for families. Boat trips operate from the harbour, while West Looe's Hannafore Point beach is good for picnics and rock-pooling.

Whitsand Bay

🏄 🌊 🏖️ ➕ 🌊 🏖️ 🅿️ 🦀 ❗

A fine, three-mile swathe of surf-fringed sand, Whitsand brings a touch of north Cornwall to this stretch of coast – just take heed of the signs warning of rip

currents, steep access and the risk of being cut off at high tide. Lifeguards patrol the beaches, of which Tregonhawke and Tregantle are best for families.

Cawsand & Kingsand

🏄 🌊 🏖️ 🌊 🏖️ 🅿️

These pretty twin villages on the Rame Peninsula have small beaches of sand and shingle. There are rock pools at Kingsand and boat hire (kayaks, dinghies and windsurfers) at Cawsands.

Out & about Southeast Cornwall

Action stations

Adrenalin activities
Adrenalin Quarry
Lower Clicker Rd, Menheniot, PL14 3PJ, T01579-308204, adrenalinquarry. co.uk. Easter-Sep daily 1000-1800; Oct-Easter, call for times. Zip wire (no age limit) and Giant Swing (minimum age 5) £12.50 for first ride, £7 for second ride, £50 family. Not all thrill rides in Cornwall involve surf – the zip wire at Adrenalin Quarry accelerates you to speeds of 40 mph over a 490-m-long cable suspended 50m above a lake. And, if that doesn't get your heart thumping, try the three-person Giant Swing, plunging towards the lake, experiencing a brief moment of zero gravity.

Boat trips
Fowey Cruise
Town Quay, Fowey, T07775-685941, foweycruise.com. Apr-Oct daily. Pottering around Fowey Harbour for 45 minutes is a great way to see local attractions like St Catherine's Castle and the house in waterside Bodinnick where Daphne du Maurier wrote the first of her novels. Longer cruises go upriver to Lerryn, passing Fowey docks, the villages of Golant and Cliff and Ethy Quay, where Kenneth Grahame may well have sought inspiration for Wlnd in the Willows. You can also voyage to Lostwithiel, landing at the medieval Town Quay, or to

Charlestown with its Shipwreck and Heritage Centre (see page 173). Just six miles east of Fowey, the historic fishing village of Polperro takes about an hour to reach by boat, passing seabird nesting cliffs and the stunning duo of Lantic Bay and Lantivet Bay where it's not unusual to spot basking sharks or dolphins.

Fowey Town Quay Boat Hire
Fowey, T07989-991115, fowey-boat-hire.co.uk. Apr-Oct 1000-1800. Explore the tidal creeks of the River Fowey. Self-drive boats take up to five passengers.

Mevagissey-Fowey Ferry
Lighthouse Quay, Mevagissey, T07977-203394, mevagissey-ferries. co.uk. Apr-Oct daily from 1000. Return fares £14 adult, £8 child. Taking around 35 minutes to link two of Cornwall's most charismatic ports, the 50-seat Bessie James often has encounters with dolphins and basking sharks. Ask the crew for a map of walks around Fowey (the ferry docks at Whitehouse Quay) or the 45-minute amble to Heligan Gardens if you are going to Mevagissey.

Boats operating from **Looe** are chalked up on quayside boards and include daily two-hour mackerel fishing trips on the Boscastle Lass (T07887-

875726), Carrie Jane (T0785-339 1090, fishing-cornwall. co.uk) and Swallow (T07831-616316), birdwatching on the Mystique II (T07900-472252, mystiquefishing.com) and glass-bottom boat trips around Looe Island (T01503-263747).

In **Mevagissey**, you can hire self-drive motorboats, book a cruise around Mevagissey Bay or join a mackerel-fishing trip. Check the boards on the harbourfront for times and fares.

Canoeing
See page 172.

Cycling
Pentewan Valley Cycle Hire
West End, Pentewan, PL26 6BX, T01726-844242, pentewanvalleycyclehire.co.uk. Daily 0900-1700. Adult bike £14/day, child's bike £9/day, tag-a-long £8/day. Pedal north from Pentewan on National Cycle Route 3 (mixture of traffic-free and on-road) to St Austell or branch off south to the Lost Gardens of Heligan and Mevagissey (all traffic-free). The Eden Project (see page 178) is also within reach.

Go-karting
Kartworld
Menheniot, PL14 3PJ, T01579-347229, kartworldcornwall.co.uk.

Easter-Oct daily from 1000, Nov-
Easter Sat-Sun from 1000. Infant
carts (ages 6 and under) from £1,
Bambini karts (ages 7-9) £20/30
minutes, Junior karts (ages 10-15)
£22, Adult karts £30.
Racing tracks for all ages,
including an 800-m circuit
(maximum speed 40 mph) and
an infant circuit for children six
and under (using 5-mph, coin-
operated karts).

Horse riding
Polmartin Riding
Polmartin Farm, nr Herodsfoot,
PL14 4RE, T01503-220428,
polmartinfarm.com. Call for rates.
BHS-approved riding school in
beautiful countryside.

Multi-activity
Active 8
Liskeard, T01579-320848,
activecornwall.co.uk.

Surfing
Discovery Surf School
Bigbury-on-Sea, Devon, TQ7 4AS,
T07813-639622. £38/2-hr lesson.
This Devon-based operator offers
surf lessons at Tregonhawke
Beach and Tregantle Beach on
Whitsand Bay.

Watersports
Fowey Maritime Centre
Fowey, PL23 1BE, T01726-833924,
foweymaritimecentre.com.
A full-blown, RYA-accredited
sailing school with less intense
dinghy sailing courses for kids.
The centre also runs week-long

The harbour at Looe.

family sailing holidays during
the summer months aboard a
Beneteau 40.7 Challenger yacht,
exploring the south coasts
of Devon and Cornwall and
incorporating RYA qualifications.

Polkerris Beach Company
The Pilchard Store, Polkerris, PL24
2TL, T01726-813306, polkerrisbeach.
com. Sailing or windsurfing
taster session £39, RYA sailing or
windsurfing course £150, supervised
sailing or windsurfing £8/hr plus
£16-30 equipment rental, stand-up

paddle surfing tuition £25/hr, sit-on
kayak hire £9-14/hr.
This small centre is right on the
beach and offers personalized
tuition in windsurfing, sailing
and stand-up paddle surfing.
If you're not sure what to do,
try one of the 90-minute taster
sessions which includes a short
demonstration on land before
getting straight out on the
water. You can also rent sailing
dinghies, windsurfers and kayaks.
For great snacks, try the Polkadot
Café (see page 185).

Up a creek with a paddle
– kayaking at Lerryn.

Paddle power

Encounter Cornwall
Downs Hill, Golant,
PL23 1LJ, T01208-832104,
encountercornwall.com.
2-hr evening sundowner paddles,
Jun-Aug, £20 adult, £10 child;
3-hr Creeks & Backwaters or
Harbours & Beaches trips £25 adult,
£12.50 child (under 16);
Single kayak hire £20/half day,
£30/day; double kayak hire
£30/half day, £45/full day.
Children under 18 must be
accompanied by an adult.

Fowey Kayak Expeditions
Passage St, Fowey, PL23 1DE,
T01726-833627, foweyexpeditions.
co.uk, foweykayakhire.co.uk.
River Expeditions (May-Sep)
£25 person (under-8s free);
single kayak hire £8/hr, £18/half
day, £22/day; double kayak hire
£12/hr, £28/half day, £36/day.

'Believe me, my young friend, there is nothing – absolutely nothing – half so much worth doing as simply messing about in boats.' Of course, Ratty was spot on when he shared this nugget of wisdom with Mole in *The Wind in the Willows*. Moments later their boat struck the bank, but that didn't dent their enthusiasm for a jolly day out on the river.

Kenneth Grahame's children's classic was partly inspired by his holidays at Fowey, and now it's a simple matter to follow in the wake of Mole and Ratty by joining a canoeing trip on the river.

The antithesis to north Cornwall's surf scene, canoeing on the River Fowey is a relaxed affair – gentle paddling along sheltered creeks, water chuckling under your kayak's hull and picnics on the riverbank. It's also the best way to see the estuary's wildlife, which includes otters, egrets and kingfishers.

One of two canoeing operators on the river, Encounter Cornwall is based in the idyllic hamlet of Golant – an ideal place for novices to refine their paddling technique in stable open-cockpit or sit-on kayaks. Longer trips venture into the main Fowey Estuary, stopping perhaps for a look around the riverside settlements of Lerryn or St Winnow before nosing about in Woodgate Pill in search of kingfishers. With a whole day on the river (and some canoeing experience under your life vest), you could easily make it down to Fowey and Polruan, paddling in the shadow of huge ocean-going ships moored in the harbour. After lunch on a deserted beach, canoe back to Golant on a rising tide – a fantastic river adventure covering around 10 miles.

Fowey Kayak Expeditions offers guided five-hour canoeing trips upstream from Fowey, with about two and a half hours on the river and the rest of the time exploring Lerryn and Golant. If you're feeling independent and free-spirited, both operators also offer kayaks for hire – however, this is not recommended for beginners.

Charlestown Shipwreck & Heritage Centre

Charlestown, PL25 3NJ, T01726-69897, shipwreckcharlestown.com. Mar-Nov daily 1000-1700. £5.95 adult, £3.50 child (under 10s free). As close to a real-life treasure chest as you'll ever get, this wonderfully cluttered museum showcases artefacts from over 150 shipwrecks, including the *Titanic*, *Mary Rose* and *Lusitania*. You can also board the lifeboat *RNLB Amelia* and scurry through a tunnel (once used for transporting china clay) to a terrace overlooking Charlestown's docks where two square-rigged sailing ships are moored. Backtracking through the tunnel, you find yourself walking through a lifesize diorama of early 19th-century Charlestown buildings, including a harbour cottage,

blacksmith and cooper (barrel maker). This is followed by various maritime-themed displays – the old diving suits and diving bells will have children goggle-eyed, while the section charting the history of the RNLI is a must-see. There are a few hands-on gizmos, but nothing more high-tech than tapping out SOS on a morse code machine. The remainder of the museum is largely cabinets bursting with shipwreck paraphernalia. There's plenty of fascinating stuff here – but there's a lot of it, so be sure to equip children with I-Spy sheets (available at the entrance) to help buoy their enthusiasm levels.

Cotehele House & Quay

St Dominick, nr Saltash, PL12 6TA, T01579-351346, nationaltrust.org. uk. Garden daily from 1000; house and mill Mar-Nov Sat-Thu (mill daily) from 1100. Check website for rates. Calstock ferry, T01822-833331.

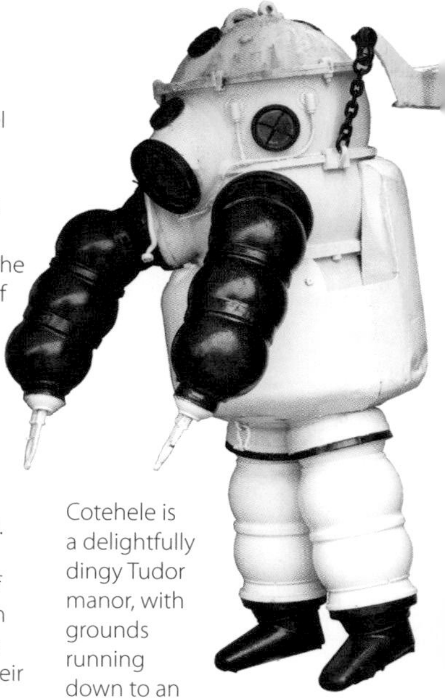

Cotehele is a delightfully dingy Tudor manor, with grounds running down to an old quay on the River Tamar that can be reached by ferry from Calstock. A short walk downriver, the watermill has workshops featuring a blacksmith, carpenter, saddler and wheelwright. So, where to begin? If a family fun activity is running (usually Mondays, Tuesdays and Wednesdays during August), then make a beeline for the

Cotehele House.

Education Room. Otherwise, collect Tracker Packs or quiz sheets for the children and head for the manor house.

Little altered since its completion by the Edgcumbe family around 1539, Cotehele House is remarkably well preserved. The main hall is adorned with armour and weapons (and some whale jaw bones by the fireplace), while ancient tapestries festoon the walls of the dining room and bedrooms – infusing them with a perpetual, musty twilight, as if time really has stood still here for five centuries. Children will be kept busy trying to spot details in the tapestries for their quiz sheets. Ask one of the friendly and engaging National Trust volunteers if you need a clue – they'll also point out other features like the spy holes or 'squints' for peeping onto rooms below.

Outside, the formal gardens have views over the valley and conceal medieval treasures like the dovecote and stewpond (for keeping carp). It's a steepish walk through beautiful woodland down to Cotehele Quay, where a discovery centre has scale models recreating the scene in the 19th century: coal, limestone and market produce being loaded onto barges for transport down the Tamar River. One of them – the *Shamrock* – is moored outside, but you can't go aboard. Instead, children will be happy exploring the Shipping Office, playing coits, practising knots and scribbling yarns at the craft desk. The quay is a lovely spot for a picnic and there's also a café selling ice creams.

The Lost Gardens of Heligan
Pentewan, PL26 6EN, T01726-845100, heligan.com. Apr-Sep daily 1000-1800; Oct-Mar, daily 1000-1700; tearoom daily from 0930. £11 adult, £6 child (5-16), £29 family, free entry to shop and tearoom.
Any child who's read *The Secret Garden* will be intrigued by Heligan which seems to sprout straight from the pages of Frances Hodgson Burnett's classic novel about a hidden, neglected garden nurtured back to life. Remember, though, that Heligan is now a large, working garden and conservation project – don't expect any fanciful forays into fairy-themed playgrounds or other children's attractions.

Instead, let your imagination run wild as you follow boardwalks through tunnels of banana palms and bamboo in the subtropical Jungle and discover natural sculptures on the Woodland Walk. See if you can spot the Giant's Head – montbretia sprouting in orange-tipped plumes from his head – or the mesmerising Mud Maiden, cloaked in ferns and ivy. Don't miss Horsemoor Hide – part of Heligan Wild – which combines traditional wildlife-spotting (overlooking a bird feeding area, wildlife pond, meadow and woodland) with live CCTV footage of bats, birds and badgers. You can even use remote-controlled cameras to zoom in on whatever turns up. Nuthatches and woodpeckers often visit the nut feeders, while kingfishers occasionally stake out the pond.

Heligan's Northern Gardens are festooned with flowers, fruit and veg (including poo-powered pineapple) and there's an excellent tearoom serving soups, roast lunches and snacks. At the entrance, Lobbs Farm Shop (see page 184) is the place to pick up local produce.

The *Shamrock* at Cotehele Quay.

Lost and found – Heligan's treasures include (from top left) a water cherub in the Italian Gardens, old-fashioned tools in the Vegetable Garden, a secret doorway in the Melon Yard, the Mud Maiden, Jungle Garden, Flower Garden and Giant's Head.

Out & about Southeast Cornwall

More family favourites

Amazing Cornish Maize Maze
Smeaton Farm, Pillaton, Saltash PL12 6RZ, T01579-351833, amazingcornishmaizemaze.co.uk. Jul-Sep daily 1030-1700. £6 adult, £4.50 child (3-16), £19 family. Frighteningly fiendish maze with a different theme each year, plus farm trail, play area and café.

Fowey Aquarium
Town Hall, Fowey. May-Dec 1000-1700. £2 adult, £1.50 child (3-13). Built in 1950 by a local fishmonger, Fowey's dinky aquarium relies on fishermen and local anglers for stocking its tanks. You never know what the latest 'live catch' might be, but chances are you'll see conger eel, cuckoo wrasse, dogfish, mullet and lobster. A touch pool allows children to get to grips (gently) with crabs and starfish.

The Monkey Sanctuary
Murrayton, Looe, PL13 1NZ, T0844-272 1271, monkeysanctuary.org. Easter-Sep, Feb & Oct half term, call for opening times. £8 adult, £5 child (5-15), £25 family.
Beating the drum for primate welfare, this inspired centre provides a stimulating home for capuchin and woolly monkeys – many of them confiscated as illegally kept pets. Keepers give talks and workshops throughout the day. You can help to make enrichment toys for the monkeys, explore a wildlife trail

and bat cave, and tuck into award-winning vegetarian food at the Tree Top Café – proceeds of which go to the sanctuary's charity, Wild Futures.

Mount Edgcumbe
Cremyll, Torpoint, PL10 1HZ, T01752-822236, mountedgcumbe. gov.uk. Apr-Sep Sun-Thu 1100-1630. £7.20 adult, £3.75 child (5-15), £12.50 family; house and Tamar cruise tickets £11 adult, £7 child. The grand family home of the Edgcumbes, restored to its 18th-century splendour, is surrounded by formal gardens and the wider (free-to-enter) country park – see page 166.

Polperro Heritage Museum of Smuggling & Fishing
The Warren, Polperro, T01503-273005, polperro.org. Mar-Oct daily 1000-1800. £2 adult, £0.50 child. With its narrow lanes, wonky houses and higgledy-piggledy harbour, Polperro was always destined to become a tourist trap – but you can see a more gritty side to the village at this small museum with its 19th-century photos, ship models and artefacts. Walk or take a horse-and-cart or tram down to the village from the car park, passing Cornwall's Fairy Kingdom, the Chocolate Dream Company, model village and galleries, tea rooms and cafés galore. The museum is tucked away in the old pilchard factory by the harbour. See if you can

Fowey Aquarium.

also find the House on Props, then walk out to the harbour entrance, past the old Sail Loft, to see the lighthouse.

Porfell Wildlife Park
Trecangate, nr Lanreath, PL14 4RE, T01503-220211, porfell.co.uk. Apr-Nov daily 1000-1800 (plus weekends Feb-Apr). £9.50/adult, £6.50 child (3-13), £29 family.
A peaceful, laid-back park with lemurs, meerkats, tamarins, zebras and other furry favourites, plus a children's farm, woodland walks, café, picnic area and Maasai Village where you can learn how animals and humans coexist in the Great Rift Valley.

Restormel Castle
Nr Lostwithiel, PL22 0EE, T01208-872687, english-heritage.org.uk. Apr-Nov daily from 1000. £3.60 adult, £2.20 child (5-15). Battle imaginary dragons, rescue maidens in distress and strut your stuff, just like Edward the Black Prince did when he visited this splendid keep – now a ruined shell ripe for a picnic.

Restormel Castle.

Tamar Valley Donkey Park
St Ann's Chapel, Gunnislake, PL18 9HW, T01822-834072, donkeypark. com. Apr-Sep, daily from 1030; call for winter opening. £6.95 person (under-2s free), £25 family.
Feed and pet donkeys, ponies, goats, sheep, pigs, rabbits and guinea pigs. You can also ride the donkeys or horse around in the play barn.

Trewithen Gardens
Grampound, nr Truro, TR2 4DD, T01726-883647, trewithengardens. co.uk. Mar-Jul daily 1000-1630. £8.50 adult, children under 12 free.
Renowned for its magnolias and camellias, this historic private estate has tranquil woodland walks, picnic areas and a tea room selling local produce.

Wheal Martyn
Carthew, St Austell, PL26 8XG, T01726-850362, wheal-martyn.com. Year round daily from 1000.
£9 adult, £5 child (6-16), £24 family. Ever wondered what those 'white mountains' are as you drive past St Austell? The story of china clay mining is revealed at this country park through historical trails, interactive displays and a platform overlooking a working pit.

Rain check

Cinemas
White River Cinema
White River Place, St Austell, T01726-66301.
Vue
Barbican Leisure Park, Shapters Rd, Coxside, Plymouth, T01752-222241.

Indoor play & amusements
Kidzworld
Stadium Retail Park, Par Moor Rd, St Austell, PL25 3RP, T01726-815553, kidzworlduk.co.uk. Apr-Sep daily 1000-1900, Oct-Mar Tue-Sun 1000-1900. £6.50 adult, £10.45 child (3-12). Vast play zone with Skytrail aerial course, Lasertag, digital climbing wall, dodgems, mini golf, sand and water play, rollerskating, soft play for toddlers and babies and a tropical-themed restaurant.

Indoor swimming pools
Lux Park Leisure Centre
Coldstyle Rd, Liskeard, PL14 3HZ, T01579-342544, tempusleisure.org.uk.
Polkyth Leisure Centre
Carlyon Rd, St Austell, PL25 4DB, T01726-223696, tempusleisure.org.uk.
Saltash Leisure Centre
Callington Rd, PL12 6DJ, T01752-840940, tempusleisure.org.uk.

Museums & aquariums
Fowey Museum
Town Hall, Fowey. Easter-Oct Mon-Fri 1030-1630. £1 adult.
Lostwithiel Museum
Fore St, Lostwithiel. Easter-Sep Mon-Sat 1030-1630. Free.

Visit The National Marine Aquarium
Just across the border in Devon, the UK's largest aquarium (T0844-893 7938, national-aquarium.co.uk, year round daily from 1000, £12.75 adult, £8.75 child (4-15), £37 family) is easy to reach from southeast Cornwall. Start in the Plymouth Sound zone with its rock pool critters, before exploring the kelp forests of the British Coasts exhibit, modelled on Eddystone Reef. Next is the Atlantic Ocean zone with a 2.5-million-litre tank containing sharks, barracuda and stingrays, jacks and tarpon – circling a full-sized replica of a sunken World War II seaplane. The final zone, Blue Planet, showcases marine life from around the world and includes a huge Great Barrier Reef tank – home to a loggerhead turtle that was washed up at Sennen Cove in 1990.

Don't miss The Eden Project

Bodelva, nr St Austell, PL24 2SG, T01726-811911, edenproject.com. Year round daily from 1000 (car parks open 0900 during summer school holidays). On the door entry £23.50 adult, £10.50 child (5-16); online tickets up to 15% off; reduced prices if you walk, cycle or take public transport £19.50 adult, £6.50 child, £24 family, children free.

Bulging from an old china clay pit like a giant string of silvery frog spawn, Eden's vast biomes have become an icon, not just of British tourism, but of sustainability. Visiting this hallowed shrine to vegetation has almost become a rite of family holidays in Cornwall – a peat-free pilgrimage that's right up there with surfing and Stein's fish 'n' chips. And it's hardly surprising. Not only is the Eden Project immensely fun and educational for kids, but it also reconnects them with the environment, plunging them into an earthy succession of habitats, from jungle to global veggie patch.

Zig-zagging along paths below the visitor centre, most people make straight for the Rainforest and Mediterranean Biomes, but don't overlook the outdoor space – it's riddled with shortcuts, hideaways, stepping stones, spy-holes and sandpits. You might also bump into a Pollinator, one of Eden's resident interpreters who act as guides and impromptu storytellers. Everything you need for building a den can be found in the play area. And, of course, everywhere you look you'll see real plants, growing, flowering, fruiting and generally giving your senses a thorough workout.

Brace yourself for the Rainforest Biome. Littl'uns might wilt in the hot and humid atmosphere, so take your time and make use of the water fountains scattered throughout this record-breaking greenhouse (240 m long, 110 m wide and 50 m high). As well as identifying tropical fruits and spices, you'll find out, through imaginative displays, how rubber, chewing gum and cola drinks are derived from rainforest plants. There's also a waterfall and jungle settlement to discover, while sharp-eyed explorers might spot a tree frog.

The Mediterranean Biome is just as mesmerising with its cork and citrus plantations, grape vines and perfume garden. There's a lot to see at the Eden Project, but try to leave a good hour or two for tinkering about with the interactive exhibits in The Core educational centre. The elaborate nut-cracking machine is addictive, while the Plant Engine reveals the importance of leaves. You can also fly over the biomes on a 660-m zip wire, or visit during winter when the Eden Project is transformed into a wonderland of ice skating and Christmas markets.

Natural cycle

Cycle to the Eden Project and you not only fast-track through entrance queues and get a discount on admission tickets (see left), but you also help to reduce traffic congestion and feel really good about yourself. The **Clay Trails** cycle route (directions and maps on the Eden project website) links Bugle with the Eden Project along four miles of easy, mainly level gravel track (there's one moderate climb), passing woodland and a picnic shelter overlooking some lakes. A more challenging five-mile route between Wheal Martyn and the Eden Project offers panoramic views of St Austell Bay and the clay mines. You can access both trails from National Cycle Network Route 3, which runs through Bodmin and St Austell. If you need bikes, contact Pentewan Valley Cycle Hire (see page 170) or Jungle Cycle Hire (Bugle, T01726-852204).

Hot stuff – the luxuriant Rainforest Biome.
Above: lavender fields, a jungle settlement
and a big machine to crack a small nut.

Visiting this hallowed shrine to vegetation has almost become a rite
of family holidays in Cornwall – a peat-free pilgrimage that's right up
there with surfing and Stein's fish 'n' chips.

Pick of the pitches

Bay View Farm

St Martins, Looe, PL13 1NZ, T01503-265922, looebaycaravans.co.uk. May-Sep. £10-22/pitch, £25-40/snug.

Unzip your tent and gaze straight across Looe Bay from this wonderful coastal farm that's also home to seven shire horses. Three wooden camping snugs (sleeping two adults and two children) can be rented.

Camping Caradon

Trelawne, Looe, PL13 2NA, T01503-272388, campingcaradon.co.uk. Apr-Oct. £13-23.50/pitch, plus £3 extra adult, £2 extra child.

Close to Looe, Polperro and Talland Bay, this family-run park has a games room, playground and club house. There's also a handy bus stop outside the park's entrance.

Carlyon Bay Camping Park

Carlyon Bay, PL25 3RE, T01726-812735, carlyonbay.net. Apr-Sep, £13-27/pitch (2 adults), plus £5-6 extra adult, £4-5 extra child (3-15).

Just two miles from the Eden Project and a short walk to the beach, this spacious site has a heated swimming pool, playground and crazy golf.

Court Farm

St Stephen, nr St Austell, PL26 7LE, T01726-823684, courtfarmcornwall. co.uk. Apr-Sep. £8-11/pitch, plus £1-2 extra person.

Perfect for starry-eyed campers, this small and very peaceful site, deep in the Cornish countryside, has an astronomy telescope.

East Crinnis Camping & Caravan Park

Lantyan, East Crinnis, PL24 2SQ, T01726-813023, crinniscamping. co.uk. Easter-Oct. £12-20/pitch, plus

£3 extra person, yurts and log cabins from £375/wk.

A leafy, well-landscaped park with its own fishing pond, East Crinnis makes a good base for exploring south coast beaches, as well as the Eden Project and the fishing villages of Mevagissey and Fowey.

Heligan Woods

St Ewe, Mevagissey, PL26 6EZ, T01726-842714, heliganwoods.co.uk. Jan-Nov. Call for rates.

Beautifully landscaped park next door to the Lost Gardens of Heligan, with 16 luxury holiday homes and 90 pitches.

Highertown Farm Campsite

Lansallos, PL13 2PX, T01208-265211, nationaltrust.org.uk. Easter-Oct. £4-5 adult, £2-2.50 child (2-12).

Quiet, rural and within easy walking distance of the beautiful

beaches of Lantivet and Lantic Bay, this basic campsite has stunning coastal views.

Penmarlam Caravan & Camping Park

Bodinnick, nr Fowey, PL23 1LZ, T01726-870088, penmarlampark. co.uk. Apr-Oct. £6.50-11/pitch, £5-8.50 adult, £2-3 child (3-15).

⚓ 🏕 🅿 ♿ 🔥 🍴 🛒 🐕 WC ⚡

Located on the east bank of the Fowey River, this tidy site has great views and easy access to Fowey on either the Bodinnick or Polruan ferry.

Pensagillas Farm

Grampound, TR2 4SR, T01872-530808, pensagillas-park.co.uk. £10-17.50/pitch, rental tents £25.

⚓ 🏕 🚿 🐕

A short drive from Mevagissey and the Lost Gardens of Heligan, this rural site has a farm trail, fishing lakes and livery stables (should you choose to take your horse on holiday). For no-fuss camping, you can also rent ready-pitched tents, complete with beds and cooking gear.

Treveague Farm

Gorran, PL26 6NY, T01726-842295, treveaguefarm.co.uk. Apr-Oct. £9-22/pitch (2 adults), plus £2 extra person. Cottages from £430/wk.

⚓ 🏕 🅿 ♿ 🔥 🍴 🛒 🐕 ⚡ 🛁

The perfect spot for wildlife lovers, Treveague Farm has a state-of-the-art hide with night vision cameras allowing you to watch the nocturnal antics of badgers and foxes. Everything from peregrine falcons to hummingbird hawk moths have been recorded at the farm; and there's a resident expert on hand to take you on nature walks. Treveague has wonderful coastal views, with footpaths leading to Gorran Haven, as well as the secluded Vault and Hemmick beaches. The farm's restaurant serves organic produce, and a storyteller visits during peak season to recount traditional folk tales.

Holiday parks

Killgarth Manor
Polperro, PL13 2JQ, T0844-847 1356, hoseasons.co.uk.

Looe Bay Holiday Park
St Martins, PL13 1NX, T0844-335 3450, parkdeanholidays.co.uk.

Meadow Lakes Holiday Park
Hewas Water, PL26 7JG, T01726-882540, meadow-lakes.co.uk.

Par Sands Holiday Park
St Austell Bay, PL24 2AS, T01726-812868, parkleisure.co.uk.

Pentewan Sands Holiday Park
Pentewan, PL26 6BT, T01726-843485, pentewansands.com.

River Valley Holiday Park
London Apprentice, St Austell, PL26 7AP, T01726-73533, rivervalleyholidaypark.co.uk.

Tencreek Holiday Park
Looe, PL13 2JR, T01503-262447, dolphinholidays.co.uk.

Tregoad Park
St Martin, nr Looe, PL13 1PB, T01503-262718, tregoadpark.co.uk.

Trelawne Manor
Looe, PL13 2NA, T0844-847 1356, hoseasons.co.uk.

Seaview International
Boswinger, nr Gorran Haven, PL26 6LL, T01726-843425, seaviewinternational.com.

Sun Valley Resort
Pentewan, PL26 6DJ, T01726-843266, sunvalleyholidaypark.co.uk.

Whitsand Bay Fort
Millbrook, PL10 1JZ, T01752-822597, whitsandbayholidays.co.uk.

The campsite at Treveague Farm, with views towards Gorran Haven.

Sleeping Southeast Cornwall

Cottages

Bosinver Farm Cottages
See pages 18-19.

Cornhill Farm Cottages
St Blazey, Par, PL24 2SP, T01726-815700, cornhillfarmcottages.co.uk. £360-670/wk.
Just a short walk from the Eden Project, these converted stone barns are on a small, family-run farm with plenty of friendly animals to become acquainted with, from saddleback pigs to miniature Shetland ponies.

Crylla Valley Cottages
Notter Bridge, nr Saltash, T01752-851133, cryllacottages.co.uk. Call for rates.

The garden games, adventure play area, wildlife walks and complimentary baby equipment are just one half of the deal at Crylla Valley Cottages. Stay here and you also get free membership of a local country club, with its indoor pool, children's fun zone and sauna.

Fox Valley Cottages
Lanlawren Farm, Trenewan, PL13 2PZ, T01726-870115, foxvalleycottages.co.uk. £315-1165/wk.
Sitting pretty in seven acres of unspoilt countryside, three miles west of Polperro and a mile from Lansallos beach, this group of 11 holiday cottages has the added bonus of an indoor swimming pool, spa and sauna.

Green Acres Cottages
Penpillick, Par, PL24 2RU, T01637-839544, greenacrescottages.co.uk. £550-1225/wk.
A luxurious development of 10 stone cottages with stunning countryside views, Green Acres has an indoor pool, sauna and small 'garden' farm.

Tredethick Farm Cottages
Tredethick, Lostwithiel, PL22 0LE, T01208-873618, tredethick.co.uk. Call for rates and availability.
The owners of these nine traditional cottages (mostly clustered around a courtyard) have stopped at nothing to make this a rural paradise for children. Feeding the animals is almost a daily routine – and it's followed by pony riding on Monday and Wednesday mornings. The play barn has practically its own beach with 10 tons of sand: enough to satisfy the most stringent of sandcastle connoisseurs. There's also a wendy house, slide, giant trampoline, ride-on tractors and a football pitch. The farm trail, meanwhile, is your ticket to exploring fields and woods, or joining a footpath leading to the riverside hamlet of St Winnow. Then there's the farm shop with local treats like organic ice cream, Cornish fudge, elderflower pressé and – music to most parents' ears – ready-made meals. You see, it's not just kids that are made a fuss of at Tredethick Farm. Grown-

ups also get their fair share of goodies – from the well-equipped cottages to the comfy sofas, fresh-ground coffee and magazines in the soft play area.

Fowey.

Best of the rest

Adventure Cornwall
Lombard Farm, nr Fowey, PL23 1NA, T01726-870844, adventurecornwall. co.uk. Houses Feb-Oct, £580-1680/wk; yurt Mar-Oct, £460-960/wk; tipi Jun-Sep, £530-960.
Proof that the action isn't always confined to Cornwall's north coast, Adventure Cornwall runs canoeing trips on the River Fowey and rock climbing on Bodmin Moor from its base at Lombard Farm. As well as two contemporary cottages (both sleeping six), there's a five-berth yurt with wood burner and hot tub, plus a large tipi for overnight camps. Fowey is within easy walking distance, while a more adventurous 50-minute hike will take you to rarely crowded Lantic Bay.

Deer Park
Forest Holidays, see page 16.

Cottage agents
See also page 186.

Fowey Harbour Cottages
T01726-832211,
foweyharbourcottages.co.uk.

Looe & Polperro Holidays
T01503-265330,
looeandpolperroholidays.co.uk.

Also recommended
Honicombe Manor Resort
St Ann's Chapel, PL17 8JW, T01822-832583, honicombemanor.co.uk.

Mount Brioni
Looe Hill, PL11 3JN, T01503-250251, cornwall-self-catering-holidays.com.

Notter Mill
Notter Bridge, Saltash, PL12 4RW, T01752-843694, nottermill.co.uk.

Valleybrook
Lansallos, PL13 2QE, T01503-220493, valleybrookholidays.com.

Splashing out

Fowey Hall Hotel
Fowey, PL23 1ET, T01726-833866, foweyhallhotel.co.uk. Call for rates.
Going posh with kids only works when you find a luxurious hotel devoid of pretentiousness, where staff are able to engage with life forms lower than navel height and where the term 'child friendly' doesn't in fact mean 'child friendly but we'd really rather not, thank you.' Does such a place exist? Yes. In fact, there's a whole chain of them called Luxury Family Hotels and one of them sits proud above Fowey Estuary with views to Polruan and the open sea. A 19th-century mansion that was thought to be the inspiration for Toad Hall in *The Wind in the Willows*, Fowey Hall is set in five acres of gardens and is just a short stroll from Readymoney Cove and the town of Fowey. Facilities include an OFSTED-registered den for children under eight, a playroom for older kids and an indoor pool. Rooms are large and indulgent (although you'll need a suite if you have two children) with everything on hand – from DVDs to baby equipment – to make your stay hassle-free. Fine food and an Aquae Sulis Retreat add the finishing touches.

Eating Southeast Cornwall

Local goodies

Cornish Orchards Farm Shop

Westnorth Manor Farm, Duloe,
PL14 4PW, T01503-269007,
cornishorchards.co.uk. Easter-Nov.
Mon-Fri 1000-1700, Sat 0930-1230.
Cider, apple juice, elderflower
pressé, honey and preserves.

Lobbs Farm Shop

Heligan, St Ewe, PL26 6EN, T01726-
844411, lobbsfarmshop.com. Year-
round Mon-Fri 0930-1730 (1700 in
winter), Sat-Sun 1030-1630.
This fabulous farm shop at
Heligan Gardens (see page 174)
has meat and cheese counters,

Lobbs Farm Shop.

Market days

Callington Farmers' Market
Town Hall, Friday 0900-1300.

Grampound Produce Market
Village Hall, Saturday 0930-1230.

Liskeard Farmers' Market
Moorswater Industrial Estate,
every other Friday 1000-1200.

Lostwithiel Farmers' Market
Community Ctr, Friday 1000-1400.

Mevagissey Farmers' Market
West Wharf, Sunday 0900-1300.

Truro Farmers' Market
Lemon Quay, Saturday 0900-1600.

fruit, vegetables, dairy products,
bread, jams, chutneys, biscuits,
ice cream, smoked fish and
other local produce – much of it
sourced from the owner's Kestle
Farm (30-minute tours available
during spring and summer). The
farmhouse kitchen produces
freshly cooked quiches, pork
pies and seasonal salads, while
the adjacent Countryside Barn
has displays on farming.

Purely Cornish Farm Shop

St Martins, nr Looe, PL13 1NX,
T01503-262680, purelycornish.co.uk.
Stock up on cheese, clotted
cream, pasties and other local
produce and enjoy a light meal,
organic coffee or smoothie
at the Chillout Bar. The Purely
Cornish Deli in East Looe,
meanwhile, is the place to go
for pick-and-mix hampers.

Taste of the Westcountry

Fore St, St Cleer, Liskeard,
PL14 5DA, T01579-345985,
tasteofthewestcountry.co.uk.
Year round, daily 0900-1800.
Local seasonal fruit and
vegetables, sausages and
burgers for the barbecue,
pasties, bread, cakes, cheeses,
ice cream, jams and chutneys.

Fish & chips

A quality chippie, **The Other
Place** (Fore St, Fowey) is hard to
beat. **Trebonney** (Fore St, Roche,
St Austell) also has an excellent
reputation. In Mevagissey, try the
The Big 'Un (Olivers Quay).

Quick & simple

Crooked Inn

Saltash, PL12 4RZ, T01752-848177,
crooked-inn.co.uk.
Traditional pub with family
dining room, children's play area
and farmyard pets.

House on the Props

Polperro, PL13 2RE, T01503-272310,
houseontheprops.co.uk.
Propped up on timbers from
the *Maverine*, wrecked nearby
around 1700, this teetering tea
room serves breakfasts, lunches
and afternoon teas. Try the
scrummy home-baked cakes.

Lerryn River Stores

Lerryn, T01208-872375.
Cream teas, sandwiches, ice
cream and anything else you
might need for a picnic on the
green overlooking the creek.

Louis' Tea Rooms

Kit Hill Country Park, Callington,
PL17 8AX, T01579-389223.
Treat yourself to a Cornish cream
tea after hiking up Kit Hill (see
page 167).

Pinky Murphy's Café

North St, Fowey, PL23 1DB, T01726-
832512, pinkymurphys.com. Mon-
Sat 0900-1700, Sun 0930-1600.
Colourful, cool and quirky, Pinky
Murphy's serves the legendary
FatBoy hot chocolate (£2.95), as
well as some great soups, meat
and veggie platters, ciabattas,
paninis and baguettes.

Polkadot Café

Polkerris, PL24 2TL, T01726-813306, polkerrisbeach.com.
Part of the sporty Polkerris Beach Company (see page 171), the Polkadot Café serves Treleavens ice cream, pasties, home-made cakes and other local snacks.

Rashleigh Inn

Polkerris, PL24 2TL, T01726-813991, therashleighinnpolkerris.co.uk. Daily, meals served 1200-1500, 1800-2100.
Eat inside or out at this 300-year-old boathouse right on the beach. Fresh seafood a speciality.

Sams

Fore St, Fowey, PL23 1AQ, T01726-832273, samsfowey.co.uk.
The kids' menu at this lively, fun eatery really hits the spot, with home-made burgers, lasagne, calamari, fish, mussels, shell-on prawns, chicken and a wicked pudding just £6.95 for two courses. Sams also has a beach café (T01726-812255) in the old lifeboat station at Polkerris, serving fresh pizzas and seafood.

Talland Bay Beach Café

Talland Bay, PL13 2JA, T01503-272088, tallandbaybeachcafe.co.uk. Easter-Oct daily.
This chirpy little café sits right above the beach at Talland Bay – a perfect spot for a cream tea, pasty, fresh crab sandwich or home-made cake.

The Wheel House

West Quay, Mevagissey PL26 6UJ, T01726-843404, wheelhouse.me.uk. Daily from 0900.
Formerly a net loft, this harbourside restaurant has a well-deserved reputation for sublime seafood. The all-day menu features tasty starters like hot crab pot with avocado and parmesan (£8), while mains (around £8-13) include old favourites like Cornish fishcakes, cod and chips and Fowey River mussels. Starters on the evening à la carte menu range from panfried calamari (£6.50) to seared St Austell Bay scallops (£8.50). Main courses start at around £12.

Also recommended
Wreckers

Charlestown Harbour, PL25 3NJ, T01726-879053, wreckers.me.uk. Daily from 1000.
More of the same from the owners of the Wheel House (see above), Wreckers serves breakfasts, cream teas, lunch snacks and an excellent range of dinner dishes.

Q @ The Old Quay House

Fore St, Fowey, PL23 1AQ, T01726-833302, theoldquayhouse.com. Lunch daily May-Sep and weekends Oct-Apr; dinner daily.
Relaxed yet stylish, Q spills out onto a terrace overlooking the Fowey Estuary. Local ingredients from land and sea are given a Mediterranean zing. The dinner menu is £30 for two courses or £37.50 for three courses.

Trawlers

The Quay, East Looe, PL13 1AH, T01503-263593, trawlersrestaurant.co.uk. Tue-Sat from 1830.
Fine dining with a view of the harbour, Trawlers is predominantly a fish restaurant and has a daily changing menu. Expect to pay around £25 for a two-course meal, which might well include culinary delights like roasted monkfish wrapped in pancetta with caramelized butternut squash and creamed leeks or crispy-skin sea bass with a lobster thermidor sauce.

Also recommended
Austell's

Beach Road, Carlyon Bay, PL25 3PH, T01726-813888, austells.co.uk.
Fresh, locally-sourced food served in a contemporary setting.

Cornish cream teas were traditionally served with a sweet white bread roll, rather than a scone. Nowadays, there are all kinds of variations, including 'Thunder and Lightning' where a scone is topped with clotted cream and honey or golden syrup.

The Roseland

Where exactly this Area of Outstanding Natural Beauty begins and ends is a little hazy but, for the purposes of this book, it's the stretch of coast between Dodman Point and St Mawes. You'll know you've reached the Roseland Peninsula when hedgerows start to press in on either side, grass sprouts along the middle of the road like a green mohican and the lane fizzles out in a sleepy fishing village or deserted cove.

Get your bearings

Dangling like a loose thread from the A390 between Truro and St Austell, the A3078 is the only main road into the Roseland. It's just one of the ways, however, of reaching St Mawes, the peninsula's harbour town on the estuary opposite Falmouth. Joining two ends of the B3289, the car- and passenger-carrying **King Harry Ferry** (T01872-862312, falriver.co.uk) takes 10 minutes to rattle across a narrow neck of the Fal – and in doing so saves you a 27-mile loop via the A390

Walk this way

If you or your children get a sense of déjà vu at St Anthony, it's probably because the lighthouse here featured in the animated television series *Fraggle Rock*. Guiding ships into Falmouth Harbour (and away from the Manacles reef), the lighthouse is not open to the public, but there are still some fascinating walks at this westernmost tip of the Roseland Peninsula. Just beyond the car park and holiday cottages are the remains of fortifications where big guns once swept the approach to the Carrick Roads. During the Second World War, a Battery Observation Point was built to monitor the position of enemy ships. You can find it by following the rock-cut ditch path where gun-control officers and signallers once scurried to their posts. Duck inside the concrete bunker and peep through the narrow slit. The views are amazing, stretching from St Mawes Castle across the estuary to Pendennis Castle and beyond to Gyllyngvase beach, Maenporth beach and the Helford rivermouth. Look carefully and you should just make out the Goonhilly satellite dishes pimpling the Lizard. Of course, most children will be more interested in sighting a Nazi U-boat sneaking into the harbour or a full-blown Spanish Armada. In reality, you're more likely to see container ships, oil tankers, yachts, fishing boats and perhaps a Royal Navy Fleet Auxillary ship or destroyer. A short stroll beyond the Observation Point is a bird hide overlooking cliffs above an inaccessible shingle beach. By now your spying skills should be so well-honed that fulmars and even peregrine falcons may fall within your sights.

St Anthony Head
T01872-862945, nationaltrust.org.uk. Year round daily. Free admission.

and A3078. If travelling by foot, the **St Mawes Ferry** (T01326-741194) plies the Carrick Roads, linking Falmouth and St Mawes in just 20 minutes. Once in St Mawes, head to the **Roseland Visitor Centre** (The Square, TR2 5AG, T01326-270440, stmawesandtheroseland.co.uk) for ferry times, walk leaflets and other information.

Dawdling along the waterfront at St Mawes is pleasant enough – the quayside bakery serves proper pasties or children can fritter some pocket money on the stoneware sculptures of seals and puffins in the Waterside Gallery. The main attraction here, though, is **St Mawes Castle** (see page 188) – a short walk along the seafront. Don't forget shrimping nets as there are some good rock pools along this stretch of coast at low tide. You could also try crabbing off the harbour wall (crab lines are for sale in the post office stores).

You'll know you've reached the Roseland Peninsula when hedgerows start to press in on either side, grass sprouts along the middle of the road like a green mohican and the lane fizzles out in a sleepy fishing village or deserted cove.

When the tide turns, Towan Beach is ripe for rock-pooling.

Let's go to... The Roseland

Castles & kayaks

Sharing guard duties with Pendennis Castle (see page 192) across the estuary, **St Mawes Castle** (T01326-270526, english-heritage.org. uk, Apr-Nov Sun-Fri from 1000, Nov-Mar Fri-Mon from 1000, £4.50 adult, £2.70 child) is one of the best preserved and most elaborately decorated of Henry VIII's coastal fortresses. A quiz sheet is available to help children appreciate the castle's strategic role in defending the crucial anchorage of the Carrick Roads from French and Spanish fleets. Rather embarrassingly, the castle – though virtually impregnable from the sea – was hopelessly prepared for a land attack during the Civil War. The castle's Royalist commander took one look at the advancing Parliamentarians, ducked briefly as a warning cannon ball whistled overhead, then promptly surrendered.

One of the best ways to admire St Mawes Castle is from the sea and, although the Falmouth ferry passes beneath its ramparts, you can take a more leisurely look by hiring a sea kayak. **St Mawes Sit-on Kayaks** (The Quay, St Mawes, TR2 5DG, T07971-846786, stmaweskayaks.co.uk, Easter-Sep daily 0900-1700) has easy-to-paddle double kayaks (children under 16 must be accompanied by an adult) for £20 for up to two hours, £30 for a four-hour session or £40 for a whole day. Try to hire one of the Peekaboo kayaks (same rates), which have a clear panel built into the hull, allowing you to gaze at the fishes as you paddle. Although sit-on kayaks are extremely stable, you should only venture around St Anthony Head in calm sea conditions. Otherwise, stick to the sheltered Percuil River (separating St Anthony Head from St Mawes) or head up the Carrick Roads to St Just in Roseland, stopping at beaches as you go.

Hit the beach

The nearest good beach to St Mawes is **Towan** – an easily overlooked cove reached by a short walk across fields from the National Trust car park at Porth Farm (on the road between St Anthony and Portscatho). A mixture of coarse sand and pebbles, it is fringed by the sheltered, turquoise-waters of Gerrans Bay and has rock pools at low tide.

Further west, **Pendower** (or Carne) is a mile-long sandy beach overlooked by the exquisite **Nare Hotel** (T01872-501111, narehotel.co.uk), where you might prefer to pop in for a seafood lunch or afternoon tea at the Quarterdeck Restaurant rather than splash the kids' inheritance on an overnight stay (doubles cost from £270 per night, suites from around £480).

A stunning two-mile cliff walk around Nare Head leads to the tiny fishing hamlet of **Portloe** (also reached by narrow lanes). There's a small shingle cove here at low tide.

Next along the coast are the hidden twin-beauties of **East** and **West Portholland**. You can park at either, but East Portholland has the bigger sandy beach (only exposed as the tide ebbs) and the delightful Journey's End Café, which serves snacks and drinks from the back door of a cottage on the seafront.

Nearby, **Caerhays** (Porthluney Cove) has a beach shop and café, plenty of sand at low tide and a grassy area for retreating to at high tide. Tucked away behind the bay, the castellated mansion of **Caerhays Castle** (T01872-501310, caerhays.co.uk) has lovely gardens to explore.

From Caerhays, it's a squeeze to get down the lanes leading to **Hemmick Beach** – you're better off parking at Penare and walking to this idyllic sandy cove nestled in the lee of Dodman Point.

Canvas & cottages

A short walk from sandy coves, **Trewince Farm** (Portscatho, TR2 5ET, T01872-580430, trewincefarm.co.uk, May-Sep, £12-19) has just 25 pitches – most with sea views. For an equally splendid location, but with holiday park facilities, try **Seaview International** (Boswinger, PL26 6LL, T01726-843425, seaviewinternational.com, Apr-Oct, camping pitches £10-42, static caravans £245-1150/wk).

A haven for wildlife and a paradise for children, **Pollaughan Cottages** (Portscatho, TR2 5EH, T01872-580150, pollaughan.co.uk, year round, £390-1950/wk) sit pretty on a 22-acre farm. Dragonflies and moorhens make a beeline for the wildlife pond, while kids make a fuss of the two donkeys, four pygmy goats and assorted chickens, ducks and sheep. There's also a soppy black labrador called Bryher, a trampoline, tennis court, safely fenced nature pond and a pick-your-own veggie patch. Porthcurnick Beach, meanwhile, is just a 20-minute stroll away. Choose one of three well-equipped, open plan cottages (sleeping up to six) or opt for the three-bedroom wing of the Victorian farmhouse.

For other self-catering cottages on the Roseland, try **Roseland Holiday Cottages** (T01872-580480, roselandholidaycottages.co.uk).

Splashing out

Designed with families in mind, the **Rosevine** (Portscatho, TR2 5EW, T01872-580206, rosevine. co.uk, £1000-2550/wk) is a classy coastal retreat consisting of a Georgian house divided into 12 family apartments and suites (with one or two bedrooms, a sitting and dining area and kitchen), as well as a couple of smart self-catering cottages, sleeping up to eight and with their own private gardens. The Rosevine's restaurant is superb, while a deli service provides breakfast boxes, packed lunches and freshly prepared supper dishes that you can heat up for a quiet meal in. Rosevine also hits the spot with its excellent facilities: a children's den, indoor pool and wooden play area to name a few. The hotel overlooks Gerrans Bay and has a sandy beach just 140 m from its garden gate.

Grab a bite

Hidden away in the old pilchard fishing village of Portscatho, **Ralph's** (T01872-580702, daily 0700-1900) does a roaring trade in pasties and also stocks a good range of locally caught seafood and other Cornish produce. The working water mill at

From top: St Mawes Ferry; fishing nets and flip-flops; pygmy goat at Pollaughan Farm; digging at Towan; view across Hemmick beach.

Melinsey (nr Veryan, T01872-501049, melinseymill. co.uk) is a peaceful spot for a light lunch or cream tea. There are willow scultpures on display and a lovely walk alongside the mill pond. In St Mawes, stock up on picnic supplies or indulge in a lunch platter or cream tea at **Café Chandlers** (The Quay, T01326-270998, cafechandlers.co.uk). For traditional pub fare, try the **Victory Inn** (T01326-270324, victory-inn.co.uk).

Falmouth

A shipshape mix of historic port, working harbour and Victorian seaside resort, Falmouth makes a great day out – no matter what the shipping forecast. Rainy days might send you scuttling for the brilliant National Maritime Museum, while fair weather raises all kinds of possibilities, from ferry trips along the Fal Estuary to landlubbing on Falmouth's string of sandy town beaches. In fact, once you begin uncovering the wealth of attractions in and around this mighty deepwater refuge (Cornwall's very own Sydney Harbour), you might well be tempted to drop anchor and base yourself here for extended shore leave.

Get your bearings

Ditch the car. It's more fun (and kinder on Falmouth's congested roads) to arrive by ferry. Flying the flag for car-free travel throughout the Fal Estuary, **Fal River Links** (falriver.co.uk, see also pages 192 and 194) represents several ferry operators shuttling back and forth between Falmouth and St Mawes, Flushing, Mylor Yacht Harbour, Trelissick Garden and Truro. One of the most innovative services is the **Falmouth Park & Float** (May-Sep Mon-Fri, first boat 1000, last boat 1740). Leave your car at Ponsharden (just off the A39 as you approach Falmouth), then hop on a ferry that will whisk you straight to **Custom House Quay**, a short swagger from the National Maritime Museum. All-day Float Passes cost £16 for one car and up to seven passengers. Falmouth's other main ferry dock is the nearby **Prince of Wales Pier** where the **visitor information centre** (T01326-741194, falmouth.co.uk) can be found.

Wise up to the sea

National Maritime Museum
Discovery Quay, Falmouth, TR11 3QY,
T01326-313388, nmmc.co.uk. Daily 1000-1700.
£11 adult, £7.60 child (6-15), £31 family.

The next best thing to messing about in boats on the sea, this outstanding museum is awash with nautical nuggets. Start your voyage of discovery in the **Main Hall** where an airborne flotilla (suspended on wires from the ceiling) includes three Olympic-gold-winning yachts. The 1866 steam launch *Waterlily* sits sedately beneath them, while the **Survival Zone** stirs things up with epic tales of endurance at sea – don't miss the *Edna Mair*, a tiny dinghy in which the Robertson family survived for 38 days in the Pacific after their yacht sank. The **Nav Station** gallery has plenty of interactive gizmos for mini-skippers (steer a boat against the tide and make for the safe harbour); the **Quarterdeck** explores how the design of boats has been adapted for hunting, fishing or sport; the **Cornwall Galleries** are full of yarns about smugglers, shipwrecks and pilchard fishing, while **The Hold** has a different exhibition most years (the theme 'Search and Rescue' will run until 2015). Don't forget to climb to the **Look Out** with its panoramic views over Falmouth Harbour, or to immerse yourself in the **Tidal Zone**, which provides a mesmerizing window on the harbour's marine life, from mullet to barnacles (stand there long enough and you'll see the tide rise and fall). To prevent certain mutiny be sure to take plenty of 50p coins – you'll need them at the **Waterfront**, where radio-controlled yachts can be steered across an indoor pool that's ingeniously strafed by an artificial breeze. For a breath of real sea air, step outside onto the **Museum Pontoon** to see which historic boats have called into port. The museum also has a waterside café and a gift shop overflowing with books, model boats and other maritime nicknacks.

Witchcraft – model boats 'fly' through the National Maritime Museum as if by magic. Right: the museum's Tidal Zone.

Let's go to... Falmouth

Fine art & fortresses

Largest and most intact of Cornwall's castles, **Pendennis Castle** (Castle Dr, TR11 4LP, T01326-316594, english-heritage.org.uk, year round daily from 1000, £6.70 adult, £4 child (5-15), £17.40 family) squats on a headland just to the east of Falmouth Docks and offers superb views across the estuary to its partner castle at St Mawes (see page 188). Originally built by Henry VIII to guard the harbour against the threat of French and Spanish warships, the fort is now a military time capsule with Tudor guns, First World War guard house and Second World War tunnels. It's an exciting place to explore, with activity sheets, workshops and events for children during the summer holidays.

Equally family-friendly, the **Falmouth Art Gallery** (The Moor, TR11 2RT, T01326-313863, falmouthartgallery.com, year round Mon-Sat 1000-1700, free admission) has been a recipient of the *Guardian* newspaper's Kids in Museums award. There's nothing hushed or stuffy about this place. Noise is positively welcomed and there are activities for children of all ages, including babies.

Gyllyngvase Beach.

Hit the beach

Closest to the town centre, **Castle Beach** is overlooked by Pendennis Castle and is a good spot for rock pools and a picnic. Next door is **Gyllyngvase**, Falmouth's most popular beach with a Blue Flag Award, safe swimming and lots of facilities, including toilets, lifeguard, deckchair hire, lost child centre and the Gylly Beach Café (see opposite). The sand here is just the right consistency for satisfying sandcastles. Follow the coast path west over the headland and you will find **Swanpool Beach**, a sheltered sand and pebble cove with crazy golf and a café. Just

Pendennis Castle.

inland is Swanpool Nature Reserve where you can see ducks, swans and the occasional kingfisher on a brackish lagoon. A mile south of Falmouth, **Maenporth** is a sandy beach sheltered from the wind by low cliffs and offering watersports such as sea kayaking and windsurfing.

Take to the water

Orca Sea Safaris (Discovery Quay, TR11 3QY, T01326-214928, orcaseasafaris.co.uk, daily, minimum age 6) runs wildlife cruises from Falmouth in its fast, 12-seat RIB. The one-hour Bay Discovery (£24 adult, £16 child, £75 family) zips across Falmouth Bay in search of seals and seabirds. The two-hour Coastal Explorer (£39.50 adult, £28 child, £125 family) ventures further afield, giving you a better chance of dolphin and basking shark sightings.

Offering summer boat trips on the luxurious *Moyana* from either Falmouth or St Mawes, **Helford River Cruises** (falriver.co.uk) passes Pendennis Castle, Trebah Gardens and Port Navas on its route to Frenchman's Creek. See page 190 and 194 for other Fal River Link services.

To take control of the helm yourself, make your way to Mylor Yacht Harbour where **Mylor Boat Hire** (Mylor, TR11 5UF, T01326-377745, mylorboathire.co.uk) has a veritable armada for hire, from family motorboats and traditional sailing yawls to zippy RIBs. Expect to pay around £30 per hour or £100 per day for a six-person motor boat.

Further up the estuary, **Loe Beach Boat Hire** (Feock, TR3 6SH, T01872-864295, loebeach.co.uk) can kit you out with various sail-, paddle- and

Falmouth Harbour

motor-powered craft, and also has an RYA Watersports Centre.

Cornish Diving School (Bar Rd, Falmouth, TR11 4BN, T07885-771282, cornishdivingschool. co.uk) offers pool-based Bubblemaker courses for small fry as young as eight, while the **Falmouth Surf School** (Woodlane Close, Falmouth, TR11 4QU, T01326-212144, falmouthsurfschool.co.uk) takes board riders in search of Cornwall's best waves (day-long safaris cost £30). A half-day session (£25) will get you up and standing, while full-day tuition (£40) will perfect your jump-up. There are also 'family taster' sessions lasting one and a half hours (£80 for a minimum of four people). At just £15, the school holiday Grommet Course for nine- to 13-year-olds is excellent value.

If your grommets are also into raft building, coasteering, kayaking, sailing and windsurfing, sign them up for the Kids' Club at **Elemental UK** (Swanpool Beach, T01326-318771 or 07795 480474, elementaluk.com, weekends and school holidays, £18/half day, £30/full day).

Check in

Falmouth Beach Resort Hotel (Gyllyngvase Beach, T01326-310500, thefalmouthbeach.co.uk, call for rates) offers versatile accommodation, including family suites, two self-catering apartments and a three-bed cottage. Facilities include babysitting, early mealtimes for children and a swimming pool.

For holiday cottages in and around Falmouth, check out **Falmouth Holiday Rentals** (T01872-264441, falmouthholidayrentals.co.uk).

Grab a bite

A crisp, battered crust above the rest, **Harbour**

Lights Fish & Chips (Arwenack St, T01326-316934, harbourlights.co.uk) has a takeaway and sit-down restaurant with great views of the harbour. Also enjoying a prime waterfront location, **Pizza Express** (Maritime House, T01326-318841, pizzaexpress.com) overlooks Discovery Quay near the National Maritime Museum.

For Falmouth's ultimate seaview meal, however, the **Gylly Beach Café** (Cliff Rd, T01326-312884, gyllybeach.com) is right on Gyllyngvase Beach. The Gylly's clean, minimalist style makes it feel like there's nothing between you, the beach and the ocean. Watch the waves, the ships moored offshore and the distant lighthouse on St Anthony's Head, while you tuck into a varied menu that includes Full Cornish breakfasts, lunch snacks (fish cakes, burgers, mussels, home-made sandwiches etc) and dinner mains (from around £13) such as Cornish rib-eye steak. For more upmarket dining, try **Hooked on the Rocks** (T01326-311886, hookedcornwall.com) at Swanpool Beach.

Falmouth Beach Resort Hotel.

Let's go to...

Truro

Let's face it. The vast majority of families on holiday in Cornwall are unlikely to put Truro on their 'must do' list. The capital of the Duchy of Cornwall just seems to get in the way, particularly if you're trying to drive to Falmouth or the Lizard on the A39 and get snarled up in traffic on its outskirts. Don't be too hasty, however, in wanting to bypass Cornwall's only city. Not only does Truro have a magnificent cathedral and the county's best museum, but it can also be the staging post for adventures downriver.

Get your bearings

It can be a nightmare trying to park in Truro, so leave your car at the park-and-ride (Langarth Park on the A390 at Threemilestone). Buses stop at the Royal Cornwall Museum and Victoria Square, from where it's a short walk along St Nicholas Street and Boscawen Street to reach the **tourist information centre** (T01872-274555, tourism.truro.gov.uk). Cut through Cathedral Lane to reach Truro's fine Gothic pile, or head down Lemon Street to the local produce and Fairtrade market or **Plaza Cinema** (T01871-200 3304). Leading from Lemon Street, Back Quay provides access to the theatre, **Hall for Cornwall** (T01872-262466, hallforcornwall.co.uk).

City highlights

Free to enter, the **Royal Cornwall Museum** (River St, TR1 2SJ, T01872-272205, royalcornwallmuseum. org.uk, Mon-Sat 1000-1645) has a busy schedule of family events, including treasure trails, craft activities and storytelling. You can also pick up Explorer Backpacks (£1) to help kids interpret the exhibits in the main gallery where 5000 years of Cornish history are revealed. The Bonython Gallery has displays on Cornish habitats and wildlife with a special discovery area for families, while the Rashleigh Gallery is all-a-glitter with minerals and gems. Upstairs, there's a small gallery with a quirky collection of Egyptian artefacts, including the 2500-year-old mummy of Ast Tayef Nakht. The River Street Café in the museum's lobby has a good selection of sandwiches and paninis, as well as soup, home-made cakes, fresh fruit juices, smoothies and Roskilly's ice cream.

You can't miss **Truro Cathedral** (St Mary's St, T01872-276782, trurocathedral.org.uk, Mon-Sat from 0730, Sun from 0900, free admission). The Neo-Gothic landmark (built from Cornish granite between 1880 and 1910) has a spire rising 76 m above the street. Inside, there are spectacular vaulted arches and stained glass windows.

City escapes

Departing from Truro's Town Quay, **Enterprise Boats** (T01326-374241, falriver.co.uk, call for family rates) provides a seasonal ferry link between the city and Falmouth (or St Mawes), stopping en route at **Trelissick Gardens** (Feock, TR3 6QL, T01872-862090, nationaltrust.org.uk, year round daily from 1030, £7.20 adult, £3.60 child, £18 family). With woodland spilling down to the estuary shore, this tranquil garden has two circular walks. Neither takes more than about 45 minutes, so you've got plenty of time for a stroll before hopping on the next Falmouth-bound ferry.

Above: Barbed message – the Royal Cornwall Museum bristles with intriguing exhibits, including this Stone Age arrowhead.

Neo-Gothic marvel –
Truro Cathedral.

Grown-ups' stuff Cornwall

Inroads

Getting there
By car Reach the end of the M5 near Exeter, then it's decision time – either take the **A30**, looping north of Dartmoor, and enter Cornwall just before Launceston (your best option if you're heading for the north coast or far west), or take the **A38**, dipping below Dartmoor and crossing the Tamar Bridge (£1 toll eastbound only) into South Cornwall. If you fancy a detour through North Devon, you could also reach Cornwall by taking either the A361 or A377 to Barnstaple before picking up the **A39** Atlantic Highway (breezing into Cornwall just north of Bude). You can also join the A39 at junction 27 of the M5.

The A30 shoulders the heaviest load of traffic, but it is dual carriageway most of the way to Penzance, with single-carriageway sections at Temple, near Bodmin, and also between Carland Cross (where the A39 goes south to Truro) and the Three Burrows roundabout (where you can head south on the A390 to Truro or north on the A3075 to Newquay). Peak-time delays are likely at these locations – try to avoid travelling on Fridays (1500-1800) or Saturdays (1000-1700).

By coach Falmouth, Newquay, Penzance, St Austell, St Ives, Truro and most other main centres in Cornwall are served by **National Express** (T08717-818178, nationalexpress.com), with connecting services from Bristol, Birmingham and London.

By ferry Chain ferries shuttle back and forth across the Tamar between Devonport and Torpoint every 10 minutes at peak times. The fare – only payable eastbound – is the same as using the toll bridge (see left). Contact **Tamar Crossings** (tamarcrossings.org.uk) for more details.

By plane Several airlines serve **Newquay Cornwall Airport** (newquaycornwallairport.com), including **easyJet** (easyjet.com) from Liverpool and London Southend; **Flybe** (flybe.com) from Belfast, Edinburgh, Inverness, Isle of Man, Liverpool, London Gatwick, Manchester, Newcastle and Norwich and **Skybus** (islesofscilly-travel.co.uk) from the Isles of Scilly.

By train Operated by **First Great Western** (T08457-000 125, firstgreatwestern.co.uk), the direct London Paddington to Penzance service takes between five and six hours, calling at Liskeard, Bodmin, Par, St Austell, Truro, Redruth, Camborne, Hayle and St Erth (see page 198 for branchline connections). Expect to pay around £90 for an adult return fare, £50 for a child (5-15), but check online for special offers.

Getting around
Public transport timetables can be downloaded from cornwallpublictransport.info.

By bicycle Cornwall has several excellent cycling trails, including the **Camel Trail** (see page 46), the **Coast to Coast Trail** (page 80) and the **Mineral Tramways Mining Trails** (page 80) centred around Camborne and Redruth.

Click ahead
Useful travel planning websites include: theaa.com, nationalrail.co.uk, rac.co.uk, seat61.com and traveline.info.

A30 pit stops

A386 junction Fuel (north- and southbound).
B3257 junction Fuel and Subway (southbound only).
B3274 junction Fuel (north- and southbound).
B3275 junction Fuel, Premier Inn and McDonalds (northbound only).
A39 junction Fuel (accessible north- and southbound).
A390/3075 junction Fuel and Starbucks (north- and southbound).
A3074/3301 junction Fuel, Travelodge, McDonalds, Boots Midnight Pharmacy, M&S, Next, Costa Coffee (north- and southbound).
Penzance outskirts Morrisons, McDonalds, 24-hour Tesco (including fuel).

Isle be bound (getting to the Scillies)

Isles of Scilly Travel (T0845-710 5555, ios-travel.co.uk) operates Skybus services to the islands, Monday-Saturday, from Exeter, Land's End and Newquay, using Twin Otter and Islander aircraft carrying up to 19 people. Expect to pay around £70 one-way for an adult, £55 for a child (2-15) and £19 for an infant (under 2) departing from Land's End Airport, or £100/83/30 for day returns. The *Scillonian III* (book through Isles of Scilly Travel) sails throughout the summer (Mon-Sat, plus occasional Sun departures) leaving Penzance at 0915 and arriving at St Mary's around 1200. Expect to pay around £42 one-way for an adult, £21 for a child (2-15) and £11 for an infant (under 2), or £35/18/9 for day returns (a family day-trip ticket costs around £75). Air & Sea Day Trip tickets cost around £72 for an adult, £50 for a child (2-15) and £25 for an infant (under 2).

By bus All operators offer free travel for under-fives.
First Group (T0845-600 1420, firstgroup.com) has a FirstDay Cornwall ticket (£7.20 adult, £5.50 child, £12.40 family) allowing unlimited travel throughout Cornwall. For unlimited travel on **Western Greyhound** (T01637-871871, westerngreyhound.com) choose the Day Explorer (£8.50 adult, £5.50 child, £17 family)

Truro's park and ride (T01872-279270, parkfortruro.org. uk) operates from Langarth Park, Threemilestone (A390), Monday-Saturday 0700-1900.

The **Ride Cornwall** one-day travel pass is valid on all rail and most bus services within Cornwall and between Cornwall and Plymouth for £10 adult, £7.50 child, £20 family, Mon-Fri after 0900 and Sat-Sun anytime.

By car Car hire is available from **Avis** (Newquay Airport, T08445-544 9396; avis.co.uk), **Cornwall**

Car Hire (Newquay, T01637-850971, cornwallcarhire.co.uk), **Enterprise** (Penryn T01326-373355, enterprise.co.uk), **Europcar** (Newquay Airport, T01637-384 3415, europcar. co.uk), **Hertz** (Newquay Airport, T0843-309 3053, hertz.co.uk) and **St Ives Car Hire** (T0845-057 9373, stivescarhire.co.uk). For ultimate surf chic (or just a great family touring holiday), hire a VW campervan from **Cornwall Campers** (T01872-571988, cornwallcampers.co.uk). Weekly rates start at around £500.

By ferry There are 16 ferry services in Cornwall. A network of ferries, boats, buses and trains, **Fal River Links** (T01872-861915, falriver.co.uk, see also page 186) is a one-stop shop for car-free travel in the Falmouth area. Services include: **Enterprise Boats** (T01326-741194) linking Truro, Falmouth, St Mawes and Trelissick Gardens; **Falmouth Park & Float** (see page 190),

🚌 Scenic bus rides

First buses:
35 Falmouth–Mawnan Smith–Helford Passage–Glendurgan and Trebah–Constantine–Gweek–Flambards–RNAS Culdrose–Helston.

81B Plymouth–Torpoint Ferry–Sheviock–Crafthole–Seaton–Hessenford–East Looe–Polperro.

300 Penzance–Newlyn–Porthcurno–Land's End–Sennen Cove–St Just–Botallack–Geevor Tin Mine–Zennor–St Ives–Carbis Bay–Marazion–Penzance.

Western Greyhound buses:
524 Heligan Gardens–St Austell–Mevagissey–Fowey.

547 Newquay–Perranporth–Hayle–Gwithian–St Ives.

556 Newquay–Porth–Watergate Bay–Tregurrian–Newquay Airport–Mawgan Porth–Porthcothan–Constantine Bay–St Merryn–Harlyn Bay–Padstow.

584 Wadebridge–Rock–Polzeath–Port Isaac–Camelford

595 Wadebridge–Camelford–Tintagel–Boscastle–Bude.

The South West Coast Path is the only way to reach Nanjizal cove near Land's End.

King Harry Ferry (T01872-862312, see page 186) saving 27 miles on the road trip between St Mawes and Falmouth, and **St Mawes Ferry** (T01326-741194) crossing the Fal between St Mawes and Falmouth.

Other fun (and useful) ferry routes to try include Calstock–Cotehele Quay (page 173), Mevagissey–Fowey (page 170) and Padstow–Rock (page 56).

By foot You can plan short forays on the 630-mile **South West Coast Path** by logging onto the official website, southwestcoastpath.com.

By plane Scenic flights over the Penwith Peninsula and to the Isles of Scilly are available at **Land's End Airport** (T01736-788771, landsendairport.co.uk).

By train Scenic branch lines (greatscenicrailways.com) include **St Erth–St Ives**, following the shores of the Hayle Estuary and St Ives Bay with stops at Lelant and Carbis Bay; **Truro–Falmouth**, a half-hourly service linking Perranwell and Penryn; **Par–Newquay**, a route joining the north and south coasts, and **Liskeard–Looe**, an hourly service through the Looe Valley. Buses run to the Eden Project from St Austell station and Helston from Redruth station.

Family holiday operators
Footsteps of Discovery (T07899-928131, footstepsofdiscovery.co.uk) runs family survival weekends where you learn all the basics – from fire lighting to building a shelter.

Outdoor Adventure (T01288-362900, outdooradventure. co.uk) operates a residential outdoor centre overlooking Widemouth Bay, near Bude. Family holidays are available here during July and August and cost around £625 per week for adults and £500 per week for children (eight to14), including accommodation, meals, equipment, instruction, evening entertainment and local transport. You can choose from activities ranging from surfing and coasteering to archery, abseiling and orienteering.

➲ **Kids'** gear

Stock up on family travel essentials at lioninthesun.com, muddypuddles. com, nomadtravel.co.uk and sun-togs.co.uk.

Cottages agents

Cornwall wide – see individual chapters for local agents.

Blue Chip Holidays
bluechipholidays.co.uk

Child Friendly Cottages
childfriendlycottages.co.uk

Classic Cottages
classic.co.uk

Cornish Cottage Holidays
cornishcottageholidays.co.uk

Cornish Cottages
cornishcottagesonline.com

Cornish Gems
cornishgems.com

Cornish Traditional Cottages
corncott.com

Cornwalls Cottages
cornwallscottages.co.uk

Duchy Holidays
duchyholidays.co.uk

English Country Cottages
english-country-cottages.co.uk

Helpful Holidays
helpfulholidays.com

Hideaways
hideaways.co.uk

National Trust Holiday Cottages
nationaltrustcottages.co.uk

Powells Cottage Holidays
powells.co.uk

Premier Cottages
premiercottages.co.uk

Southwest Holiday Cottages
southwestholidaycottages.com

Toad Hall Cottages
toadhallcottages.co.uk

Welcome Cottages
welcomecottages.com

West Country Cottages
westcountrycottages.co.uk

Which map?

Ordnance Survey (ordnancesurvey. co.uk) produces a general touring map of Cornwall (Tour 1). For more detail, choose a Landranger map; for walking and other activites go for an Explorer map.
Landranger maps:
190 Bude & Clovelly
200 Newquay & Bodmin
201 Plymouth & Launceston
203 Land's End & Isles of Scilly
204 Truro & Falmouth

Explorer maps:
101 Isles of Scilly
102 Land's End
103 The Lizard
104 Redruth & St Agnes
105 Falmouth & Mevagissey
106 Newquay & Padstow
107 St Austell & Liskeard
108 Lower Tamar Valley & Plymouth
109 Bodmin Moor
111 Bude, Boscastle & Tintagel
112 Launceston & Holsworthy

Online resources

Further information
BBC Cornwall
bbc.co.uk/cornwall

Cornwall Tourist Attractions
cata.co.uk

Cornwall County Council
cornwall.gov.uk

Cornish Food & Drink
foodfromcornwall.co.uk

Cornish Mining World Heritage Site
cornish-mining.org.uk

English Heritage
english-heritage.org.uk

Forestry Commission
forestry.gov.uk

Gardens of Cornwall
gardensofcornwall.com

National Trust
nationaltrust.org.uk

Royal National Lifeboat Institution
rnli.org.uk

South West Coast Path
nationaltrail.co.uk

South West Lakes Trust
swlakestrust.org.uk

Surfing Great Britain
surfinggb.com

Sustrans
sustrans.org.uk

Surf forecast
magicseaweed.com

Tide tables
tidetimes.org.uk

Environmental groups
Blue Flag beaches
blueflag.org

Coast One Planet Tourism
coastproject.co.uk

Cornwall Wildlife Trust
cornwallwildlifetrust.org.uk

Duchy of Cornwall
duchyofcornwall.org

Environment Agency
environment-agency.gov.uk

Isles of Scilly Wildlife Trust
ios-wildlifetrust.org.uk

Marine Conservation Society
mcsuk.org

Natural England
naturalengland.org.uk

RSPB
rspb.org.uk

Surfers against Sewage
sas.org.uk

Grown-ups' stuff Cornwall

There's something for all ages in Cornwall, from nappy-bound beach blobs shovelling sand into their mouths, to strutting surf-dude teens trying to stay cool after being dumped by a wave.

Babies (0-18 months)
Renting a cottage or holiday caravan gives you the flexibility and independence to maintain those all-important baby-care routines. Look for properties that provide baby gear to save you having to pack cots, sterilisers etc. For a spot of adult relaxation, several family-friendly hotels offer crèches or baby-listening services. **Baby Friendly Boltholes** (babyfriendlyboltholes.co.uk) is a good place to start.

Child's play – Praa Sands.

Weever fish.

☷ This hurts
Cornwall is generally very safe. Most serious accidents happen when people ignore warnings from beach lifeguards (see page 5) or stray too near cliff edges. You should also be wary of weever fish, buried in sand at the low-water mark on North Cornwall beaches with just five poisonous spines protruding from their backs. The sting can be excruciating. Submersion in very hot water is the best treatment. Better still, wear wetsuit boots when in the sea at low tide.

Toddlers/pre-school (18 months-4 years)
Make sure your cottage or holiday park is as toddler-proof as possible with enclosed gardens, fenced-off pools, stair gates etc. Days on the beach demand vigilance with this age group, but they can also burn off energy in more carefree situations, such as one of Cornwall's farm parks – many of which have soft play areas.

Kids/school age (4-12 years)
These are probably the best years to take kids on a camping holiday – it's still an adventure for them and they can help out with basic chores, like fetching water. Cornwall has stunning campsites – some a barefoot stroll from the beach. King Arthur and his knights often storm onto junior school curriculums, so a visit to Tintagel is a must. You can also exercise young minds at historic properties owned by the National Trust and English Heritage, or at one of Cornwall's gardens, zoos or aquariums. A great way to enforce beach safety, surf lessons usually have a minimum age of eight.

Teenagers (13 years+)
Cornwall can be very cool. Teens will thrive at north coast surf resorts like Bude and Newquay with their non-stop beach sports, trendy beach cafés and designer shops, while quieter locations like Fowey will suit active types passionate about learning to sail. Some holiday parks and hotels have special clubs and activities for teenagers (far more preferable to Newquay's nightlife). Renting a large property which you can share with friends who also have teenagers is often a good way to keep teen strops at bay.

Single-parent families
Check with attractions to see if they offer single-parent family admission (cheaper than the normal family rate based on two adults and two children). With their organized activities and onsite entertainment, holiday parks are a good way to meet up with other families. **Single Parent Fun** (singleparentfun. com) has plenty of suggestions for days out and things to do, while **Cornwall Council** (cornwall. gov.uk) organizes Father and Son

◑ Shop ahead
Before you leave home, order fresh, local Cornish produce and other food essentials online at food4myholiday.com and it will be delivered direct to your holiday cottage (and even put in the fridge) ready for your arrival.

★ **Holiday** heaven

Offering the UK's widest choice of self-catering holidays, **Hoseasons** (hoseasons.co.uk) has around 50 lodge and park properties to choose from in Cornwall, from the lively Holywell Bay and stylish Mullion Cove Lodges to the laid-back Sea Acres. There's also a great range of holiday cottages.

Weekends at its four outdoor education centres (see below).

Special needs

Several holiday operators, such as Gwel an Mor near Portreath and Pollaughan Farm on the Roseland Peninsula have accommodation specially designed for wheelchair users. **Disability Cornwall** (disabilitycornwall.org.uk) is a good source of information, while **Walks with Wheelchairs** (walkswithwheelchairs.com) provides free information on routes that are suitable for those that use a wheelchair.

Dog owners

Visit Cornwall (see page 203) produces a leaflet detailing dog-friendly beaches and attractions. See also visitcornwall.com.

☺ **Active** tykes

In Cornwall there are outdoor education centres (cornwall.gov.uk) at Carnyorth (nr St Just, T01736-786344), Delaware (nr Gunnislake, T01822-833885), Porthpean (nr St Austell, T01726-72901) and St Just in Roseland (T01326-270885).

✚ **Beach** safety

Beach lifeguards patrol popular beaches during the main season. **Red and yellow flags** show lifeguarded areas – the safest place to swim, bodyboard and use inflatables. **Black and white chequered flags** show areas for surfboards and other non-powered craft – never swim or bodyboard here. **Orange windsocks** show offshore winds, so never use an inflatable when the sock is flying. **Red flags** mean danger! Never go in the water when the red flag is flying under any circumstances. See also page 5.

Grown-ups' stuff Cornwall

Essentials

Baby supplies
Truro Mothercare, Pydar St.

Camping supplies
Fraddon Nevisport, Kingsley Village.
Penzance Millets, Market Jew St.
St Agnes Aztec Leisure, Trevellas.

Doctors & medical centres
Bude The Stratton Medical Centre, Hospital Rd, Stratton, EX23 9BP, T01288-352133.
Falmouth Trescobeas Surgery, Trescobeas Rd, TR11 2UN, T01326-315615.
Helston Helston Medical Centre, Trelawney Rd, TR13 8AU, T01326-572637.
Mevagissey Mevagissey Surgery, River St, PL26 6UE, T01726-843701.
Newquay The Health Centre, St Thomas Rd, TR7 1RU, T01637-850002.
Penzance Bellair Clinic, Alverton Rd, TR18 4TA, T01736-575500.
Redruth Manor Surgery, Forth Noweth, TR15 1AU, T01209-313313.
St Austell The Park Medical Centre, Bridge Rd, PL25 5HE, T01726-73083.
St Ives The Old Stennack School, Stennack, T01736-793333.
St Just Cape Cornwall Surgery, Market St, TR19 7HX, T01736-788306.
Tintagel Tintagel Medical Centre, Bossiney Rd, PL34 0AE, T01840-770214.
Truro Tregony Surgery, Well St, Tregony, TR2 5RT, T01872-530483.

Hospitals
The following hospitals have A&E departments:
Bodmin Bodmin Hospital, Boundary Rd, PL31 2QT, T01208-251300.
Bude Stratton Hospital, Hospital Rd, Stratton, EX23 9BP, T01288-320100.
Falmouth Falmouth Hospital, Trescobeas Rd, TR11 2JA, T01326-434700.
Fowey Fowey Community Hospital, Green Lane, PL23 1DU, T01726-832241 (minor injuries).
Launceston Launceston General Hospital, Link Rd, PL15 9JD, T01566-765650 (minor injuries).
Newquay Newquay Hospital, St Thomas Rd, TR7 1RQ, T01637-893600 (minor injuries unit only).
Penzance West Cornwall Hospital, St Clare St, TR18 2PF, T01736-874000.
Redruth Cambourne Redruth Community Hospital, Longreach House, Barncoose Terrace, TR15 3ER, T01209-318000.
St Austell St Austell Community Hospital, Porthpean Rd, PL26 6AD, T01726-291100.
Truro Royal Cornwall Hospital Trust, Treliske, TR1 3LJ, T01872-250000.

Pharmacies
Bodmin Day Lewis, Dennison Rd.
Bude Boots, Belle Vue.
Camelford Boots, Market Place.
Falmouth Boots, Market St.
Fowey Boots, Fore St.
Hayle Boots, Penpol Terrace.
Helston Steven Hall, Trelawney Rd.

Launceston Day Lewis, Broad St.
Looe Looe Pharmacy, Fore St.
Mevagissey Boots, Fore St.
Newquay Boots, Bank St; Drury's, Chester Rd.
Padstow Boots, Market St.
Penzance Boots, Market Jew St.
Redruth Boots, Fore St.
St Agnes Boots, Vicarage Rd.
St Austell Day Lewis, Victoria Place; Boots, Fore St.
St Ives Leddra, Fore St.
St Just Ramsay Pharmacy, Fore St.
St Mawes St Mawes Pharmacy, Kings Rd.
Saltash Lloyds, Fore St.
Tintagel Alliance, Fore St.
Torpoint Boots, Fore St.
Truro A J Reed, Frances St; Boots, Pydar St.
Wadebridge Day Lewis, Jubilee Rd.

Surf supplies
Newquay Ann's Cottage, Fistral Beach.
St Agnes Finisterre, Wheal Kitty Workshops.
Truro Cornish Surf Company, Carnon Downs Garden Centre.

Supermarkets
Bodmin ASDA, Launceston Rd; Co-operative, St Mary's Rd; Morrisons, Priory Rd; Sainsbury's, Dennison Rd.
Bude Co-operative, Lansdowne Rd; Co-operative, Burn View Rd; Morrisons, Stucley Rd.
Camborne Lidl, North Roskear Rd; Tesco, Wesley St.
Camelford Co-operative, High St.
East Looe Co-operative, Fore St; Spar, Bayview Rd.

Falmouth ASDA, Jennings Rd; Co-operative, Ponsharden Industrial Estate; Lidl, Falmouth Rd; Tesco, Killigrew St.
Hayle Lidl, Loggans Mill.
Helston Lidl, Penzance Rd; Somerfield, The Parade; Tesco, Clodgey Lane.
Launceston Co-operative, Western Rd; Co-operative, Newport Industrial Estate; Lidl, Hurdon Rd; Tesco, Tailstocks Rd.
Liskeard Morrisons, Plymouth Rd.
Lostwithiel Co-operative, Quay St.
Newlyn Co-operative, The Strand.
Newquay Co-operative, Oakleigh Terrace; Lidl, Treloggan Rd; Morrisons, Treloggan Rd; Sainsbury's, Fore St; Somerfield, Fore St.
Padstow Tesco, Sarah's Lane.
Penzance Lidl, Western Promenade; Morrisons, Eastern Way; Tesco, Branwell Lane.
Perranporth Co-operative, Station Rd.
Port Isaac Co-operative, New Rd.
Redruth Morrisons, Agar Road, Pool; Tesco, Tolgus Hill.
St Austell ASDA, Cromwell Rd; Lidl, East Hill; Tesco, Daniel Lane.
St Ives Co-operative, The Stennack; Tesco, St Ives Rd.
St Just Co-operative, Market Sq.
Saltash Waitrose, Tamar View.
Truro Marks & Spencer, Lemon Quay; Sainsbury's, Treyew Rd; Somerfield, Victoria Sq; Tesco, Garras Wharf.
Wadebridge Co-operative, Jubilee Rd; Lidl, Eddystone Rd; Tesco, West Hill.
West Looe Spar, Princes Sq.

Cornwall Tourist Board
VisitCornwall, Pydar House, Pydar Street, Truro, TR1 1EA.
T01872-322900
F01872-322895
Email: enquiries@visitcornwall.com
visitcornwall.com.

Tourist information centres
Bodmin Shire Hall, Mount Folly, PL31 2DQ, T01208-76616, bodminlive.com.
Boscastle The Harbour, PL35 0HD, T01840-250010, visitboscastleandtintagel.com.
Bude The Crescent, EX23 8LE, T01288-354240, visitbude.info.
Camelford North Cornwall Museum, The Cleave, PL32 9PL, T01840-212954.
Falmouth Prince of Wales Pier, TR11 3DF, T01326-741194, falmouth.co.uk.
Fowey South St, PL23 1AR, T01726-833616, fowey.co.uk.
Hayle Hayle Library, Commercial Rd, TR27 4DE, T01736-754399.
Isles of Scilly Hugh Town, St Mary's, T01720-424031, simplyscilly.co.uk.
Launceston White Hart Arcade, Broad St, T01566-772321, visitlaunceston.co.uk.
Liskeard Forester's Hall, Pike St, PL14 3JE, T01579-349148, liskeard.gov.uk.
Looe The Guildhall, Fore St, East Looe, PL13 1AA, T01503-262072, visit-southeastcornwall.co.uk.
Lostwithiel Liddicoat Rd, PL22 0HE, T01208-872207.
Mevagissey St Georges Sq, PL26 6UB, T01726-844440.

Newquay Marcus Hill, T01637-854020, visitnewquay.org.
Padstow Red Brick Building, North Quay, PL28 8AF, T01841-533449, padstowlive.com.
Penzance Station Approach, TR18 2NF, T01736-335530, purelypenzance.co.uk.
Perranporth St Pirans Rd, TR6 0BH, T01872-575254, perranporthinfo.co.uk.
Redruth Cornwall Centre, Alma Place, TR15 2AT, T01209-216760, visitredruth.co.uk.
St Agnes Vicarage Rd, TR5 0TL, T01872-554150.
St Austell Bypass Service Station, Southbourne Rd, PL25 4RS, T01726-879500, visitthecornishriviera.co.uk.
St Just Library, Market St, TR19 7HX, T01736-788165.
St Ives Guildhall, Street an Pol, TR26 2DS, T0905-252 2250, stivestic.co.uk.
St Mawes Roseland Visitor Centre, Millennium Rooms, The Square, TR2 5AG, T01326-270440, stmawesandtheroseland.co.uk.
Tintagel Bossiney Rd, PL34 0AJ, T01840-779084, visitboscastleandtintagel.com.
Truro Boscawen St, TR1 2NE, T01872-274555, tourism.truro.gov.uk.

Toys & beach gear
Mullion Cornish Kites, Meaver Rd.
Newquay Venus, Tolcarne Beach.
Padstow Dukeswood, Duke St.
Port Isaac The Gullery, Fore St.
St Austell Adeba Toys, Truro Rd.
St Ives Fabulous Kids, Fore St.

Index

A

Abbey Garden 154-155
abseiling 44, 81
Amazing Cornish Maize Maze 176
Annet Island 150
aquariums 57, 69, 84, 176, 177
archery 44, 64

B

babies 200
Barbara Hepworth Museum and
   Sculpture Garden 124
basking sharks 100, 110, 192
beachcombing 137, 159
beaches; see individual entries
beach games 22
beach safety 5, 201
Bedruthan Steps 74-75
bike hire 46, 80, 111
birdwatching 4, 7, 72, 111, 122, 130,
   132, 159
Blue Hills 86
Blue Reef Aquarium 84
boat trips 24, 43, 44, 58, 80, 110, 124,
   132, 133, 136, 148, 151, 158-159, 166,
   170, 186-187, 190, 190, 192, 194
Bodmin 46, 60
   Town Museum 60
Bodmin & Wenford Railway 63, 65
Bodmin Beacon 62
Bodmin Moor 31, 60-65
Bodrifty 101
Booby's Bay 74
books 23
Boscawen-un Stone Circle 101
Boscastle 26, 31, 36-37
Bossiney Haven 39
bowling 49, 86, 113
Bryher 150
Bude 31, 33
   Castle Heritage Centre 49
bus routes 197

C

Cadgwith 129
Cadgwith Cove 130

cafés 54-55, 58, 72, 92-93, 120, 125,
   145, 154, 184-185, 189, 193
Caerhays 188
   Castle 188
Camel Estuary 47, 56
Camelford 34
Camel Trail 31, 46-47, 56, 60
campsites 50, 58, 64, 87, 116-117, 125,
   142-43, 150, 152, 180-181, 188
canoeing 43, 44, 64, 172
Cape Cornwall 104
Carbis Bay 124
Cardinham Woods 60, 62, 63
Carlyon Bay 168
Carnglaze Caverns 65
Carruan Farm 53
Castle Beach 192
Cawsand 169
Chapel Porth 78
Charlestown 165, 168
   Shipwreck & Heritage Centre 173
Cheesewring Trail 62, 63
Chocolate Factory & Craft Centre 141
China Clay Country Park;
   see Wheal Martyn
Chysauster Ancient Village 101
cinemas 49, 86, 113, 141, 177, 194
climbing 44, 64
coasteering 43, 44, 81, 193
Coast to Coast Trail 80
Constantine Bay 71, 72, 74
Cornish Birds of Prey Centre 86
Cornish Mines and Engines;
   see East Pool Mine
Cornish Seal Sanctuary 129, 138
Cotehele House & Quay 165, 173-174
cottages 52, 58, 64, 88, 118, 125, 144,
   152, 182, 189, 199
Courtroom Experience 60
The Cove 156
Coverack 129, 133
crabbing 24, 26-27, 71, 129, 132,
   164, 166
Crackington Haven 31, 33, 39
Crantock Beach 78
Crealy Great Adventure Park 84-85
Crooklets 38
cycling 43, 46-47, 62, 64, 80, 111, 159,
   170, 196

D

Dairyland Farm World 84
Daymer Bay 34, 42, 57
dog owners 201
Dozmary Pool 34
Duckpool 38

E

Eastern Isles 150
East Looe 166, 169
East Pool Mine 86
Eden Project 165, 178-179

F

Falmouth 165, 190-193
   Art Gallery 192
farmers' markets; see markets
farm shops 53, 58, 64, 91, 119, 184
fish & chips 54, 56-57, 92, 120, 146,
   184, 193
Fistral Beach 78
The Flambards Experience 129, 139
Fowey 26, 165, 167, 183
   Aquarium 176
Future World @ Goonhilly 139

G

Geevor Tin Mine 99, 100, 112-113
Gew-Graze; see Soapy Cove
Gillan Creek 133
Glendurgan 144
Godrevy Head 69, 72
Godrevy Lighthouse 78
Godrevy Towans 78
go karting 80, 170-171
Golant 172
Golitha Falls Nature Reserve 62, 63
Goonhilly Downs 129
Gorran Haven 165, 168
Great Bay 156-57
Great Western Beach 77
Gunwalloe Church Cove 132, 137
Gweek 129
Gwithian Sands 68, 71, 72, 79
Gwithian Towans 71, 79

Gwynver Beach 102-103
Gyllyngvase 192

H

Harbour Beach (St Ives) 124
Harbour Cove (Padstow) 58
Harlyn Bay 71, 74
Hawker's Cove 58
Hayle Sands 79
Hayle Towans 79
Helford Estuary 72, 129
Helford Passage 129, 133
Helford River 192
Heligan Gardens; see Lost Gardens of
   Heligan
Hell's Mouth 72
Helman Tor 62
Helston 129
Hemmick Beach 188, 189
Hidden Valley Discovery Park 67
holiday parks 51, 88-89, 117, 143, 181
Holywell Bay 69, 78
   Fun Park 78, 84
horse riding 43-44, 80-81, 111, 136-
137, 159, 171
hotels 90, 118, 143, 152, 154, 183,
189, 193
The Hurlers 63

I

ice cream 24, 53, 58, 91, 119, 145
Isles of Scilly 99, 148-159
   Museum 149
   Wildlife Trust 149

K

kayaking; see sea kayaking
Kennack Sands 129, 133, 142-143
King Arthur's Great Halls 34
Kingsand 169
kite flying 24, 34, 72
kitesurfing 81
Kit Hill Country Park 167
Kynance Cove 4, 128, 129, 132-133

L

Lamorna Cove 106
Land's End 99, 102-103
   attraction 113
Lanhydrock 65
Lantic Bay 168-169
Lanyon Quoit 101
Lappa Valley Railway 84-85
Launceston 66-67
   Castle 66
   Steam Railway 66-67
Lerryn 165
Levant Mine & Beam Engine 113
Lizard 129
Lizard Lighthouse 131, 139
   Heritage Centre 139, 140
Lizard Point 131
Loe Bar 130
Looe; see also East Looe 26, 160-161,
   165, 166, 167
   Island 166
Lost Gardens of Heligan 165, 174-175
Lostwithiel 165
Lundy Bay 34
Lusty Glaze Beach 77

M

mackerel fishing 58, 110, 170
Maenporth 192
maps 199
Marazion 99, 107
Marconi Wireless Station 132
markets 53, 91, 119, 145, 184
Mawgan Porth 69, 75
Mawnan 129
Mevagissey 26, 165, 166, 167
   Museum 166
   Sealife Aquarium 166
Minack Theatre 106, 113
Mineral Tramways 80
Monkey Sanctuary 176
Mother Ivey's Bay 74
Mount Edgcumbe 165
Mousehole 23, 99, 101
   Wild Bird Hospital 101
Mullion 129
Mullion Cove 129, 132, 133

multi activity 44, 81, 137, 171
Museum of Witchcraft 37, 49

N

Nanjizal 94-95, 106, 198
National Lobster Hatchery 57
National Marine Aquarium 177
National Maritime Museum 165, 191
National Seal Sanctuary; see Cornish
   Seal Sanctuary
Neolithic remains 101, 167, 194
Newlyn 99
New Mills Farm Park 67
Newquay 69, 76-77, 78
   Zoo 85
North Cornwall Museum 49
Northcott Mouth 38

O

The Old Post Office 49
orienteering 44

P

Padstow 26, 46, 56-59
Paradise Park 85
Par Sands 168
pasties 119
Pendower 188
Pendennis Castle 192
Penhale Sands 78
Penlee House Gallery & Museum 113
Pentewan 165, 168
Pentreath Beach 131
Penzance 99
Perranporth 69, 72, 78
Perran Sands 78, 107
Poldark Mine 141
Poldhu Cove 132
Polkerris 168
Polperro 26, 165, 207
   Heritage Museum 176
Polruan 165
Polzeath 31, 40-41, 57
Porfell Wildlife Park 176
Porteath Bee Centre 53
Port Gaverne 31, 33, 41

Index

Porth Chapel 106
Portheras Cove 104-105
Porthcothan 74
Porthcurno 1, 99, 106, 108-109
  Telegraph Museum 106, 113
Porthgwarra 106, 107
Porthgwidden 124
Porth Joke 78
Porthleven 130
Porthmeor Beach 124-125
Porthminster Beach 124, 126-127
Portholland 188
Porthpean 168
Porthtowan 68, 78
Port Isaac 26, 31, 33, 34, 41
Portloe 188
Port Quin 31, 33, 41
Portreath 69, 71, 72, 79
Praa Sands 107
Prideaux Place 57
Priest's Cove 104
Prussia Cove 107

Q

quad biking 81

R

Rame Peninsula 165
Readymoney Cove 168
residential holidays 44, 198
restaurants 55, 58, 93, 121, 125, 146-
  147, 185, 193
Restormel Castle 176
Rick Stein 56-57, 59
Rock 31, 42, 56
rock-pooling 24, 25, 71, 107, 159
rock climbing; see climbing
The Roseland 186-189
RNAS Culdrose 129, 130
Roskilly's 145
Royal Cornwall Museum 194

S

sailing 44, 64, 81, 159, 171, 193
Samson 150
sand castles 22

scuba diving 137, 193
sea kayaking 24, 44, 64, 81, 137, 172,
  188, 193
seal watching 72, 110, 124, 158-159
St Agnes 69
  Museum 72, 124
St Agnes (Isles of Scilly) 148-149, 150
St Anthony Head 187
St Austell 165
St George's Cove 57
St Ives 99, 122-127
  Bay Line 122
  Museum 124
St Just 99
St Martin's 150, 156-157, 158
St Mary's 148-149, 150, 151, 158
St Mawes 165, 187
  Castle 187, 188
St Michael's Mount 99, 114-115
St Nectan's Glen 34
Sandy Mouth 38-39
Screech Owl Sanctuary 86
Sennen Cove 2, 23, 99, 102-103
Siblyback Lake 63, 64
single-parent families 200
Slaughterbridge 34
snorkelling 24, 159
Soapy Cove 134-135
soft play centres 86, 124, 141, 177
special needs 201
Springfields Fun Park 86
stand-up paddle boarding 171
surfing 24, 45, 58, 82-83, 111, 124,
  171, 193
Summerleaze 34, 38
Swanpool Beach 192
swimming pools 49, 86, 141, 177

T

Talland Bay 169
Tamar Lakes Watersports Centre 44
Tamar Otter & Wildlife Centre 67
Tamar Valley Donkey Park 177
Tate St Ives 124
Tehidy Country Park 72
Tintagel Castle 30, 31, 33, 48-49
tipi holidays 51
toddlers 200

Tolcarne Beach 77
Towan Beach (Newquay) 76-77
Towan Beach (Roseland) 188
Treasure Park 85
Trebah Gardens 129, 140-141
Trebarwith 31, 33, 39
tree climbing 81
Tresco 150
Trethorne Leisure Park 67
Trevathan Farm Shop 34, 53
Trevaunance Cove 78
Trevigue Wildlife Conservation 49
Trevone Bay 74
Trevose Head 69
Trewidden Garden 113
Trewithen Garden 177
Treyarnon Bay 74
Truro 165, 194-195
  Cathedral 194-195

W

Wadebridge 46
walks 48, 60, 62, 72, 100, 102-103, 130,
  131, 137
Watergate Bay 69, 71, 72, 75
waterskiing 44, 58
Wayside Museum 113
weever fish 200
The Western Rocks 150
Wheal Martyn 177
Whitesand Bay 98, 102-103, 104, 106
Whitsand Bay 165, 169
Widemouth Bay 31, 39
wildlife safaris 81, 159
windsurfing 44, 64, 81, 137, 171, 193
Wonder Years Toy Experience 49

Y

youth hostels 88, 118

Z

Zennor 100
zip wire 81, 170

Cliff-top vigil at Polperro.

Credits

Footprint credits

Text Editor: William Gray
Picture Editor: William Gray
Layout & production: William Gray
Maps: Kevin Feeney

Publisher: Patrick Dawson
Managing Editor: Felicity Laughton
Advertising: Elizabeth Taylor
Sales and Marketing: Kirsty Holmes

Print

Manufactured in Spain by GraphyCems.

Footprint Feedback

We try as hard as we can to make each Footprint guide as up to date as possible but, of course, things always change. If you want to let us know about your experiences – good, bad or ugly – then don't delay, go to footprinttravelguides. com and send in your comments.

Photography credits

All photographs by the author William Gray, except the following:
Bosinver Farm Cottages: p18-19
Gooseham Barton Cottages: p52
Paradise Park: p85 (lorikeet)
Shutterstock: p3 (bucket and spade), p7 (sand), p21 (kite), p29 (sea urchin), p35 (Port Isaac), p37 (Boscastle), p42 (Daymer Bay), p47 (Camel Estuary), p53 (honey bee), p58 (Padstow), p63 (Golitha Falls), p65 (Bodmin Railway), p76 (Towans Beach), p84 (sea horse), p86 (East pool Mine), p95 (scallop), p114 (St Michael's Mount), p119 (pasty), p124 (Barbara Hepworth Museum), p125 (Porthmeor Beach), p126-127 (Porthminster Beach), p130 (helicopter), p133 (Mullion Cove), p145 (cows), p161 (pebbles), p166 (East looe), p166 (Mevagissey), p170 (mackerel), p171 (Looe), p177 (Restormel castle), p177 (National Marine Aquarium), p183 (Fowey), p185 (scone), p192 (Pendennis Castle).

Publishing information

Footprint Cornwall with Kids, 2nd edition
© Footprint Handbooks Ltd, April 2014

ISBN 978-1-907263-86.6
CIP DATA: A catalogue record for this book is available from the British Library.

® Footprint Handbooks and the Footprint mark are a registered trademark of Footprint Handbooks Ltd.

Published by Footprint

6 Riverside Court
Lower Bristol Road
Bath BA2 3DZ, UK
T +44 (0)1225 469141
F +44 (0)1225 469461
footprinttravelguides.com

Distributed in North America by

Globe Pequot Press, Guilford, Connecticut

Acknowledgements

A family effort, this book would not have been possible (nor nearly as much fun to research) without the huge support, enthusiasm, beach critiques, ice-cream tasting and tent-pitching skills of Joseph and Eleanor Gray, and their mother, Sally. The author would also like to offer special thanks to VisitCornwall for their valuable advice and support.